Merger in Daylight

Merger in Daylight

The Economics and Politics of European Merger Control

Damien Neven
Robin Nuttall
and Paul Seabright

Centre for Economic Policy Research

The Centre for Economic Policy Research (CEPR) is a network of more than 180 Research Fellows, based primarily in European universities. CEPR coordinates its Fellows' research activities and communicates their results to the public and private sectors. CEPR is an entrepreneur, developing research initiatives with the producers, consumers and sponsors of research. Established in 1983, CEPR is already a European economics research organization with uniquely wide-ranging scope and activities.

CEPR is a registered educational charity. Grants from the Leverhulme Trust, the Esmée Fairbairn Charitable Trust, the Baring Foundation, the Bank of England and Citibank provide institutional finance. The ESRC supports CEPR's dissemination programme and, with the Nuffield Foundation, its programme of research workshops. None of these organizations gives prior review to CEPR's publications nor necessarily endorses the views expressed therein.

CEPR is pluralist and non-partisan, bringing economic research to bear on the analysis of medium- and long-run policy questions. CEPR research may include views on policy, but the Executive Committee of CEPR does not give prior review to its publications and takes no institutional policy positions. The opinions expressed in this volume are those of the authors and not those of CEPR.

Contents

Acknowledgements   ix
Preface   xi
Executive Summary   xiii
Executive Summary (French)   xvii
List of Tables   xx
List of Figures   xxi

1   Introduction   1
   1.1   The purpose of this study   1
   1.2   What the Merger Regulation has done   4
   1.3   Outline of this book   5
   1.4   Some background hypotheses   9
   Notes   13

2   The analysis of mergers   15
   2.1   Introduction   15
   2.2   What is market power?   17
   2.3   Why does market power matter?   32
   2.4   Methods for assessing the impact of a merger on market power   45
   2.5   The implementation of procedures   63
   Appendix 2.1   Speed versus accuracy in merger control: a simple model   67
   Notes   73

3 The merger decisions of the European Commission   76
   3.1 Introduction   76
   3.2 Definition of a concentration   78
   3.3 Defining the relevant market   90
   3.4 Assessing dominance   101
   3.5 Efficiency: defence or offence?   116
   3.6 Remedies   117
   3.7 Concluding remarks   131
   Notes   134

4 The reactions of firms   136
   4.1 Introduction   136
   4.2 Responses to our survey   138
   Notes   149

5 The bargaining game   151
   5.1 The bargaining game   151
   5.2 Conclusions   160
   Notes   160

**6 Regulatory capture and the design of European
   merger policy**   163
   6.1 The theory of regulatory capture   163
   6.2 Regulatory capture and European merger policy   192
   6.3 Concluding remarks   206
   Notes   207

7 The procedures of merger control   214
   7.1 The EC and elsewhere: an international comparison 214
   7.2 Strengths and weaknesses of the EC's procedure   223
   Notes   226

8 Some options for change   229
   8.1 Modifications to the current procedure   229
   8.2 Institutional changes   231
   8.3 The terms of the Regulation   236
   8.4 Changes in the analysis of mergers   240
   Notes   242

Appendix I	243
Appendix II	267
Bibliography	281
Index	287
Index of European cases	295

Acknowledgements

The idea for this study came from a suggestion made by David Deacon at a May 1992 workshop on future directions for research in competition policy organized jointly by the European Centre for Advanced Research in Economics (ECARE) in Brussels and the Centre for Economic Policy Research (CEPR) in London. Initial financial support for the work came from the CEPR's research initiative on 'Market Structure, Industrial Organization and Competition Policy', which is funded by the Commission of the European Communities (CEC) under its SPES Programme. Paul Seabright would like also to acknowledge financial support from the Directorate-General for Economic and Financial Affairs of the CEC, from the UK Economic and Social Research Council research initiative on the Single European Market, and from the Institut d'Economie Industrielle at the University of Toulouse.

We would like to thank the Directorate-General for Competition of the Commission of the European Communities for permission to reproduce the statistics, diagrams and documents found in Appendices I and II.

We have received a great deal of information, help, comments and advice from Robin Aaronson, Mark Armstrong, Pierre Buigues, Mark Clough, David Deacon, Mathias Dewatripont, Claus-Dieter Ehlermann, Antonio Estache, Jonathan Faull, Nicholas Forwood, Abraham Hollander, Fabienne Ilzkovitz, Frédéric Jenny, Guy de Jonquières, Bruce Lyons, Colin Mayer, Roderick Meiklejohn, Janusz

Ordover, Sandrine Rainotte, Horst Reichenbach, Patrick Rey, André Sapir, Georges Siotis, Romano Subiotto, Susie Symes, Larry White, Colin Overbury and many members of the Merger Task Force, officials of the Bundeskartellamt, Conseil de la Concurrence and the Office of Fair Trading, and many anonymous respondents to our questionnaires. Peter Johns directed the technical production of the volume, with the collaboration of Pradeep Jethi, Martin Klopstock and Kate Millward. Florence Chauvet, Nancy De Munck, Brigitte Pernet and Pierrette Vaissade provided supremely efficient secretarial assistance. Students at the universities of Brussels, Cambridge and Toulouse took part in the experiment described in Chapter 3. Our particular thanks go to Jeremy Edwards and Jean Tirole, who made detailed comments on the whole manuscript. We have been able to respond to only some of their many suggestions for improvement, and it would be more than usually unfair for them to bear any responsibility for the shortcomings that remain.

Preface

At the end of 1989 the European Council of Ministers approved a Regulation establishing a new system of merger control for the European Community. The Regulation came into force at the end of September 1990, and in the two and a half years that followed, around 140 transactions resulted in decisions by the European Commission under the new procedures.

This is the first independent review of the EC Merger Regulation. Its origins lie in a May 1992 workshop of a CEPR initiative on 'Market Structure, Industrial Organization and Competition Policy' funded by the European Commission under its SPES programme. The workshop brought together researchers with officials from the Commission and the national competition policy offices of the member states and other European countries to establish priorities for the research programme (see the account in CEPR *Bulletin* No. 50/51). Our discussions clarified the issues raised by the Merger Regulation and the need for an economic assessment of its implementation.

This is a particularly timely contribution to the policy debate in the European Community. The Merger Regulation itself stipulates that the thresholds determining which mergers fall under the jurisdiction of the European Commission must be reviewed by the end of 1993. The evaluation here should inform the debate over changing the Regulation's scope, which should extend to all aspects of how it is in fact being applied.

Furthermore, the controversies surrounding the ratification of the Maastricht Treaty have prompted a re-examination of some of the assumptions underlying the process of European integration and hence of European competition policy. In the light of these fundamental questions, this monograph uses state-of-the-art research methodology and analysis on a wealth of data. The result is a searching examination of the political economy of merger control, with wide-ranging implications for issues such as transparency of regulation, regulatory capture, subsidiarity, and institutional design.

The authors have a subtle understanding of the legal as well as the economic context, and I have no doubt that their work will be as valuable to policy-makers and practitioners as it is illuminating to outside analysts. It is sympathetic to the difficulty of merger control yet clear on how existing procedures could be improved. CEPR is delighted to publish this monograph.

Richard Portes
26 April 1993

Executive Summary

This study suggests that the process of merger control that has been implemented in the European Community since September 1990, though impressively speedy and administratively efficient, suffers from a number of important weaknesses. In particular, it is likely that in a number of important decisions the Commission has not given adequate weight to the interests it is supposed to serve. Our conclusions are based on an evaluation of the Commission's published decisions in the light of contemporary economic research, a survey of firms who have been the object of the Commission's investigations and of their legal advisers, and an assessment of the merger control procedure and the institutions responsible for its implementation. Our study of the published decisions yields four main conclusions:

1. The analysis presented by the Commission is often based on judgments that are sketchily presented, and appeal to a variety of factors, the weight accorded to which varies from case to case in an insufficiently systematic manner.
2. The Commission has been extremely accommodating in its interpretation of jurisdiction to the wishes of firms to be treated under the Merger Regulation instead of under Article 85 and 86 procedures or by national authorities.
3. The Commission's market definitions are based on a procedure that will tend to result in excessively narrow definitions. One

result of this is that more cases than necessary appear to raise concerns about dominance, which leads the Commission often to appeal to countervailing considerations in a sometimes arbitrary manner.

4. The conditions that have been attached to certain decisions sometimes appear cosmetic and of doubtful effectiveness, particularly since they often presuppose the willing cooperation of the firms upon which they have been imposed.

These conclusions are evidence of considerable flexibility on the Commission's part. But while some degree of flexibility is both necessary and desirable, it can easily lead to a distortion of the policy of merger control in favour of special interest groups, and in particular of those firms that have the most effective lobbying power.

The results of our survey confirm this interpretation: firms and their advisers, while generally pleased with the operation of the Regulation, suggest that they feel confident of considerable bargaining power when negotiating with the Commission, as a result of which they can sometimes extract significant concessions.

The merger control procedure and the institutions charged with its implementation are unnecessarily open to manipulation of this kind. The lack of separation between the process of investigation and the process of decision means that the analysis of cases can be easily written in such a way as to attempt to justify decisions already taken on other grounds than those that follow from the analysis. The procedure is excessively opaque and can lead to unnecessary confusion and lack of accountability.

We consider a number of possible measures of reform, of which the most salient are the following:

1. In the short term, there is a case for publishing systematically the draft decisions before these are laid before the Commission. Conditions attached to decisions should also be given a systematic evaluation before the decisions are taken.

2. In the longer term, it would be highly desirable to separate the responsibility for merger notification and investigation in the hands of a separate agency, and distinguish it from the power of negotiation and decision that would rest in the hands of the Commission.

3. An explicit 'efficiency defence' allowing claims about synergies and other gains from a merger shold not be ruled out. At present,

arguments about efficiency gains appear to play some part in the procedure, without their ever being explicitly admitted and consequently without being accorded a proper and objective evaluation. Explicit consideration of potential efficiency gains would considerably improve the transparency of the procedure.

These various modifications, and particularly those that affect transparency, are in our view more important in the short term than the revision of the turnover thresholds determining the transactions that fall under the Merger Regulation.

Executive Summary (French)

Cet ouvrage suggère que le processus de contrôle des concentrations mis en place dans la Communauté Européenne, dont la gestion administrative est remarquable, souffre cependant de faiblesses importantes; en particulier, il semble que pour un certain nombre de décisions importantes, la Commission n'a pas pu défendre les intérêts qu'elle est censée représenter. Notre analyse repose sur une évaluation des décisions prises par la Commission (à la lumière des développements récents de l'économie industrielle), une enquête réalisée auprès des firmes qui ont été l'objet du contrôle et de leurs conseillers, et une évaluation de la procédure de contrôle et des institutions qui sont chargées de la mettre en oeuvre. De notre examen des décisions, on retiendra en priorité quatre conclusions.

(i) l'analyse présentée par la Commission dans ses décisions fait une large place à des jugements dont la justification est laconique. L'analyse fait appel à des facteurs variés et l'importance qui leur est accordée varie d'une manière qui peut paraître insuffisamment cohérente.

(ii) la Commission semble avoir fait preuve de bonne volonté dans son appréciation de la dimension communautaire des concentrations, de manière à assurer aux entreprises une évaluation dans le cadre de la nouvelle Réglementation plutôt que dans le cadre des articles 85/86 ou des législations nationales.

(iii) les marchés retenus par la Commission sont souvent excessivement étroits, de telle manière que de nombreuses opérations atteignent des parts de marchés importantes; dans ce contexte, l'analyse de la dominance potentielle des firmes devient hazardeuse et ouvre la porte aux jugements arbitraires.

(iv) les conditions dont la Commission a assorti ses décisions semblent parfois cosmétiques et leur efficacité peut fréquemment être mise en doute, ceci d'autant plus qu'elles supposent un certain degré de coopération de la part des entreprises concernées.

Ces résultats prêtent à penser que la grande flexibilité dont la Commission a fait preuve dans son analyse et ses jugements peut être associée à un détournement des objectifs de la Réglementation en faveur des entreprises et des intérêts particuliers dont la représentation auprès de la Commission est la plus effective.

Les résultats de notre enquête confirment cette interprétation: les entreprises concernées et leurs conseillers indiquent que leur position de négociation est favorable et que des concessions importantes peuvent être obtenues de la Commission.

La procédure de contrôle et les institutions chargées de la mettre en oeuvre ouvrent effectivement la porte à ces manipulations, ainsi, l'absence de séparation entre investigation et évaluation politique a pour conséquence que l'analyse des cas peut être écrite de manière à justifier des décisions prises par ailleurs. De manière générale, la procédure, par son manque de transparence, permet de nombreux amalgames et élude les responsabilités.

Un grand nombre de propositions de réforme sont considérées. On peut retenir les éléments suivants.

(i) Dans le court terme, on pourrait publier de manière systématique les projets de décision avant que ceux-ci ne soient présentés au collège des Commissaires. Les projets de décision pourraient également inclure une évaluation des conditions dont une décision positive pourrait être assortie.

(ii) A plus long terme, allouer au corps administratif une responsabilité exclusive pour la notification et l'investigation des cas et cantonner de manière formelle la responsabilité de la Commission à la négociation des décisions et à leur évaluation politique semble désirable.

(iii) Considérer explicitement les gains d'efficacité associés aux concentrations ne doit pas être écarté. Alors qu'ils ne sont pas censés être mentionés, les gains d'efficacité sont considérés sans que les estimations présentées par les parties concernées puissent être vérifiées. La considération explicite des gains d'efficacité est d'autant plus bienvenue qu'une plus grande transparence pourra être assurée.

Ces différentes modifications, et en particulier celles qui affectent la transparence, semble plus importantes à court terme que la révision des critères de chiffres d'affaires qui définissent les concentrations ayant une dimension communautaire.

List of Tables

Table 3.1 Market shares and decisions (in descending order of market share).

Table 3.2 Lower-bound estimates of Herfindahl–Hirschman indices (in descending order of post-merger HHI).

Table 3.3 Experimental survey of the predictability of the decision.

Table 4.1 The survey respondents.

Table 4.2 The procedure.

Tabole 4.3 The opinions of firms.

Table 6.1 Applications of the Tiebout model to regulatory centralization.

Table 7.1 Merger control procedures in various jurisdictions.

List of Figures

Figure 2.1   The allocative inefficiency of monopoly.

Figure 2.2   Monopoly with productive inefficiency as well as allocative inefficiency.

Figure A2.1   The social cost of merger, as determined by the firm's optimal choice of the private benefit of merger.

Figure 6.1   The effect on the value of a convex function of a reduction in its argument.

Figure 8.1   Division of responsibility for stages of procedure.

Figure AI.1   Notifications received.

Figure AI.2   Final decisions.

Figure AI.3   Timeliness of final decision (phase I cases).

Figure AI.4   Timeliness of final decision (phase II cases).

Figure AI.5   Geographic market definition.

Figure AI.6   Language of procedure.

Figure AI.7   Nationality breakdown.

Figure AI.8   CE12 nationality breakdown.

Figure AI.9   EFTA nationality breakdown.

Figure AI10 Cross-border cases (all countries).

Figure AI.11 Cross-border cases (CE12 = one country).

Figure AI.12 Notifications and decisions.

Figure AI.13 Type of concentration.

Figure AI.14 Referral to member states.

Figure AI.15 Suspension of the concentration.

1

Introduction

1.1   The purpose of this study

At the end of 1989, after more than a decade and a half of intermittent negotiation, the European Council of Ministers approved a Regulation establishing a new system of merger control for the European Community. The Regulation came into force at the end of September 1990, and in the two and a half years that followed around 140 transactions resulted in decisions by the European Commission under the new procedures. One case so far (the acquisition of de Havilland by Aerospatiale/Alenia) has been blocked, and a number have been modified or have had conditions imposed. The Competition Directorate of the Commission (DG-IV), which established a special Merger Task Force to handle the notification and investigation of the cases involved, has received highly favourable press comment and reactions from industry for the speed and flexibility of its procedures (about which many were sceptical when the Regulation came into force). The administrative success of the new system has increased pressure for reform of other more cumbersome procedures within the Commission; and at the end of 1992 the outgoing Competition Commissioner, Sir Leon Brittan, promised changes to the investigation procedures under Articles 85 and 86 to bring them more closely into line with those affecting mergers, provided 'an equivalent level of resources is provided throughout DG-IV'.

The time seems ripe for a review of these developments. This is true not just in the straightforward sense that any regulatory innovation needs to be studied after a certain period to see whether it is working well. The current time is particularly appropriate for at least two reasons. First, the Regulation stipulates that the thresholds determining which mergers fall under the jurisdiction of the European Commission must be reviewed by the end of 1993. An evaluation of what has actually happened during the first two and a half years could usefully inform the debate over the appropriateness of any extension in the scope of the Regulation. Secondly, and more fundamentally, there have been a number of changes in the political climate in Europe that have prompted a re-examination of some of the assumptions underlying the process of European integration, of which the Merger Regulation was one expression. One particular change has been due to the heated political discussion surrounding the ratification of the Maastricht Treaty and the expression of strong reservations about the character of European unification, not only by the population of Denmark but by significant minorities in other member states. One of its most visible manifestations has been a renewed emphasis on the virtues of decentralization, and more particularly on the principle of subsidiarity, according to which powers should be granted to the institutions of the European Community only when it has been established that they cannot be satisfactorily exercised by member states.[1]

The reaction against the growth in the power of European Community institutions has come about partly for bad reasons.[2] However, there are also some very sound reasons for questioning this growth in power. At a time when the process of European integration is creating increasing numbers of new problems and inviting new solutions, there is a danger of constitution-making by stealth, in which institutions are established and granted powers, either in response to particular needs and difficulties, or because of an onrush of goodwill towards a general process, without enough questions being asked about the uses to which such powers can and will be put in the future. To say this is not (at least, not in our case) some sort of code for wishing to reverse the process of European integration. On the contrary, the implications are more positive: it is precisely at a time when new institutions are being created that it makes sense to ask fundamental and sceptical questions about the role such institutions will play and their capacity to exercise well the powers they will enjoy.

Accordingly, in addition to discussing merger control from the traditional perspective of industrial economics, we take the principle of subsidiarity seriously as a guide to institution design and discuss the benefits of decentralization in the implementation of competition policy. We argue (in Chapter 6) that the competition between jurisdictions which is triggered by a process of decentralization is desirable to the extent that it reduces the likelihood of competition policy authorities' being 'captured' by particular interest groups. However, we recognize that international mergers involve spillovers across countries which could not easily be taken into account by decentralized authorities. We discuss alternative arrangements short of centralization which could improve on this outcome – including the explicit coordination of the policies of national authorities. We conclude, however, that these arrangements are unlikely to be effective and that some centralization in the case of merger control is warranted. Given that centralized institutions (which do not have obvious counterparts to compete against) could be more prone to capture, designing these institutions so that capture can be limited is particularly important. We therefore discuss at some length how the theory of capture can offer guidance in designing a centralized institution in charge of merger control.

There are consequently two main themes to this study. First, we look at what the European Commission has done. We review the decisions it has taken and the impact these have had on firms, in light of what economic principles suggest are appropriate methods of merger analysis. Secondly, we analyze the system that the Commission has put in place, evaluating it in light of the economic theory of capture and institution design. Most of the argument in the book is therefore directed to answering two questions: what should a merger authority do, and how can such an institution be designed in the European context to ensure that it actually does this in the face of other pressures and temptations?

Our evaluation of the implementation of the Merger Regulation rests on three kinds of evidence: we have analyzed published decisions; we have undertaken a survey of the firms and lawyers involved in cases investigated in the Regulation's first two years of operation; and we have analyzed institutional details of the current merger control procedures. From our examination of published decisions, we point to several ways in which the analysis of mergers undertaken by the Commission could be improved. We also suggest that some observed decisions can best be interpreted as the outcome of a process of negotiation between firms and the Commission, in which the Commission has come under some pressure to deviate from what at first sight would appear a natural reading of its terms of reference. This interpretation is confirmed by the results of our surveys, and underlines the need to consider in more detail the institutional implementation of merger control. Our analysis of these institutional arrangements identifies a number of shortcomings, which indeed increase the risk of the Commission taking decisions in *ad hoc* response to the political pressures of the moment rather than as part of a coherent overall policy. We conclude by discussing measures to deal with these shortcomings, distinguishing between modifications to the procedure that involve legal or institutional changes, changes in the design and responsibility of institutions, amendments to the terms of the Regulation, and improvements in the method of merger analysis.

1.2   What the Merger Regulation has done

The text of the Merger Regulation is reprinted as Appendix II to this book, and a number of its provisions are discussed in some detail in Chapter 6. For present purposes we can summarize the effect of the Regulation as threefold:

1. It establishes jurisdiction. This is done by the stipulation that 'concentrations' between parties with a combined worldwide annual turnover exceeding ECU 5 billion fall under the competence of the European Commission, provided at least two of the parties each have an EC-wide turnover exceeding ECU 250 million, and provided the parties do not conduct two-thirds or more of their EC-wide business in one and the same member state. There are some further exceptions to this rule, embodied in Articles 9, 21(3) and 22(3) (see section 6.2.2); these articles have, however, been rarely applied so far.

2. It determines criteria for judgment. In particular, it requires the Commission to block concentrations that would 'create or strengthen a dominant position'. However, subject to the jurisprudence underlying the concept of a dominant position, the Regulation does not further constrain the way in which the

analysis of dominance is performed. But it does fairly clearly limit the relevant criteria to ones relating to competition: a reference to 'technical and economic progress' is subject to the rider that it should benefit consumers and not be an obstacle to competition, and most observers have agreed that, formally at least, this effectively excludes any explicit 'efficiency defence'.

3. It establishes a timetable for decisions. In particular, cases that are deemed not to raise significant competition concerns must be cleared within a month of notification (which must itself be within one week of the triggering event[3]). Other cases can proceed to a second stage, at which a more detailed analysis is performed; for these the investigation must be completed within four months.

Appendix I shows summary statistics relating to the cases investigated under the Regulation up to 25 March 1992 (two and a half years since it came into force).

1.3   Outline of this book

The first part of the book deals with the analysis of mergers. In Chapter 2 we discuss the theoretical methodology appropriate to this task. Looking at what economic principles have to say about the analysis of market power and its remedies, we consider what tools a merger control agency should use to investigate the impact of merger proposals on competition. We also begin to tackle the issues raised by informational constraints on the agency's analysis, in particular by considering how it should trade off the two desiderata of speed of decision-making and accuracy of analysis.

Chapter 3 uses this framework to examine the decisions taken by the Commission for which published judgments exist. We ask whether the criteria used in the Commission's published analysis are consistent, either with each other or with recent economic scholarship. We reach a number of conclusions, of which the most salient are the following:

1. In many respects the Commission's procedures are insufficiently systematic, both in the sense that they are used less than consistently between cases, and in the sense that they rely

excessively on qualitative judgments and hunches where more quantitative and structured analyses are possible.

2. There are a number of sources of bias in the procedures for determining market definition, which will tend to lead on average to an excessively narrow definition of the relevant market.[4]

3. Partly as a consequence of this, the analysis of dominance is performed in a way that would be excessively lax if the market definitions had been more accurately undertaken.

4. Some of the remedies imposed on firms may do little to meet competition concerns, since they rest on optimistic conjectures about the future developments of competitive forces; some of them may be very difficult to enforce.

5. Overall, as a consequence of these features, the Commission's analyses are insufficiently transparent to allow third parties to tell with any confidence whether their judgment in individual cases has been sound. Some decisions appear somewhat arbitrary even when this could have been avoided.

6. A number of decisions are suggestive of a process of negotiation in which the firms have enjoyed a strong hand.

Chapter 4 looks at the procedure from the point of view of firms. Based on surveys of firms who have made merger proposals, and of the law firms that have advised them, we consider, first, what firms think of the procedure and the costs it imposes on them, and secondly, at whether there is any evidence that firms change their business strategies in response to the presence of the Regulation. Our most important findings are:

1. Firms are on average extremely pleased at the speed and flexibility with which the Regulation has been implemented. The costs imposed on them by the procedure are gratifyingly small when set against the value of the transactions concerned and the importance of reaching a sound decision. A number of firms nevertheless express irritation at the amount of information they are required to supply. There is some degree of national variation in the degree of satisfaction expressed, which we interpret as partly reflecting the stringency of the procedure firms would have had to undergo from national authorities in the absence of the Regulation.

2. There is no evidence at all that potential transactions have been

deterred by fear of the procedure, at least compared to the system of national merger control previously in place.

3. There is nevertheless evidence of changes to the form of transaction undertaken in a significant minority of cases, usually for reasons of 'forum shopping'.[5] While many of these changes may be cosmetic, some could impose significant distortions on business decision-making.
4. Some industrialists, and most lawyers, note that the Commission appears very keen to clear deals if at all possible. The lawyers in particular are aware that this may give them significant bargaining power with the Commission even in doubtful cases.

The evidence of Chapter 4 not only helps us to evaluate the decisions the Commission has taken, but raises important questions about the nature of the procedures from which those decisions have emerged. This leads naturally into the second part of the book, beginning with Chapter 5. Here we ask whether the theory of bargaining can explain some of the features of the observed decisions, especially the evident keenness of both firms and the Commission to seek compromise outcomes to difficult cases. We emphasize that the fact that only one case has so far been blocked is not in itself a sign that the procedures are lax: such a tendency could arise either from a weak procedure or from a stringent one that dissuades firms from undertaking transactions that have adverse consequences for market power. Nevertheless, we adduce other evidence suggesting that rather more of the compromises than is desirable have come from the Commission's side. This may partly be because the Commission has not yet been sufficiently able to make its policy credible in the eyes of firms (we discuss ways in which its ability to do so might be strengthened), and partly because the policy itself is subject to modification under various kinds of political pressure. We conclude the Commission may, by wishing to reassure firms of its willingness to clear deals if possible, have laid itself open to more manipulation than is desirable. We also note that the enthusiastic reception of the Regulation procedures by firms, while in itself an important achievement, needs supplementing by further argument before we can reach a considered judgment on the procedure as a whole. If you want to know whether the gamekeeper is doing a good job, you don't just ask the poachers.

This leads to a discussion in Chapters 6 and 7 of procedures and institutions. Chapter 6 examines the theory of regulatory capture, in particular distinguishing between responses to the phenomenon based on improved accountability, greater political independence and increased transparency. In the light of this analysis, Chapter 7 examines the actual procedures of European merger control, in the process comparing it with that in a number of other jurisdictions. We note a number of strengths of the European procedures, but conclude that as a whole they suffer from a significant lack of transparency, and that some of the features of actual decisions noted by us in the first part of the book may be partially explained by this. A lack of transparency may result in capture by the interests of large firms, particularly those with significant bases of political support in member states. We argue that increased transparency is both feasible and in the public interest; it would also be in the interest of many in the Commission itself, because it would increase the credibility of the policy that many officials genuinely wish to carry out. In the light of this discussion, Chapter 8 evaluates some possibilities for reform.

We have tried where possible in this study to avoid technical discussions where the same arguments can be expressed in a more intuitive way.[6] Most of the technical material is concentrated in Chapter 2, parts of which will probably be rebarbative to readers who are not professional economists. However, the remaining chapters ought, we hope, to be intelligible to readers familiar with economic ideas but who do not have an academic economics training - provided they are willing to skip the text at points where our attempts to be clear and intuitive have failed. Chapter 3 contains a great deal of detailed discussion of particular cases, which may be indigestible to readers who are more interested in general competition policy issues than in the details of European merger control; we have included section summaries to make it easier to extract from the chapter the messages of wider interest. By contrast, we hope that Chapters 2 and 6 in particular contain material of relevance to significantly broader issues of public policy.

In the course of the study we must inevitably assume a number of background hypotheses about the role of competition in the economy; while space prevents our defending these in depth, it is important to be explicit about what we do and do not need to assume. These hypotheses are not, however, a part of the detailed argument in the chapters that follow.

1.4 Some background hypotheses

1.4.1 *The benefits of more competitive markets*

The first underlying hypothesis that is assumed rather than explicitly defended in this book is that competition in an industrialized economy is indeed a good thing. This is a less banal point than it may sound. The theoretical arguments for competition (based on the first welfare theorem for a perfectly competitive economy with complete markets) are beside the point: it is not realistic to expect even a vigorous competition policy to lead to perfect competition. Likewise, pointing to the disastrous consequences of central planning in the East European fashion is also irrelevant, precisely because intervention on the scale needed to suppress competition so comprehensively is completely discredited. What is at issue is whether, within the overall framework of a mixed economy, more competitive markets are generally better than less competitive ones. Conventional analyses[7] of the welfare losses from monopoly have typically come up with very small magnitudes (no more than one or two percentage points of gross domestic product for the US economy). Furthermore, we know that market power is not necessarily damaging if it offsets other distortions in the economy. For instance, given what we know about the failures of credit and other financial markets to finance risky investments, monopoly profits could represent a valuable offsetting source of internally generated investment funds to offset under-investment due to acknowledged market failures in financial markets.

The case for competition is both theoretical and empirical. First, the benefits of monopoly power can accrue only if the resulting rents are realized in the form of profits and if those profits are re-invested in promising ventures. Because of failures of corporate control, monopoly power can lead to inefficiency and 'the quiet life'. In such cases, there may be no retained earnings for investment; even if there are, the temptation for managers to invest them in pet projects or to finance empire-building may be hard to resist. In these circumstances, the welfare losses associated with monopoly power will typically be much larger than the Harberger triangles of conventional theory (as we discuss in section 2.3.2). Secondly, empirical evidence suggests that, even if markets are imperfectly competitive, it may matter very much whether the number of participants in the market is one or two, or (say) half a dozen (see, for example, Bresnahan and Reiss (1991)). There is also evidence that high barriers to entry (and the consequent low risk of challenge by outsiders) may encourage productive inefficiency.

1.4.2 *The inadequacy of* laissez-faire

The second underlying hypothesis of this book is that the benefits of competition in an industrialized private-ownership economy cannot be attained by complete *laissez-faire*. We do not subscribe to the Austrian view (due to Schumpeter and Hayek among others) of the private sector as its own most effective police force, though we acknowledge the validity of many of its criticisms of naive interventionism. Even if the state refrains from imposing artificial barriers to the competitive process, it is not always realistic to expect the normal processes of greed and envy to ensure that market entry bids away the rents in monopolized activities. It is now familiar from modern industrial organization theory that free market entry may lead either to excessive or insufficient entry. Unfortunately, this kind of analysis has become increasingly complex in recent years as research has shown that the nature of competition in any market may depend as much on what cannot be observed as on what can. It is the potential as well as the actual competitors, the tacit as well as the overt collusion, the threats that are sufficiently credible not to need carrying out, that may determine whether competition is really working. Determining the 'right' degree of competition will therefore be a subtle and difficult matter, exactly the kind of judgment that modern public-choice theories of the state warn us may lead to government failure.

However, comparing the ideal degree of competition in the economy to the *laissez-faire* solution is unrealistic, because no government in history has ever undertaken complete *laissez-faire*. Governments have always intervened, usually to restrict competition, in order to share in the associated monopoly rents. They may do so either explicitly for taxation purposes or because of the asymmetry in political perceptions which means that the existing jobs and profits threatened by competition have more political clout than the potential but not yet existent jobs and profits that can be created by competition. Once the distortions of the political process are taken into account, it is much more reasonable to suggest that, in the absence of an explicit policy to the contrary, the extent of competition in a modern industrial economy will be inadequate rather than excessive. This suggests that competition authorities have a doubly difficult task. Not only must they undertake difficult discretionary judgments, using procedures that are nevertheless reasonably transparent and free from the temptations of rent-seeking. They must also, as a branch of government, seek to undo many of the biases and distortions that a government by its very nature is inclined to impose on the economy it oversees.

Rather than viewing its task as simply ensuring by administrative fiat the 'right' degree of competition in the economy, an effective competition authority has therefore to view the process much more dynamically. It must assist in the enfranchisement in the economic process of many of the interests that are naturally underrepresented in the alliance of managers and politicians that makes up the modern corporatist state. Shareholders, consumers and potential employees are three of the most important such interests. Much of the pressure for monopolization of an industrial economy, whether via mergers and takeovers or lesser forms of collaboration, comes from managers wanting to appropriate rents at the expense of these groups. Sometimes shareholders may suffer disproportionately, when the monopolization represents empire-building rather than profitable activity; sometimes it is consumers (when profitable activity extends market power); often it is potential employees, when monopolies and cartels use the security of their position to stagnate instead of to innovate and to expand. An effective competition authority is the ally of all these excluded groups, and the public interest benefits significantly from their enfranchisement.

1.4.3   *The importance of merger control*

Merger control is in some respects the most obvious focus of competition policy, simply because growth by acquisition instead of by market expansion can easily represent the lazy way to monopoly power. Mergers can offer firms the immediate freedom from the nuisance of having to compete with each other. They can thereby avoid the need to earn their monopoly power the hard way, by persuading enough customers to buy their products. Indeed, some companies appear to believe that their potential for corporate growth should override other considerations, so that public policy should be more lenient towards mergers in markets where alternatives for growth are not feasible.[8]

So our third underlying hypothesis is that merger control (including the regulation of both friendly and hostile takeovers) must be one of the central components of any credible competition policy. But mergers and acquisitions can also offer two kinds of economic benefit that market expansion cannot: first, the chance to recombine corporate assets in more efficient ways, and secondly, the ability for capital markets to monitor the performance of management and to allow new owners to replace managers whose performance is inadequate. The extent to which actual mergers have succeeded in performing either of these two functions is a matter of fierce debate, on which we touch in Chapters 2 and 6. But just as competition policy cannot ignore merger control if it is not to leave open the most tempting route of all to monopoly power, so it cannot adopt an inflexibly restrictive approach to mergers without forgoing these potential benefits.

1.4.4   *Industrial policy and economic benefits wider than competition*

It should be evident from what we have said so far that competition is, in our view, desirable only in so far as it contributes to other ends that are valued more directly. It follows that developments which diminish competition (such as some mergers) may nevertheless sometimes be desirable on balance if they bring other benefits (such as increased production efficiency, greater investment, or innovation).

The consideration of other benefits than competition does not imply, however, that competition policy is systematically at odds with the goals of industrial policy. On the contrary, well-conceived industrial policy interventions are usually motivated by particular market failures like the existence of market externalities and spillovers (as in research and development). These market failures are usually best addressed by a direct response (for instance, the use of research subsidies). Adopting a lax approach towards competition policy is at best an indirect and at worst a counterproductive response to such problems, since there is nothing to ensure that the monopoly rents it confers on firms will indeed be invested in the desired activities rather than dissipated in other ways.

There is, however, one kind of circumstance in which competition policy may conflict directly with industrial policy, and this is where there exist significant scale economies that warrant a degree of industrial restructuring (whether in growing or declining industries), but which are likely to result in increased market power. Here mergers and acquisitions may indeed be the direct response to the problem. Accordingly, it will be no surprise that in Chapter 8, we argue that an explicit procedure to trade off such benefits against the damage done to competition by certain mergers would itself have some benefits. But this does not mean that we favour an explicit 'efficiency defence' under the Regulation in all circumstances. An efficiency defence would have benefits, as we have indicated. It would also have costs, namely the risk that it would be exploited to gain approval for undesirable mergers on the basis of spurious claims about the magnitude of the efficiency gains to which they gave rise. The importance of this risk would depend, we argue, on the precise way in which an efficiency defence was implemented. Accordingly we come down in favour of an efficiency defence provided it is part of a package of reforms whose purpose would be to minimize the expected costs. But for the time being it is important to emphasize that our discussion in Chapters 2–4, while giving little explicit consideration to efficiency benefits since these are not a formal part of the criteria of analysis embodied in the Regulation, does not in any way imply that we believe competition to be the sole economic good.

Notes

1. In principle the same arguments ought to apply to decentralization within countries, but the advocates of subsidiarity have not always followed this logic through into domestic politics.
2. In France, for example, there has been an inaccurate association of the Maastricht Treaty with the difficulties created for the farming sector by the crisis of overproduction and the consequent reforms of the Common Agricultural Policy. In the United Kingdom press discussion of the 'bloated bureaucracy' of Brussels appears quite unaware that the 14,000 civil servants of the European Commission would be insufficient to staff

even a medium-sized British government department such as the Department of Transport, which had 15,300 civil servants in 1991 (source: CSO). They also represent about the same number as the total federal employees working in Washington, DC, in the year 1882. Drèze (1992), who makes the latter comparison, points out that it is important to correct for the different (and more limited) functions performed by the European Commission: 'A great majority of US federal civil servants will never have any equivalent at Brussels: for example, those who work in the postal services and, we must hope, in the Pentagon. But others work in sectors like agriculture, industry, transport, energy: there are 100,000 of them … [and] it is this figure which it is reasonable to compare to the 14,000 European civil servants' (p. 15).

3. The triggering event is whichever of the following occurs first: the conclusion of an agreement, the announcement of a public bid, or the acquisition of a controlling interest.

4. This may be offset if the unsystematic character of the procedures referred to in 1 leads to biases in the opposite direction; the extent to which this is true of actual judgments is harder to ascertain.

5. Almost all changes appear to have been made with the intention of increasing the likelihood of being treated under the Regulation, in order to avoid either Article 85/86 procedures or investigation by national authorities.

6. We have not been able to avoid the usual scholarly apparatus of footnotes and references as much as some readers might have wished. However, in a study like this one, where we have undertaken a great many interviews with individuals, many of whom wished to remain anonymous, we trust that there will be enough rumour and gossip in the footnotes to compensate.

7. Beginning with those performed by Harberger (1954); for more recent evidence, see Scherer and Ross (1990, pp. 668–72).

8. For instance, a memorandum issued by Nestlé protesting at the Commission's procedures in the investigation of its acquisition of Source Perrier complains that the Competition Directorate 'should not prevent any more than is necessary the growth of industries by acquisition. This is sometimes the only means of expansion open to firms in slowly-growing markets' (Nestlé SA: 'Defauts Fondamentaux dans les Procédures de la Direction Generale pour la Concurrence de la Commission Européenne', 22 July 1992).

2

The analysis of mergers

2.1 Introduction

In this chapter we set out some basic principles to guide the evaluation of the Merger Regulation which is performed in the ensuing chapters. We begin by asking what can be learned from economic theory about the way in which mergers ought to be analyzed, leaving until Chapter 6 issues about the nature of the institutions that can or should be established to perform such an analysis. As we indicated in Chapter 1, public policy is concerned about mergers because of the possibility that they may enhance market power. Here we shall investigate this claim more closely, basing our analysis upon four main questions. *First*, what is market power, and how is it related to other familiar economic concepts such as market structure, as well as to the notion of dominance embodied in European Community law? *Secondly*, why and how much does the exercise of market power matter? *Thirdly*, what are the most reliable means a competition authority can use to determine whether a proposed merger will enhance market power? *Finally*, any diagnosis of market power will be imperfect, and in being undertaken will impose costs upon the economy in general and the merging parties in particular: how can the benefits of merger control in restraining the exercise of market power be evaluated against these various costs?

We shall argue first that the concept of market power is fairly simple, and is expressed by the extent to which the parties to a merger would be able to raise the prices of their products while still maintaining demand for those products (that is, by the own-price elasticity of demand for the products of the post-merger firm). However, it is usually very difficult to infer the magnitude of this elasticity of demand from observable evidence: if it were, merger control would be a straightforward matter. The armoury of procedures used by anti-trust practitioners (market definition, calculation of market shares or concentration indices, assessment of dominance and so forth) should therefore be seen as *indirect indicators* of market power, which are useful only to the extent that they provide evidence as to the magnitude of the own-price elasticity of demand for the products of the merged firm. So one of our chief tasks is to analyze exactly what the relationship is between these indirect indicators and the basic concept itself. We undertake this analysis in section 2.2.

Market power matters, we suggest, partly because it may lead to allocative inefficiency and partly because it may worsen productive inefficiency; we discuss in section 2.3 some reasons why the latter effect may be at least as important as the former. If it does matter, that provokes the natural question: what can public policy do about it? So in section 2.4 we go on to discuss the steps a competition authority can use to diagnose whether a given merger proposal is likely to enhance market power; we discuss in particular the procedures described in the Merger Guidelines of the US Department of Justice, and compare them with the procedures implicit in the European Community anti-trust practice. The EC's procedures, we argue, are less systematic than those of the Merger Guidelines. In addition, they are biased towards an overestimation of market power by ignoring a number of potential factors constraining the ability of merging firms to raise prices (though even the US procedures contain some less pronounced biases whose nature we describe).

The difficulties of diagnosis to which we draw attention suggest that merger control needs to be cautious: the authorities cannot identify with certainty which mergers should be prevented, and in the process of trying to do so can impose significant costs upon the economy. More intensive investigations can increase the reliability of the diagnosis at the expense of raising these costs. Is it possible to say anything systematic about how this trade-off should be made? In section 2.5 we argue that the financial resources required to fund a competition agency are negligible compared to the two most significant costs of merger control. These are the costs of delaying desirable corporate reorganizations, and the costs of mistaken judgments. 'Quick and dirty' procedures impose low costs of the former kind and high ones of the latter kind, compared to more rigorous investigations. We propose a simple framework in which to think about striking an appropriate balance between these two kinds of cost.

2.2 What is market power?

2.2.1 *Market power and dominance*

From the perspective of economic principles, market power is usually defined in contrast to the benchmark of perfect competition (see Tirole (1988), pp. 6–12). In a situation of perfect competition, firms selling homogeneous products cannot affect market prices; entry ensures that price, equated to marginal cost, just covers average cost and firms that attempt to sell above the market price lose all custom. That is, firms have no power over market outcomes. Provided that economies of scale do not prevail over the whole range of output and that the minimum efficient scale of production is small relative to the overall market demand, this outcome is feasible. Standard welfare analysis also demonstrates that the equilibrium of a perfectly competitive economy is both allocatively efficient (if markets are complete) and productively efficient.

By contrast, market power arises as soon as firms have the ability to raise their own price above marginal cost without losing all custom. In consequence their profit-maximizing price will lie somewhere above marginal cost. Estimating the market power enjoyed by a firm therefore requires an assessment of the extent to which that firm would be capable of increasing its price above marginal cost without losing all its customers. Unfortunately, this does not mean that competition authorities can simply use the extent to which prices charged by firms are above marginal cost as a diagnosis of the existence of market power, for two reasons. First, at any particular time, pricing at or temporarily below marginal cost might be part of a (rational) predatory action on the part of a firm, an action that, far from indicating a competitive situation, would presumably be associated with some market power. Secondly, as we discuss in section 2.3, one of the consequences of market power might well be the inflation of firms' costs (especially in circumstances where high price–cost margins are thought likely to attract the attention of the competition authorities); consequently, the observation that prices do not lie much above actual costs may disguise the fact that they do lie well above the cost levels that would prevail if the firm concerned faced significant competitive pressure. The diagnosis of market power is thus best performed with reference to the fundamental conditions (and in particular the demand elasticities) which determine the scope for raising price above marginal costs, rather than the price–cost relationship itself.

In Community law, there is no explicit reference to market power but rather to market dominance and the abuse of a dominant position. According to Article 86 of the Treaty of Rome, 'any abuse by one or more undertakings of a dominant position within the common market or in a substantial part of it shall be prohibited as incompatible with the common market in so far as it may affect trade between Member states'. Hence, it is clear that under Article 86 it is the abuse, not the mere holding, of a dominant position which is prohibited by Community law. Still, the Court of Justice has insisted that evidence of dominance should first be provided. Dominance itself is defined as 'a position of economic strength enjoyed by an undertaking which enables it to hinder the maintenance of effective competition on the relevant market by allowing it to behave to an appreciable extent independently of competitors and ultimately of consumers' (Michelin, case 322/81, ECJ 3461 (1983)). The Court has further confirmed that the ability to behave independently of competitors and customers will depend on whether competition is 'effective', so that the two concepts can be taken as equivalent. Accordingly, the concept of dominance includes (though is not exhausted by) the idea that a firm can profitably increase its price without losing its customers. It does not, however, imply that the firm actually does increase its price. And in the *Continental Can* case, the Court also explicitly stated that the determination of the relevant market was essential to establishing the presence of dominance. As a consequence, the Commission has systematically sought to establish first that firms were holding dominant positions, by analyzing the relevant market and computing the market share of defendants. In the *United Brands* and *Hoffman-La Roche* cases, the Court also adopted the view that dominance could be assessed by structural elements; the Court took the view that high market shares (above 40/50%) were sufficient evidence of dominance. As far as abuse is concerned, high prices (above long-run marginal cost) are typically considered sufficient evidence (see George and Jacquemin (1992)), though not as necessary. The presumption of both dominance and abuse can of course be rebutted in certain circumstances (as when the high market shares and high prices are the consequence of possession of intellectual property rights such as patents).

On the whole, one can therefore conclude that dominance has been interpreted as the ability to raise price without losing customers, whereas the abuse of a dominant position occurs when firms actually raise prices above long-run marginal costs. The abuse of a dominant position appears therefore to have been defined with reference to what economic theory suggests is a sufficient behavioural condition for the existence of market power, namely the presence of prices above marginal costs. But this does not make the two concepts (market power and abuse of dominance) equivalent: there can certainly be market power without abuse, and there can also – at least in the interpretation of the Court of Justice – be abuse without the exercise of market power.[1] And whereas market power is a purely behavioural concept (referring as it does to the own-price elasticity of demand facing a single firm), the notion of dominance involves reference to market structure in that it connotes an absence of alternative sources of supply.

The Merger Regulation in some ways goes beyond that natural interpretation of Article 86, in that it does not require the Commission to provide actual evidence of abuse of dominance; this would clearly not be feasible since merger control occurs before mergers take place. The Regulation prohibits any 'concentration which creates or strengthens a dominant position as a result of which effective competition would be significantly impeded in the common market or in a substantial part of it'. What is required is evidence that the merged entity would enjoy a position of dominance, since the Regulation presumes that dominance would actually be abused if achieved. Consequently the relevant jurisprudence focuses importantly on the notion of dominance, and particularly on the structural features that the Court of Justice has held to constitute evidence of dominance, such as high shares of a relevant market. It becomes important, therefore, to consider what relation these features have to the economic notion of market power.

2.2.2   *Market power and the elasticity of demand*

Intuition and casual observation suggest that market power most commonly arises when a firm produces a product that is differentiated from that of other firms (so that customers will not switch easily to competitors as the price increases), and when there is coordination of behaviour between firms (so that a price increase is accommodated by competitors). It will be useful therefore to distinguish between the elasticity of demand for a *product* (which describes what happens when the price of that product changes, holding constant the prices of other products) and the elasticity of demand faced by a *firm*, which includes also any changes in demand for the product after a price rise as a result of any induced changes in the prices of competing products.

BOX 2.1   *Market power and price–cost margins*

Consider a set of firms ($i = 1, \ldots, n$) selling differentiated products. Let p_i and q_i denote respectively the price charged by firm i and the quantity that it sells. Then $q_i(p_1, \ldots, p_1, \ldots, p_n)$ is the demand function faced by firm i. The relevant market for this analysis comprises all products which are to some extent substitutes for one another; it is the set of firms whose demand is jointly determined (as represented by the system $q_i(.)$, $i = 1, \ldots, n$). The absolute value of the elasticity of the demand for the product of firm i will be denoted:

$$h_i = -\left(\frac{\partial q_i(p_1, \ldots, p_i, \ldots, p_n)}{\partial p_i}\right)\left(\frac{p_i}{q_i}\right) \tag{2.1.1}$$

Notice that this elasticity is in principle a function of all prices. In particular, it is contingent on the set of prices set by competitors. We can also define the cross-price equivalents of h_i

$$h_{ij} = -\left(\frac{\partial q_i(p_1, \ldots, p_1, \ldots, p_n)}{\partial p_j}\right)\left(\frac{p_j}{q_i}\right) \tag{2.1.2}$$

Each such elasticity expresses the proportionate change of demand for product i following a proportionate change in the price of a competing product. We assume that firms operate with a fixed cost F_i and a constant marginal cost c_i.

The profit of firm i (Π_i) is then simply written as:

$$\Pi_i = q_i(p_1, \ldots, p_i, \ldots, p_n)(p_i - c_i) - F_i \qquad (2.1.3)$$

Differentiating (2.1.3) with respect to p_i yields the first-order condition:

$$p_i - c_i = \frac{-q_i}{(\partial q_i/\partial p_i) + \Sigma_j[(\partial q_i/\partial p_j)(\partial p_j/\partial p_i)]} \qquad (2.1.4)$$

Dividing through by p_i and rearranging terms, one can derive the margin that will be charged by firm i, namely:

$$\frac{(p_i - c_i)}{p_i} = \frac{1}{e_i} = \frac{1}{[h_i + \Sigma_j h_{ij}(\partial p_j/\partial p_i)(p_i/p_j)]} \qquad (2.1.5)$$

What this equation says is that the proportionate price–cost margin is equal to the reciprocal of e_i, defined as the absolute value of the own-price firm elasticity of demand. This elasticity is determined as the own-price elasticity of demand for product i (h_i), and a sum of terms each composed of the product of the proportionate change in the price of a competing product j as a result of the change in price of product i (which represents the extent to which pricing behaviour is coordinated across firms) and the cross-price elasticity of demand of product i with respect to the price of that product j (which represents the extent to which competing products are substitutes for that of firm i).

Box 2.1 makes this distinction more precise by formalizing the argument. We begin by considering a very simplified description of competition between n firms selling single products that are to some extent differentiated from each other. We assume for the time being that firms' costs are given (and therefore that they do not vary with the degree of market power enjoyed by the firms), and that they are represented by a fixed cost F_i and a constant marginal cost c_i for any firm i. We also assume a simple static model so that we can ignore such issues as predatory pricing. Then we show in Box 2.1 that the proportionate price–cost margin charged by a profit-maximizing firm will be equal to the reciprocal of the absolute value of the own-price elasticity of demand faced by that firm, and that elasticity itself has two components: the own-price elasticity of demand for the product,[2] and the sum of the indirect proportional changes in demand for the firm's product as a result of changes in the prices set by other firms. In words:

Own-price firm = Own-price product
demand elasticity demand elasticity

+

$$
\text{Sum of:} \left\{
\begin{array}{l}
\text{Cross-price elasticities} \\
\text{of product demand w.r.t.} \\
\text{competing products}
\end{array}
\right.
\times
\left.
\begin{array}{l}
\text{Proportional change} \\
\text{in prices of competing} \\
\text{products divided by} \\
\text{proportional change in} \\
\text{original product price}
\end{array}
\right\}
$$

The sign of the cross-price elasticities will be positive if products are substitutes, and the induced changes in price of competing products will be positive if firms coordinate behaviour and negative if they compete aggressively. This means that, since the own-price product demand elasticity is negative, a coordinated response by other firms (which makes the net indirect demand effect positive) will *offset* the direct demand effect, and the elasticity of firm demand will be lower in absolute value than the elasticity of product demand. Conversely, if other firms' response is aggressive, the elasticity of firm demand will be higher in absolute value than the elasticity of product demand.

A number of useful observations can already be made from this formulation:

1. First, it clearly indicates in what precise sense the source of market power is the elasticity of demand faced by the firm. In turn, both a high degree of product differentiation (which lowers the own-price elasticity of product demand) and a high degree of coordination of firm behaviour (which makes the indirect demand effect offset the direct demand effect) will lead to a high potential price–cost margin. This formulation also reveals that the market power enjoyed by firms with identical output and prices (and hence market shares) can vary a great deal according

to the reactions they anticipate from their competitors. Firms which face potentially accommodating competitors will be able to maintain higher margins.

2. Assessing the market power which would be enjoyed by a new entity resulting from a merger requires an evaluation of the elasticity of firm demand that this new firm *would actually face*. This may be quite different from the elasticity of product demand for the products produced by the two firms, and indeed even from the elasticity of firm demand faced originally by each of the merging parties.

3. The way to think about the effect of a merger on market power is to consider the difference between the response of demand to a price increase by a single firm and the response of demand when two firms that have merged simultaneously raise prices by the same amount. The formulation suggests, *first*, that the absorption of particularly rivalrous firms in a merger will lead to large increases in market power, since negative price responses will vanish in the firm elasticity faced by the merged entity (see, for instance, Kwoka (1989)). *Secondly*, if the parties were previously rivalrous, then the impact of the merger on their market power is greater if their products are close substitutes, since the negative price responses were previously amplified by large cross-price elasticities of demand. *Thirdly* (and conversely), if the parties previously coordinated prices closely, the impact of the merger is greater if their products are not close substitutes, since the positive price responses were previously damped by small cross-price elasticities.

4. The decomposition of a firm's elasticity of demand into a product elasticity of demand and a term representing the indirect effect of changes in competitors' pricing behaviour yields a distinction which can be usefully related to the practice of a number of anti-trust authorities in distinguishing between 'demand-side substitutability' and 'supply-side substitutability'. In section 2.4 we shall discuss more precisely how the US and EC authorities have actually made use of demand- and supply-side substituta-bility, but unless we indicate otherwise we shall always use the terms in the following sense: demand-side substitutability refers to the tendency of customers to switch away from a product after a rise in its price, *the prices of all other substitute products remaining unchanged*; while supply-side substitutability refers to

any additional change in the firm's demand that may come about *through any reaction in the pricing behaviour of competitors.*

5. In addition to distinguishing two different kinds of substitutability, anti-trust authorities typically define a 'relevant market'. How is this related to the formulation above? First of all, note that the products which are relevant to the determination of the market power of any given firm include all those whose cross-price elasticity of demand with the original product is non-zero. Typically, however, a 'relevant market' for anti-trust purposes will include not all products with non-zero cross-price elasticities, but only a subset of these products. This is defined as the smallest subset such that a uniform proportionate rise in price of all products within the market (a rise of 5% above marginal cost in the exercise performed by the US federal authorities) would just be profitable. This appears to be a discrete approximation to the ideal question, which is whether such a price margin above marginal cost represents the *profit-maximizing* margin for a firm that controlled the relevant market. In terms of elasticities, the procedure for answering the latter question can be represented as follows (taking a 5% price–cost margin as an illustration). First, take the product (or products) concerned in the case and calculate the absolute value of the own-price product elasticity of demand. This will be equal to the own-price *firm* elasticity of demand if there is no coordination (the benchmark case where there is no price response from other firms). If this is less than 20 (the reciprocal of 5%), the product by itself already constitutes the relevant anti-trust market (in which therefore the firm has a monopoly position). If the elasticity is greater than 20, choose the product with which it has the largest cross-price elasticity of demand and set the proportional change in price of that product in response to the original price change equal to one. Then recalculate the absolute value of the firm elasticity of demand, and if this is still greater than 20, repeat the procedure until a value of 20 or less is attained.

We discuss in section 2.4.2 below some respects in which the discrete approximation (is a 5% price rise just profitable?) to this ideal question (is 5% the profit-maximizing margin?) can be misleading, and also the fact that competition authorities in practice have tended to overlook the importance of supply substitution in answering it.

6. The 'relevant market' thus defined will be smaller than the set of all products that are to some extent substitutes for the original product. Indeed, this must be so, for if the hypothetical price rise is to be only just profitable, there must be some degree of substitution away from the products within the relevant market (whose prices *ex hypothesi* all rise by the same proportion) and consequently towards some other products outside the market. It would be misleading, therefore, to think that the relevant market as it is defined by competition authorities consists of the only relevant substitutes for the product in question. Instead the way to think of the relevant market is as representing the minimum set of products over which a firm would have to have monopoly control before it could be sure of exercising a given degree of market power.

2.2.3   *Market power and market shares*

However a market is defined, it is useful to consider how the market power that can be exercised by a given firm varies with its share of that market. In order to explore this question more precisely, we must abandon the assumption we have made up till now that each firm produces a single product. Then the intuition that larger market shares imply greater market power can be expressed in the following way. Let a given market (however defined) consist of a certain number m of differentiated products. We can use the formula above to compare the market power of a firm producing j of these m products with one producing some larger number k (including the original j). The firm producing j products will face an own-price firm elasticity determined by the (aggregate) own-price product demand elasticity for the j products, offset by two indirect demand responses – one due to any induced price change in the remaining $m - j$ products, multiplied by the cross-price elasticities between those $m - j$ products and the original j; the other due to the corresponding price change in any products *outside* the defined market. The firm producing k products will enjoy a market power that differs from the former only in that the prices of the extra $k - j$ products it produces will be coordinated perfectly with the prices of the original j so as to maximize profits. So any price increase that is profitable for the firm producing *j* products must be at least as profitable for that producing *k*, and consequently the profit-maximizing price rise will be at least as great (and strictly greater unless the firm producing *j* products already anticipated perfect coordination from the prices of its competitors).

What this tells us is that, unless there is already perfect coordination between firms in a market, increasing market shares will increase market power. This is hardly surprising: if a monopolist enjoys maximum market power in a given market, it is only natural that, the closer any firm is to being a monopolist in that market, the more market power it will enjoy. Unfortunately, this reasoning does not by itself tell us anything about how *fast* market power increases with market share. To do this we must specify more precisely the relevant cross-price elasticities, and also the extent to which there is coordination between competitors.[3] Box 2.2 explores a special case in which the own-price firm elasticity of demand is a negative linear function of the market share, and the sensitivity of the elasticity to market share itself depends linearly on the proportionate response of competing firms to a price change. The more closely competitors are expected to match a price change, the less the own-price firm elasticity of demand declines with market share (in effect, coordination means that firms already have a great deal of market power at low market shares). The conditions for this linear case are admittedly somewhat special.[4] However, it does indicate what factors one should look for in assessing the relevance of market shares in the more general case. The most that can be claimed with reasonable confidence is that market power increases with market share, but it will do so less than proportionately if there is already significant coordination between firms in the market. And it is a consequence of the same reasoning that the degree of market power associated with any given market share varies greatly according to how much price coordination there is between competitors: the more symmetric is the anticipated response, the greater is the resulting market power at any given market share. So mergers may give rise to fears about increased market power on two grounds: first, that by increasing market shares they may increase market power, to a degree that varies according to the amount of price coordination already present between firms; and secondly, that by reducing the number of effective competitors in a market they may make price coordination itself easier to achieve.

BOX 2.2 *Market power and market share: a linear special case*

We assume that the demand for differentiated products can be derived from a CES sub-utility function for a representative consumer, following Smith and Venables (1988). Using the same notation as Box 2.1:

$$U(.) = q = (\Sigma \ a_i^{1/\beta} \ q_i^{\beta - 1/\beta})^{\beta/\beta - 1} \quad (2.2.1)$$

where β denotes the elasticity of substitution between differentiated products. This sub-utility function can be interpreted as a quantity index (q); a dual price index (p) can be derived as:

$$p = (\Sigma a_i^{1/\beta} \ p_i^{1 - \beta})^{1/1 - \beta} \quad (2.2.2)$$

Consumer demand can be derived from a two-stage budgeting procedure. We assume that the indirect utility obtained from the consumption of the differentiated good is iso-elastic:

$$V = q^{1 - \mu/(\mu - 1)} \quad (2.2.3)$$

Demand for the quantity index (q) is first obtained (using Roy's identity) as:

$$q = p^{-\mu} \quad (2.2.4)$$

and (given total expenditure on the differentiated goods) the demand for any particular differentiated good q_i is then given as:

$$q_i = p_i^{-\beta} a_i p^{\beta - \mu} \quad (2.2.5)$$

Finally, let w_i denote the average proportionate price change by competitors in response to a price change by firm i. This need not be interpreted as a direct behavioural variable; what matters is that it represents the conjecture by firm i about the extent to which, if it changed its own price, its competitors would follow suit. In these circumstances, Smith and Venables show that the absolute value of the own-price firm elasticity of demand facing firm i is given by:

$$e_i = \beta - (\beta - \mu)[w_i + (1 - w_i)s_i] \quad (2.2.6)$$

where s_i is the market share of firm i. In the benchmark case where no price response is expected from competitors (the Bertrand conjecture) this yields:

$$e_i = \beta - (\beta - \mu)s_i \qquad (2.2.7)$$

Note that, while the elasticity is linear in the market share, the sensitivity of market power to market share will vary considerably according to the elasticity of substitution across products within the industry. Since this is likely to vary from one industry to another it will make the use of market shares to approximate market power fairly sensitive to particular industry conditions.

2.2.4 *The market-wide effects of a merger*

So far we have considered the effects of a merger on market power by examining the various components of the own-price firm elasticity of demand that would be faced by the merged entity. In practice, of course, information about these components (specifically, about own- and cross-price elasticities of demand for individual products as opposed to product groupings) is often very difficult to obtain,[5] though it is becoming easier for consumer products through the use of bar-coding in retail outlets (see our discussion in section 2.4.1 below). Information about the degree of price coordination in a market is even harder to find, and must inevitably rest on a degree of guesswork. These factors together mean that in practice competition authorities usually find themselves forced to make inferences about the market power of the merged entity on the basis of the pre-merger market shares of the merging parties.

Besides the imprecise character of the relationship between market shares and market power that was discussed above, there is a further difficulty in using this procedure. This is that a merger that enhances market power may lead to a rise in price and reduction in output by the merged firm (though this may be offset by any cost reductions associated with the merger). This means that simply adding up the pre-merger market shares of the parties may lead to an overestimate of the likely post-merger market share. It also means that a merged firm's competitors will themselves be affected (usually favourably, though not always) by the merger. Indeed, Stigler (1950) argued that firms which do not participate in a merger may benefit even more than the participants. This presumption has been confirmed by the analysis of Salant *et al.* (1983). In a more general environment, Farrell and Shapiro (1990) also find that competitors can in general be expected to benefit from a merger, though not necessarily more than the participants. Nevertheless, Boyer (1992) shows that when mergers lead to lower costs for the participating firms, competing firms may have reason to fear being priced out of their markets. All these findings suggest that an analysis of the merger's overall impact on market power should not ignore market-wide effects.

Both German and US anti-trust law take market-wide aspects of merger control at least nominally into account. In German law, for instance, there is a presumption of collective dominance if five or fewer enterprises together have a market share of two-thirds or more (Heidenhain (1991)). A similar presumption is found in the Mergers Guidelines of the US Department of Justice, where mergers are assessed according to their impact on the Herfindahl–Hirschman index (HHI), which is defined as the sum of the squared market shares of the firms in the market. Values of the HHI may range from zero to 10,000 (if the market shares are measured in percentages) or from zero to one (if they are measured in fractions). The rationale for using the HHI is a simple one: if (and it is a big 'if') the market power enjoyed by any one firm is proportional to its market share, then the 'average' or market-wide price–cost margin is in turn proportional to the value of the HHI.[6] More specifically, the average margin, as a proportion of the margin that would be enjoyed by a monopolist, is equal to the HHI (when shares are measured in fractions). Consequently the absolute margin itself is given by the HHI divided by the aggregate elasticity of demand for all the products in the relevant market taken together. So if the 'relevant market' has been defined as one in which a monopolist could support a given price–cost margin (say 5%), the actual average margin can be found by simply multiplying this figure by the HHI.

To say that market-wide factors are considered through the use of collective dominance criteria or the HHI does not imply that the market-wide *results of the merger* are fully taken into account. In particular our analysis has indicated that the market share used to estimate post-merger market power should be the likely post-merger market shares, not simply the ones that prevail before the merger. As we discuss below, the US procedure makes some attempt to do this. But even if it can be done, mechanical use of criteria such as the HHI can give quite misleading results. For instance, the fact that average margins are proportional (under special circumstances) to the HHI does not mean that a merger that preserves or enhances the symmetry of market shares across competitors is more likely to be innocuous than one which creates asymmetries, even though the former will lead to lower values of the HHI. The reason is that symmetry of market shares may increase the ease of price coordination between competitors by reducing the degree of uncertainty each one faces about the cost and demand conditions facing the others; this will increase average market power even at given levels of the HHI.

It is difficult to predict with confidence the likely impact of a merger on price coordination between competing firms. For instance, symmetry may enhance coordination, as suggested above; alternatively, asymmetry may increase the ability of a single dominant firm to act as a price leader (Sleeuwagen (1986)). It might instead be argued that ease of coordination is related more to the number of firms in a market than to the disparities in market shares. The argument stems from the observation that the complexity of coordination rises with the combinatorial of the number of firms (in terms of the information flows, for instance). To the extent that a merger significantly reduces the number of major firms in a market, it might improve firms' ability to coordinate. Recent evidence by Bresnahan and Reiss (1991) suggests that industrial performance is related to the number of firms in an industry, with market power a problem only when the number of firms is five or less. One interpretation of these findings is that price coordination becomes very difficult when there is a larger number of significant market participants: consequently, concern over the impact of a merger on the probability of coordination might be warranted only when the merger is likely to leave five competitors or less.

The EC Merger Regulation does not explicitly include or exclude any presumption of the relevance of market-wide effects. It is nonetheless restricted by the definition of dominance as put forward in previous decisions of the Court of Justice, which has led the Commission to focus usually on single-firm market shares as a measure of dominance. The recent decision in the case of *Nestlé/Perrier* suggests, however, that the Regulation can be used to control oligopolistic dominance (see Chapter 3). In addition, the Commission's investigations have sometimes sought to take account of the impact of a merger on the incentives for coordination.

There is one final kind of market-wide effect that deserves explicit consideration, and this is the possibility that one merger may give rise to incentives for further mergers in the industry. In the United States, Section 7 of the Clayton Act is used to evaluate mergers. According to this legislation, a merger is considered illegal if it 'tends to create a monopoly'. This has been interpreted fairly broadly (at least initially) to the extent that potential incentives for further mergers which could arise from a particular merger under review have been considered. For instance, in the *Brown Shoe* case,[7] the merger was ruled illegal even though the market share of the merged entity did not exceed 5% because of the concern that 'if a merger achieving 5% control were approved,... (it) ... might be required to approve further merger efforts by Brown's competitors seeking similar market shares'. This reasoning has been called the 'incipiency doctrine'.

This ruling suggests that the Supreme Court was primarily concerned about legal precedence. Yet it raises the issue whether in principle a particular merger can enhance the profitability of additional mergers. It has indeed been observed that mergers typically happen in waves (see Caves (1991)). Anderson and Neven (1992) have attempted to explain such phenomena by showing that a shock to cost or demand parameters which makes one merger profitable (and does not initially affect the profitability of others) can actually trigger a merger wave. Their model implies that dynamic effects associated with a merger might be a proper concern of public policy. However, the incipiency doctrine is hardly the appropriate response. It does not link the decision to an evaluation of the actual likelihood of dynamic effects, and it fails to distinguish the point at which these dynamic effects begin to have harmful consequences. All is required is that current judgments on the dominance associated with market shares not be bound tightly to past rulings.

2.2.5 *Market power and concentration: overview*

The analysis presented above suggests that the use of concentration measures to assess the likely market power of a proposed merger may sometimes be an unavoidable consequence of the limited information available to competition authorities. Some positive relationship between market concentration and market power is to be expected – but the precise nature of the relationship will vary significantly across industries according to a number of factors including the degree of product differentiation and the scope for coordination between competitors. The simple analysis presented so far also ignores other factors such as market entry, potential competition or the existence of countervailing buyer power which may discipline the behaviour of existing firms. These factors will be discussed in section 2.3.

Scepticism about reliance on any simple relationship between concentration and market power is further reinforced by the absence of strong empirical support for such a relationship (see Schmalensee (1987b) or Fairburn and Geroski (1992)). However, it is more reasonable (especially in the light of findings such as those of Bresnahan and Reiss (1991)) to use market shares and other measures of concentration at least to identify the *absence* of market power, given that markets with significant numbers of small firms are unlikely to find price coordination easy. Mergers that do not lead to significant concentration levels can be approved quickly; high concentration levels can be used to create a presumption of market power which can then be explored in a more detailed investigation. To see what factors should be examined in such an investigation we shall need to consider more carefully the welfare costs of market power.

2.3   Why does market power matter?

2.3.1   *Trading off allocative efficiency and productive efficiency*

The familiar objection on efficiency grounds to the exercise of market power is that, by raising prices above marginal cost, it leads to allocative inefficiency. Figure 2.1 shows the diagram familiar from many economics textbooks, in which the loss of Marshallian consumer surplus due to monopoly pricing is composed partly of a transfer of profits to producers and partly of a deadweight loss. This deadweight loss can be thought of as the total benefits forgone by those consumers who value a product at more than its marginal cost of production, but whose custom a firm with market power is willing to dispense with in order to be able to charge the rest of its customers a higher price.

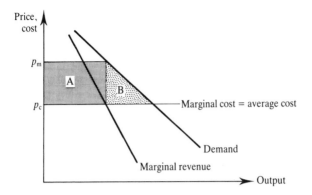

Figure 2.1 The allocative inefficiency of monopoly: p_m = monopoly price, p_c = competitive price; $p_m > p_c$; A = transfer of profits from consumers to monopolist, B = deadweight loss.

Matters become slightly more complicated once we take into account the possibility that firms may differ in their costs of production. When this is so, market power may be the undesirable consequence of a competitive advantage accruing to low-cost firms, a phenomenon which is in itself desirable because it lowers average costs of production in the industry. We can then think of the welfare consequences of market power as involving a trade-off between the losses due to allocative inefficiency and the gains accruing to increased productive efficiency. Box 2.3 explores this trade-off more precisely for the special case where market power is proportional to market share, in the spirit of the model of Williamson (1968). In this case, the overall welfare loss associated with market power in the market (the loss of consumer surplus less the increase in producer profits) is inversely proportional to the value of the Herfindahl–Hirschman index and directly proportional to the market share of the least-cost firm, which is also the largest firm. The reason for this is that, as the market share of the dominant firm increases, consumer surplus falls because prices increase (market power is exercised). At the same time, the increased market share of the least-cost firm has a beneficial impact on welfare that is reflected in the resulting increase in the HHI: the reason is simply that competition rewards efficiency. Least-cost firms have a high market share, and as the share of output produced by such firms increases, more of the lost consumer surplus translates into an increase in profits.

BOX 2.3 *A trade-off between allocative and productive efficiency*

When products are differentiated, firm's price–cost margins will not in general be proportionate to their market share. We assume instead a homogeneous good model where firms' take their competitors' output as given (subject to the caveat in footnote 4 about its lack of realism). Here the price p is uniform, and the mark-up of firm i is given by:

$$\frac{(p - c_i)}{p} = \frac{s_i}{e} \tag{2.3.1}$$

where e is the own-price aggregate elasticity of firm demand for all the firms in the market taken together (this follows from the fact that a monopolist would have a market share equal to one and a mark-up equal to the reciprocal of its own-price elasticity of firm demand).

We can multiply both sides of (2.3.1) by s_i to yield the average mark-up in the industry:

$$1 - \frac{\Sigma_i \ s_i c_i}{p} = \frac{H}{e} \tag{2.3.2}$$

where H is the value of the Herfindahl–Hirschman index for the market (defined in terms of fractions rather than percentage points).

The overall profit in the industry is then given by:

$$\Pi = \frac{QH}{e} \tag{2.3.3}$$

In a situation of perfect competition, the equilibrium price in this market would be equal to the minimum value of the marginal cost (say $c_1 = \min c_i$). The loss of consumer surplus (L) associated with oligopoly is then given by:

$$L = \int_{c_1}^{p} Q(p) \ \mathrm{d}p \tag{2.3.4}$$

where $Q(p)$ is the total output. Evaluating this integral using the equilibrium margins derived above, we obtain for a constant elasticity demand curve that:

$$L \simeq \frac{pQs_1}{e} \qquad (2.3.5)$$

so that the overall welfare loss associated with oligopoly (loss of consumer surplus minus profits) is given by:

$$W = \Pi \left(\frac{s_1}{H} - 1 \right) \qquad (2.3.6)$$

According to this formulation, the welfare loss is inversely proportional to the HHI and directly proportional to the market share of the least-cost firm, which is also the largest firm.

This analysis points out the basic terms of the trade-off between allocative and productive efficiency but falls short of explicitly characterizing the kinds of merger that would be socially desirable. Farrell and Shapiro (1990) go some way towards doing so. In their model it is assumed that only privately profitable mergers will be undertaken; it is then a sufficient condition for a merger to be socially desirable that its net external effect should be positive. This external effect is the sum of the change in consumer surplus (usually negative) and the change in competitors' profits (usually positive). They show that a privately profitable but price-increasing merger will also be socially profitable so long as the initial joint market share of the merging parties does not exceed some upper limit.[8] One advantage of the analysis is that it provides a sound justification for the use of an upper limit to the market share of the merging parties to discriminate among mergers – a practice explicit in the US merger guidelines and implicit in the implementation of the European Merger Regulation. However, the restriction of the analysis to mergers with a positive external impact effectively implies that the only gains that can be traded off against a loss of consumer surplus are increases in competitors' profits; private gains to the merging parties are not considered.[9] This leaves open the question of whether and how a negative external impact of a merger should be evaluated against any potential efficiency gains to the merging parties.

In fact, a substantial empirical literature[10] has cast significant doubt on the validity of the assumption that only mergers that can be expected to be privately profitable will be undertaken. Even share price evidence often suggests that shareholders of bidder firms will at best break even and may often lose out. More detailed long-term studies of industrial performance suggest that many mergers involve substantial management problems and frequently fail to deliver the expected benefits; at the very least, it appears that the synergy effects anticipated from mergers often fail to materialize. To the extent that privately unprofitable mergers are a systematic rather than a chance phenomenon, they suggest the importance of failures of corporate control that allow the motivation of managers to diverge from that of shareholders. Whether and to what extent public policy should be concerned to alleviate such failures of corporate control is a matter we discuss in Chapter 6. What matters for the present argument is that these empirical findings suggest it may be seriously misleading to take as given the cost structure of firms in an industry. The degree of market power enjoyed by a firm may itself have an impact on its cost levels: managers who enjoy substantial product market rents may well take advantage of these to relax their efforts to minimize costs. It is many years now since Sir John Hicks remarked (in his 1935 survey of monopoly) that 'the best of all monopoly profits is the quiet life'.

This in turn implies that it may be mistaken to see productive efficiency as a gain from market power that is traded off against allocative inefficiency. Market power may worsen rather than improve productive efficiency. And a number of arguments suggest that the costs of market power through weakened productive efficiency may be at least as important as its adverse impact on allocative efficiency.

2.3.2 *Market power and productive inefficiency*

The claim that market power may raise costs of production is based on three kinds of argument. The *first* appeals to what has been called 'rent dissipation': if a monopoly position is something which firms can spend resources to establish and defend (rather than being given to them like manna from heaven), they will in principle be willing to spend anything up to the value of the monopoly profits in order to do so. Such expenditure may take various forms: advertising, research and development, investment in excess capacity or brand proliferation in order to deter entry from rival firms, lobbying to secure government quotas or licences, to name a few. Sometimes this expenditure is in itself entirely unproductive, as when it is motivated by a competition between firms for the right to exploit some pre-existent monopoly position, such as that created by a government quota (see Krueger (1974)). In these circumstances, if the expenditure takes the form of a fixed cost, then it may be expected that as much as the whole of the rectangle representing producer profits in Figure 2.1 will be dissipated, and the social cost of monopoly power will be represented by the full amount of lost consumer surplus.[11] Sometimes, however, the monopoly position is due to consumer benefits that are at least partly created by the expenditure concerned (as in the case of research and development that results in innovations); in these circumstances it would be misleading to think of all the producer profits as being 'dissipated', since they might not exist at all in the absence of a contest to gain monopoly power. The market power that is the result of advertising represents an interesting intermediate case, with much argument over whether it represents 'wasteful' expenditure or the genuine creation of consumer benefits.

The *second* reason for thinking that market power may lead to productive inefficiency is that managers and workers who wish to extract rents from the owners of the firms for which they work can do so only if those firms themselves enjoy rents from their activities in product markets. If there are no rents from market power, firms are forced by competitive pressure to minimize costs, and firms whose managers and workers do not minimize costs will be forced out of business unless they can find philanthropists to back them.[12] Conversely, to the extent that managers and workers have a degree of control over the disposition of the fruits of market power, the presence of substantial rents creates a great temptation to inflate production costs rather than to work hard for the sole purpose of handing these rents over to the firm's owners.

Such an argument depends, of course, on the fact that shareholders find it more difficult to enforce the payment of product market rents when these are disguised in the form of high costs than when they appear in the form of audited earnings. There is nothing very surprising about this, but it does suggest that the capacity of managers and workers to take product market rents in the form of high costs will itself be limited by the effectiveness of capital market monitoring of their activities. The *third* reason for thinking that market power may raise costs, therefore, is that competition in product markets may also be important for enhancing the effectiveness of capital market competition. The ability of shareholders to ensure cost minimization will be constrained both by their costs of organizing to monitor managers (in which they face a well-known free-rider problem; see Grossman and Hart (1980)) and by the difficulty of determining to what extent fluctuations in the firm's performance are due to its economic environment rather than to the activities of its managers. Competition in product markets can help to alleviate the second difficulty, since the performance of competing firms provides yardsticks against which the performance of firms can be assessed. Invoking bad luck to justify low profits may be less convincing when there are competitors in fairly similar situations who have done significantly better. This allows some possibility for incentive schemes to be structured as 'tournaments', thereby enhancing control by shareholders.

If market power leads to high costs for either of these last two reasons, then it is typically not just fixed costs but also marginal costs of production that will be higher than under competition. This will then in turn affect prices, and could substantially increase the social costs of monopoly power. Figure 2.2 illustrates. Here it can be seen that the price set by the firm facing the downward-sloping demand curve is not only higher than the competitive level, but higher even than the level it would have set to exploit its market power if it had been minimizing costs. Compared to an outcome in which there is the same degree of market power, but costs are minimized, the result is worse for two reasons: prices are higher, and a smaller proportion of the increase in prices above the competitive level translates into profits instead of being dissipated in costs.

However, some care has to be exercised before this analysis can be used to conclude as to what extent the high costs sustained by firms with market power represent social 'waste'. Some of these high costs may represent simple transfers of rent to managers or workers and may not imply inefficient resource utilization; however, distortions in input use will often be observed at the same time. For instance, Kahn (1971) describes how technological change which occurred in the airline industry through the 1960s and early 1970s interacted with collective bargaining practices to encourage a distorted use of labour; flight crew salaries for new equipment were based on the salaries that would have been earned using the less productive older equipment. This meant that benefits from increased speed of jet equipment were partially offset by basing salaries on

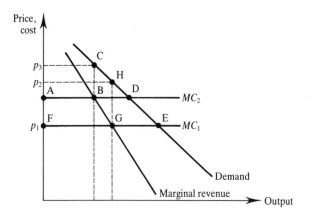

Figure 2.2 Monopoly with productive inefficiency as well as allocative inefficiency. Area GHE = deadweight loss of cost-minimizing monopoly; area ABCDEF = deadweight loss of non-cost-minimizing monopoly; area ABCDEF ≫ area GHF. Drawn assuming marginal cost equals average cost: MC_1 = marginal cost of competitive firm and of cost-minimizing monopolist, MC_2 = marginal cost of non-cost-minimizing monopolist; $MC_2 > MC_1$; p_1 = competitive price, p_2 = price of cost-minimizing monopolist, p_3 = price of non-cost-minimizing monopolist; $p_2 > p_2 > p_1$.

'pegged speed' for the aircraft (much lower than the speed planes actually flew). McGowan and Seabright (1989) provide evidence that European carriers which operated throughout the 1980s in a strongly regulated environment provided wages to their personnel which were much in excess of US levels (up to 200% for pilots), and also employed significant excess labour. Good *et al.* (1991) estimate that French carriers would have to reduce labour inputs by 23% to operate as efficiently as their US counterparts. At the same time, wages granted to the employees of French carriers were (on average) at least 50% higher than those granted by US carriers. The implication of the latter study is that rents to workers accounted for a somewhat higher proportion of the overall excess of production costs than did excessive use of labour, but that both were substantial.

In practice, it is hard to estimate empirically the extent to which production costs may be inflated due to market power. Most of the evidence relates either to the operations of utilities or to sectors in which competition has been introduced throughout the 1980s (for a survey, see Pestieau and Tulkens (1992)). Clear results emerge in at least some industries: for instance, it is found in the case of refuse collection that competition for the right to provide the service significantly enhances productive efficiency. The evidence that shareholders' monitoring of managers actually makes use of yardstick measurements provided by the presence of competing firms is, however, rather weaker (see Jensen and Murphy (1990)).

It is in the light of the insight that market power may result in inflated costs that empirical studies on the deadweight costs of monopoly power should be viewed. Most such studies have found these losses to be rather small: for instance, according to Scherer and Ross (1990), the deadweight loss attributable to monopoly pricing in the United States lies somewhere between 0.5% and 2% of GNP. It is hard to reconcile such magnitudes with the zeal of anti-trust policy – unless (as seems reasonable) the evidence of those sectors for which controlled studies have been undertaken is of wider relevance to the economy at large, and the losses in productive efficiency due to monopoly power are a significant addition to the direct deadweight costs. Ironically, monopolies that make large profits are probably to be deplored less than many of those that do not.

The insight that monopoly rents may be dissipated in high costs can also help to shed light on the significance of potential competition in diminishing the social costs of monopoly power. This is the topic of the next section.

2.3.3 *Entry and potential competition*

The theory of contestable markets (Baumol *et al.* (1988)) has changed dramatically the way in which both theorists and policy-makers view markets with a small number of competing firms. This theory has emphasized that firms may be disciplined in their market behaviour not just by their actual competitors in the market in which they operate, but also by *potential* competitors: that is, by opportunist firms who *would* set up and compete if the behaviour of firms within the market indicated the presence of rents from so doing. Such a theory could, if successful, indicate that market power may not be a serious problem even in markets where significant fixed costs of production limit the number of firms that either can or should serve the market (natural monopolies and oligopolies). The key to this reasoning lies in the distinction between *fixed* costs and *sunk* costs:

sunk costs are a special case of fixed costs of production, namely those that are not recoverable by the firm on exit from the industry. Where sunk costs of production in a market are very low, a potential entrant would be able to set up and produce in competition with existing firms; even if it were subsequently chased out again the challenge would have cost it little because it could recover most of its fixed production costs (for instance, in the form of capital equipment that kept its value on resale).

In the extreme case when sunk costs of entry to a market are zero and incumbents cannot change prices faster than entrants can set up production, the theory of contestable markets predicts that firms in a market will behave as though the market were competitive, even if they are monopolists or members of a small oligopoly. Were they not to do so, they would attract instant 'hit-and-run' entry. This theory has already made a major difference to the way in which competition authorities analyze markets: the attempt to assess barriers to entry to see whether potential competition can be relied upon as a disciplinary device has become standard practice in most jurisdictions, including the European Community. Indeed, if the extreme case of perfect contestability were thought to be empirically relevant, traditional analyses based on market shares would be completely *irrelevant*, since potential competition would be as effective as actual competition whatever the level of an incumbent firm's market share.

Unfortunately, as is well known (see Schwartz and Reynolds (1983), for example), the pure theory of contestable markets is not very robust: in particular, it relies on the assumption that entrants to a market can set up in competition with incumbents faster than the incumbents themselves can alter their prices. If this assumption does not hold, then in the presence of even very small sunk costs of entry, the presence of potential competition may have no effect at all on the behaviour of incumbent firms. Since it is unrealistic to expect sunk costs of entry ever to be precisely zero, and since in almost all industries prices can be changed more quickly than entry can be undertaken, it is therefore a matter of some importance to know whether potential competition has any significance at all as a discipline upon the behaviour of incumbent firms.

This is where the distinction between the effect of market power on profits and its effect on costs becomes important. A firm that enjoys monopoly profits but is efficiently minimizing costs has little to fear from potential entry provided it can change its prices faster than a new entrant can establish production. One that has high production costs has much more to fear, since lowering costs in response to entry by more efficient firms can be a slow and often painful business (as a number of US airlines, for example, found in the years following deregulation in 1978). Consequently, the lower are the delays and the sunk costs associated with entry and therefore the more credible is potential competition, the less willing will be the managers and workers of incumbent firms to risk enjoying the fruits of monopoly power in the form of high production costs. It may be that potential competition even raises accounting profit levels (as Morrison and Winston (1986) found for the US airline industry, for instance), since it will discipline firms' costs even more than it disciplines their prices.[13]

Consideration of the possible dependence of production costs on market power therefore vindicates at least some of the insights of contestability theory in spite of the lack of robustness of the theory in its pure form. It also suggests that in practice, potential competition should be distinguished from actual competition in the following way. Actual competition should be thought of as determining how much market power a firm currently enjoys. Potential competition should be thought of, by contrast, as affecting not how much market power it enjoys but how serious the consequences of that market power are from the point of view of economic efficiency: in particular, how much of the rents due to that market power are likely to be dissipated as high costs.

The notion of 'potential competition' has, furthermore, a somewhat broader application than just to potential entry. It can also be applied, with some modification, to the possibility that tacit collusion currently operating among firms in an oligopolistic market may break down in the future. If it does, firms who have enjoyed the fruits of that collusion in the form of high costs may be much less well placed to survive the ensuing competition than firms who have continued to keep production costs low and have instead shown high profits. The more probable is the perceived future breakdown of collusion, the harder will managers try to minimize production costs. In fact, the reduction in production costs brought about by the fear of breakdown of collusion may be interpreted as the insurance premium paid by managers to insure themselves against that future risk. And just as insurance premiums are paid in good times in return for benefits in bad times, so we should expect to see any factors that increase the probability of breakdown of collusion operate to reduce production costs (and therefore to increase reported profits) even in those circumstances in which collusion continues to be sustained. One such factor, for instance, might be the number of firms in a market: suppose that a larger number of firms increases the perceived probability that collusion will break down; then we may expect to see larger numbers of firms associated with lower production costs (and therefore, paradoxically, with higher profits in those circumstances where collusion continues to operate). Once again, potential competition has its effect not so much upon the market power enjoyed by a firm as upon the consequences of that market power for overall economic efficiency.

Finally, although considering the effect of market power on production costs provides a strong justification for investigation of the ease of entry to play a central role in the analysis of mergers, it is important that the effect of the *threat* of entry should not be confused with the effect of *actual* entry. It is not uncommon for discussion of entry by competition authorities to make little distinction between the judgment that entry is easy and therefore probable in the future, and the judgment that entry is easy and therefore that the behaviour of incumbent firms will be sufficiently restrained by the fear of it to make entry improbable in the future. Yet these two kinds of circumstance may have very different implications for efficiency. As we have indicated, the threat of entry is usually good for efficiency; actual entry may or may not be. This is no more paradoxical than the observation that the threat of imprisonment usually makes people less likely to commit crimes, while actual imprisonment typically makes them more likely to do so.

Actual entry to a market may, for the reasons we have discussed, have a beneficial impact on the degree of market power that can be exercised by the firms already in that market. But it will usually also have a cost that must be balanced against that benefit, and this consists in any duplication of the fixed costs of production already incurred by firms in the market. Note that here it is fixed costs that matter; it is irrelevant what proportion of them are sunk, since we are considering the impact of the structure of costs on the efficiency with which output is produced in the market concerned, not the extent to which the credibility of the threat of entry may be diminished by the fear of being unable to recoup capital expenditure on exit. These fixed costs may quite easily be large enough to make entry, even if profitable for the firms concerned, have a negative overall impact on efficiency within the market as a whole. Consequently, if a market analysis by a competition authority shows that entry is easy, this is not unambiguously a good thing. For example, Green and Newbery (1992) argue that the anti-competitive structure of the newly privatized electricity industry in England and Wales is likely to attract substantial new entry to the industry, which will add to excess capacity already in existence and significantly raise the industry's costs of production. In effect, members of the existing producer duopoly have no way to commit themselves credibly not to exploit their market power in the future; this makes new entry likely to be profitable (and incidentally means that the existing duopoly has no reason not to exploit its market power in the present for as long as it can). To some extent, long-term contracts can provide a means to make such a credible commitment; another way, though, would be for the industry to have been given a more competitive structure from the beginning. What this example shows is that ease of entry should not always be interpreted as mitigating the harmful effects of a merger that enhances market power. Sometimes ease of entry may exacerbate those harmful effects, especially in circumstances where the merging parties would not be able credibly to deter entry by refraining from exploiting their market power.

2.3.4 *The costs of market power: overview*

How much the exercise of market power matters will depend, as we have indicated, on a number of other features of the economy, including the mechanisms of corporate governance and control that determine the efficiency with which firms are managed. Some of these other features of the economy raise public policy issues of their own. For reasons that we shall not explicitly defend here (but that we discuss briefly in Chapter 6), we do not believe merger control should be concerned to alleviate all sources of inefficiency in the firms and the markets that are implicated in a particular merger proposal; some of these are the province of different branches of public policy, and many of them are perennial problems in the management of the firms concerned that are only incidentally relevant to the merger proposal. Mergers do, however, represent potential changes in market power with which public policy is properly concerned (as well as raising the possibility of other benefits that may offset accretions to market power). So we shall now draw on the discussion in this chapter so far to see what practical steps a merger control authority can take in the diagnosis of the likely changes in market power implied by a merger.

2.4 Methods for assessing the impact of a merger on market power

Assessing the own-price firm elasticity of demand that would be faced by a merged entity is clearly difficult, since this conditional elasticity cannot be directly observed and since, as we have discussed, it is likely to differ from the elasticity faced by the merging parties prior to the merger. Still, a reliable estimate of the elasticity faced by merging parties could go a long way towards assessing the elasticity faced by the merger. In section 2.4.1, we review some methods that can be used to estimate the elasticities faced by the merging parties. These methods require quite detailed product sales information which will often not be easily available. In such circumstances, an indirect procedure has to be employed. The procedure usually followed by merger authorities proceeds by defining a relevant market; the market share of the merged entity in that market is then estimated, and a judgment is made as to whether this market share would lead to a significant increase in market power. In some cases, explicit thresholds on market shares are used to guide the analysis, but it is understood that when actual entry or potential competition is likely to be significant, judgment will be exercised and thresholds can be revised upwards. At a very general level, this approach seems to be in line with the theoretical considerations we have presented above in so far as it tries to estimate the elasticity faced by the merged entity, using information on the relationship between market shares and market power, as well as information pertaining to particular factors which affect both the degree of market power and its likely consequences.

If the approach is fine in principle, its implementation is delicate; as we shall argue below, the procedure used to define the relevant market might matter a great deal. In addition, it is important to strike the right balance between the use of precise guidelines and the exercise of judgment. Too tight a specification of procedures could make the analysis insufficiently flexible to cope with particular cases; too discretionary an approach leaves the procedure exposed to arbitrary judgments and the risk of regulatory capture, as we discuss in Chapter 6. It is notable that the Merger Guidelines published by the US Department of Justice are significantly more detailed than the informal guidance offered by the CEC. The CEC approach is therefore potentially better tailored to particular circumstances but is also more prone to manipulation than the US approach.

2.4.1   *Direct methods*

Leaving aside the possibility of predatory pricing, if it were possible to measure the true margin between a firm's price and its minimum marginal cost of production, market power could be observed directly. Even predatory pricing is of proper concern to competition authorities only because it is likely to lead to high prices in the future (after rivals have been forced out of the market), so provided price–cost margins could be scrutinized over time they would provide all the information that was needed for the diagnosis of market power. However, the tendency we have already discussed for firms' costs to be inflated when they enjoy market power will be exacerbated if price–cost margins are used for the diagnosis: firms under investigation have a strong incentive to misrepresent their costs in order to reduce observed margins. As shown by Laffont and Tirole (1992b), external auditing of costs can help to reduce the extent of misrepresentation, but its effectiveness is limited by the verifiability of appropriate costs; it may be difficult, even for auditors, correctly to classify costs into those that would be incurred under more competitive conditions and those that would not.

Even when costs are not observable, it may still be possible to estimate econometrically the demand function faced by the firm. Such an estimation faces two major difficulties. *first*, demand and supply have to be identified. Time series (or cross-section) observations of prices and quantities represent the intersection of demand and supply, and demand has be disentangled from supply. This is commonly undertaken by specifying variables (instruments) which shift demand and cost over time. Among variables which shift demand, prime candidates are the prices of competing products. This leads us to the second difficulty, namely that the number of substitute products that might have to be introduced may be quite large. This will imply that the number of observations required to perform the estimation may become unrealistic.

These problems are serious, but not overwhelming. For instance, Hausman *et al.* (1992) provide an estimate of the demand faced by particular brands of beers. They can address the problem of identification by exploiting variations of costs across cities. They alleviate the problems associated with the number of competing products (more than 40 in the US beer market) by using a multi-stage estimation: they first estimate the demand for beer, then demand for different segments and finally the demand for particular products within each segment. By combining estimates performed at the three levels, they can derive the own-price elasticity faced by each product as well as the cross-price elasticities.

The elasticity faced by a merger and the change in price that will ensue can then be directly inferred. Since all cross-price derivatives are estimated, the elasticity faced by any combination of existing products, and therefore its potential market power, can be calculated, using the procedure we discussed in section 2.2.2. These estimates still assume that cross-price elasticities will not change as a result of the merger; some assumption will also need to be made about whether and how much the behaviour of competitors will be affected. Still, all the various indirect methods reviewed below suffer from the same shortcoming, and relative to these methods, the direct estimation of market power when feasible is clearly greatly to be preferred.

This kind of estimation is admittedly unusual. It has become possible only recently, since large data sets became available owing to computerized billing techniques in supermarkets and department stores. It uses fairly sophisticated econometric techniques. Yet it indicates that at least for some products, a direct estimate of elasticities is feasible at reasonable cost.

2.4.2   *Market definition*

2.4.2.1 *General issues*

Indirect approaches to the assessment of market power typically proceed via the definition of a 'relevant market'. In principle, a relevant market is defined as the narrowest market to which the merging parties belong and in which a hypothetical monopolist or a group of perfectly coordinating oligopolists could exert some given degree of market power; we have discussed how this is related to the decomposition of the own-price firm elasticity in section 2.2.2 above. In practice, it is defined as the narrowest market such that a given rise in prices above some benchmark level would just be profitable. Market share and other data are then used to judge how closely the behaviour of the merging parties after the merger might be expected to approximate the behaviour of the hypothetical monopolist.

The ability of a hypothetical monopolist within the relevant market to raise prices will be limited by: the tendency of customers to stop buying that monopolist's products even if the prices of other products remain unchanged (demand substitution); and any indirect effect due to changes in the pricing behaviour of firms supplying competing products (supply substitution). When considering supply substitution it will be important to distinguish changes in the pricing of existing products (which must, by definition, be outside the relevant anti-trust market), and any decision by competing firms to produce new products as a direct consequence of the increase in price. Such new products will often be *inside* the relevant market, since it is by making them close substitutes for the products whose price has risen that competitors are most likely to be able to profit from the price rise; in other words, they will involve market entry. Although in our section on market entry in 2.3.3 we argued that for most purposes entry should be thought of as determining not the level of market power but its consequences for social welfare, there may be circumstances in which competitors in neighbouring markets can begin production of products within the relevant market sufficiently quickly that their presence acts to constrain the monopolist's pricing behaviour in a way that is practically indistinguishable from ordinary supply substitution. We shall therefore distinguish between supply substitution to new products and medium-term entry according to whether the production of new products can be undertaken speedily and with minimal sunk costs. Supply substitution to new products is indeed relevant to the calculation of the *extent* of market power; medium-term entry, we have already argued, is more useful for casting light on the *consequences* of such market power.

We can summarize, then, the reduction in demand for a hypothetical monopolist's products in response to a projected price increase as having three components:

Reduction in demand for products of hypothetical monopoly	=	Demand substitution	+	Supply substitution to existing products outside the relevant market	+	Supply substitution to new products

Where, then, does the use of a particular margin (such as 5%) come in? Theoretically, the ideal procedure is the one we outlined in section 2.2.2 (point 5): one needs to hypothesize a sufficient price rise (which need not be 5% or indeed any particular number) to allow one to estimate the own-price firm elasticity of demand under progressively broader assumptions about the number of products that firm controls. The 5% margin is then used to determine the threshold elasticity at which the procedure is halted (namely, at the reciprocal of 5%). This procedure has the virtue that it does not require us to answer the question: 'raise prices 5% above what level?', since the 5% figure enters in at the stage of determining the threshold elasticity rather than for choosing the hypothetical price rise. It has two disadvantages, however: it relies on evidence (or guesswork) about point elasticities of demand for each progressively broader product definition, and it fails to take into account the possibility that some components of both demand and supply substitution (especially the production of new products) may not vary continuously with the price rise but may be triggered discontinuously once the price rise reaches a certain level. In practice, therefore, the relevant thought experiment is to see what is the narrowest market definition such that a price rise of 5% above the estimated competitive price is just profitable. Note that this will not necessarily give the same answer as the ideal procedure: for example, a 5% price rise might be just profitable, but a 2% price rise might be the *profit-maximizing* price rise. Nevertheless, for practical purposes it seems a reasonable approximation.

It is important, however, to emphasize once again that all three components of the reduction in demand for the hypothetical monopolist's products are potentially relevant to the assessment of the relevant market. Any procedure that ignores any of these components is liable to be biased. If the omitted components are positive in sign (because competitors' price responses are aggressive, for instance) the bias will lead to underestimating the own-price firm elasticity of demand, and consequently *over*estimating the degree of market power that the hypothetical monopolist would actually enjoy. It will therefore bias the procedure towards unnecessarily narrow market definitions. The opposite is true for omission of components with negative sign (due to accommodating price responses by competitors, for instance). Consideration of these sources of bias is important because, as we now discuss, both the US and the European procedures ignore some of these components.

2.4.2.2 *The US procedure*

The market definition procedure embodied in the Merger Guidelines of the US Department of Justice (1992) focuses on two particular dimensions of definition: product market and geographic market. A relevant market is defined as the narrowest combination of a set of products and a geographic area such that if all the production capacity in that product set that is located within the geographic area were owned by a single firm (a 'hypothetical monopolist'), that firm could profitably raise price by at least some percentage (usually 5%) above some benchmark price (usually the pre-merger price) for a significant non-transitory period of time.

Market definition in the US procedure takes into account solely demand substitution. Supply substitution does play a part in the procedure, but not at the market definition stage. It comes in when the authorities identify the firms whose participation in the relevant market needs to be taken into account – in other words, for the calculation of the turnover in the market and consequently the market share that can be attributed to the merged parties. Taking supply substitution into account for calculating market shares has a sound theoretical rationale. We emphasized that the appropriate market share information to use was the likely post-merger share of the merged entity, and that this would often be lower than the sum of the parties pre-merger market shares, because of both demand and supply substitution. The appropriate estimate of post-merger market shares should indeed therefore be based upon projections of shares that take into account such substitution. However, this argument applies to a market that has been correctly defined as the narrowest market in which a hypothetical monopolist could actually exercise market power, and supply substitution affects (as we have shown) the ability of the hypothetical monopolist to do so in a way that the market definition should take into account. In other words, estimating supply substitution to calculate likely post-merger market shares is not an alternative to using supply substitution at the market definition stage: supply substitution should be taken into account *at both points*.

To do so does not involve double counting, as the following simple example shows. Suppose the relevant market defined using demand substitution alone is 'winter shoes'. Demand substitution into the neighbouring product ('winter boots') would not on its own render a 5% price rise unprofitable, but suppose an aggressive price response from the producers of winter boots can be expected which would force producers of winter shoes to price competitively. If the relevant market is defined as winter shoes, calculation of the post-merger market shares will take into account any price response by existing winter shoe producers who are not party to the merger, as well as any rapid entry by winter boot producers into winter shoe production. But it will not take into account supply substitution due to aggressive pricing of winter boots, which will be deemed irrelevant since the latter have been excluded from the relevant market. Accordingly, the definition will wrongly suggest that a hypothetical monopoly producer of winter shoes alone could exercise market power. Defining the market as 'winter footwear', by contrast, will at least ensure that a market has been identified in which market power could in principle be exercised. The supply substitution taken into account in market definition will in this case include only substitution from outside the footwear market altogether, which we can assume would be unimportant. The likely behaviour of winter boot producers, by contrast, is now an instance of supply substitution *within* the market and is indeed relevant to the assessment of dominance that could be exercised by the merged firm.

Until the US Guidelines were revised in April 1992, there was a second potential source of bias in the US procedure, due to the use of pre-merger prices as the benchmark price for the 5% hypothetical increase. Such a procedure could introduce a bias in favour of wide market definitions when the merging parties are either already large or participants in a collusive oligopoly. In such circumstances prevailing prices would already reflect margins embodying considerable market power, and the correct market (as determined by a competitive benchmark) might fail the 5% test simply because the firms within it were already charging margins as high as a monopolist would wish to charge. For instance, in the well-known *Cellophane* case,[14] the US Supreme Court held that Du Pont did not have significant market power. This decision has been criticized[15] on the following grounds: Du Pont was initially charging high prices (and margins), having a high market share in the cellophane market itself. In assessing the relevant market, the Court included a number of potential substitutes, which were only substitutes because the price of cellophane was very high. The market definition was thus rather large, Du Pont's market shares fell below appropriate thresholds and no violation of the Sherman Act was found.

The recent revision of the US Merger Guidelines has stated that prevailing prices should still be used unless pre-merger circumstances are strongly suggestive of coordinated interaction, when a price more reflective of the competitive price will be estimated. Accordingly, the bias identified above could very well disappear under the new guidelines; however, it remains to be seen how in practice competitive price benchmarks will be determined.

Some have argued (White (1987)) that using pre-merger rather than competitive prices as a benchmark is appropriate because merger control is concerned only with any worsening of current performance. This view depends on the argument that mergers do no damage providing they occur between parties who are already colluding to sufficient effect. Such an argument might be shortsighted (see Schmalensee (1987a)): for the sake of illustration, consider some duopolists who at present collude perfectly in the market for salt. The current procedure might lead one to consider seasoning as the relevant market, and consequently to approve a merger between them. A potentially unstable duopoly where the exercise of market power depends on collusion would as a result be replaced by a solid monopoly.

2.4.2.3   *The European Commission's procedures*

The European Commission does not codify its procedures in guidelines like those of the US Department of Justice (DOJ). Its procedures must consequently be inferred from its actual decisions, as well as from its annual reports on competition policy which provide something of a background to those decisions. In Chapter 3 we attempt to use decisions under the Merger Regulation to infer the implicit procedures in this way. Here we give a brief characterization of the implicit EC procedures, based not only on our own inferences but on the work of Fishwick (1989) and Fishwick and Denison (1992), who have analyzed the Commission's practice in investigations under Articles 85 and 86 of the Treaty of Rome.

The Commission does not use a single stated definition of the relevant market. The relevant market is broadly defined as 'those products which are regarded as interchangeable or substitutable by the consumer, by reason of the products' characteristics and their intended use' (CEC (1992), p. 378). This definition is close in spirit to that of the DOJ but is rather less precise; it also emphasizes product characteristics and their intended use in the practical assessment of substitutability.

According to Fishwick and Denison (1992), the European practice in market definition is based entirely on demand substitution. Our own analysis in Chapter 3 below suggests that the practice is not entirely consistent, but supply substitution is certainly not always or even usually considered at the market definition stage. Furthermore, unlike in the US case, supply substitution is not used, as far as we can tell, in the calculation of post-merger market shares, which appear to be based on the current turnover of participants in the market rather than projected post-merger turnover; it seems to be used rather as a kind of qualitative adjustment to any judgment that may be made on the basis of market shares alone.

The European practice is also significantly less explicit about the degree of market power implicit in any particular market definition. While there is nothing sacrosanct about 5% or indeed any other number, the choice of a particular margin helps in the US procedure to ensure that the thought experiments are carried out in a way that is reasonably consistent between one case and another.

An important difference between the European and the US procedure is that, under the European procedure, product and geographical markets appear to be defined sequentially rather than simultaneously. The definition of the relevant market in the US guidelines makes it fairly clear that the product market and geographic market are such that, taken together, they satisfy the 5% rule. This interpretation is supported by Willig (1991), who writes that the processes of product and geographic market delineation are carried out 'simultaneously, in principle'. The extent to which this procedure is adhered to in practice is somewhat less clear; for instance, the Merger Guidelines do at times refer to one dimension independently of the other (p.16, for example). But whether product and geographic dimensions are determined simultaneously or sequentially matters a great deal: a sequential treatment (such as that employed by the Commission) might lead to an excessively narrow market definition.

Why should this be? Consider, for example, a sequential procedure such that the product market and geographic market definitions *individually* just satisfy the 5% rule. This means that a 5% rise in the price of the defined product in all geographic regions would lead to substitution away from the product *towards other products outside the defined product market* that was just insufficient to render the price rise unprofitable. Likewise, a 5% rise in the price of all products in the geographic market would lead to substitution *towards other locations outside the defined geographic market* that was just insufficient to render the price rise unprofitable. However, if the 5% price rise had taken place just for the product and geographic markets concerned, there would have been substitution towards *both* other products *and* other locations simultaneously. Unless by sheer coincidence the customers who would have substituted away towards other products were exactly the same as those who would have substituted away towards other locations, the total demand substitution towards both other products and other locations will exceed that in either dimension separately. So a 5% price that was just profitable under the sequential procedure will no longer be profitable under the simultaneous procedure. At the extreme, if *none* of the customers who would have substituted towards other products were the same as those who would have substituted towards other locations, the total substitution under the sequential procedure would be only half that under the simultaneous procedure. Then the estimated elasticity of demand faced by the merging parties would be only half the true value, leading to a market definition that was much too narrow.

In practice the extent of the bias will depend on the extent to which the willingness to trade off price and product characteristics is likely to be correlated (across the population of consumers) with the willingness to trade off price and location. If it is found that the consumers with particular tastes for product characteristics are concentrated geographically, the overestimate will tend to be large. For instance, consider the market definition for a quality item sold by a firm located in Rome. One might argue that consumers in the north of Italy attach a relatively high value to quality and accordingly are unlikely to switch easily to lower-quality items as prices are increased. Keeping locations constant, the consumers who switch away to lower-quality products will be mainly Southerners. Keeping products constant, the consumers who will switch away will be mainly Northerners. The resulting market definition might thus be excessively narrow.

We have noted that the US procedure involves a potential source of bias in its failure to take supply substitution into account at the market definition stage. The direction in which this will bias market definition depends on how likely competitors are to react accommodatingly: if aggressive supply substitution is to be expected the procedure would be biased towards excessively narrow markets. The European procedure involves the same source of bias, as well as two others. First, it compounds the neglect of supply substitution by not considering it in the estimation of post-merger market shares in the manner in which this is done in the United States. Secondly, by delineating product and geographic markets sequentially rather than simultaneously it risks defining markets excessively narrowly. The extent to which this is borne out by an examination of actual decisions will be explored in Chapter 3.

2.4.2.4 *Sources of relevant information*

We have noted also that the CEC's procedures are less precise than those of the US federal authorities. Complete precision is of course unattainable, but there are ways in which precision can be improved. We consider briefly two such ways: econometric estimates of demand for product groups, and customer surveys.

In principle, the demand faced by a hypothetical monopolist controlling a group of products that is a candidate for being the relevant market can be assessed using econometric techniques (see Scheffman and Spiller (1987)). One can estimate a relationship between the quantity sold in the candidate market, a price index for the products in the market, and the prices of substitute products outside the candidate market. Since all these prices are determined simultaneously, they need to be estimated by the technique of instrumental variables (as in our discussion of direct methods in section 2.4.1). The price in the candidate market can be instrumented by some proxy for marginal cost, whereas variables which shift the demand of competing products can be used for their prices.

The result of this estimation does not, however, provide a true estimate of the own-price firm elasticity of demand that would be faced by a hypothetical monopolist in the candidate market. The data on which the estimation is performed has been generated in an environment where firms in the candidate market were competing against one another. The elasticity estimated from this data may be quite different from that of the residual demand that a dominant firm would face for at least two reasons. First, the reactions of competitors outside the candidate market may be more accommodating towards a dominant firm than towards a collection of competitors. This will reduce the elasticity faced by a monopolist relative to that estimated econometrically. Secondly, a dominant firm might raise prices and reduce output. This will reinforce the bias towards overestimating the elasticity which would be faced by a monopolist. As a consequence, the estimated monopoly margin (for any market) will be lower than the true margin, and the market definition will be biased in favour of large markets. The procedure will thus tend to underestimate market share and to allow too many mergers. However, it is in principle possible to avoid such biases by adjusting the estimated elasticity for the difference in the market share at the sample mean and that of a monopolist, and by considering a differential response on behalf of firms outside the candidate market.[16]

Even if estimates of market demand curves should be interpreted cautiously, and should possibly be corrected in a systematic way, they still provide a reasonable first approximation of the market power that a dominant firm would enjoy – a very useful one in the absence of other systematic methods. The data requirements for such econometric procedures should not be exaggerated; indeed, the necessary information should be available to most companies as part of the routine activities of market monitoring. The econometric techniques involved are also very common and far less sophisticated than those used in the direct estimations of market power discussed in section 2.4.1.

When econometric techniques to estimate residual demand cannot be used, market definition can draw on customer surveys. In principle such surveys should attempt to assess both the reaction of customers and the reactions of firms outside the candidate market to a potential price increase. The reports of respondents to surveys cannot necessarily be taken at face value, of course: potential competitors might have a vested interest in trying to make sure that the merger is allowed if they believe they will profit thereby; accordingly, they might exaggerate the aggressiveness of their potential reply in order to guarantee that a wide market will be chosen. Conversely, if they felt threatened by the merger they might underreport their own willingness to react aggressively. Customers are likely to share this tendency for underreporting when asked about the extent to which they would switch to an alternative product in response to a price increase. They may, however, be less aware of the fact that their answer might affect the outcome of the merger review (at least as far as consumer products are concerned).

The design of consumer surveys may also matter. Consumers may find it harder to assess the extent to which their consumption would fall in response to a price increase, in the absence of clearly stated alternatives. They may find it easier to imagine the extent to which they would substitute into other named products, so that the survey may appropriately specify these alternatives. But when the number of potential substitutes is large, it may be difficult to specify a manageable list, without knowing roughly the appropriate market definition in the first place. Nevertheless, these difficulties should not be exaggerated. Surveys may be particularly valuable as a means of choosing between a short list of alternative market definitions that has already been drawn up on more qualitative grounds.

Short of consumer surveys, market definition may rely simply on product characteristics. This is the approach adopted by the CEC in most cases. By comparison with the alternatives discussed above, it relies solely on judgment to infer elasticities, and not on observed or reported behaviour by customers and competitors.

2.4.3   *Assessing dominance*

The extent to which various measures of concentration reflect potential dominance was discussed in sections 2.2.3 and 2.2.4. We emphasized that some link between concentration and market power is to be expected but that a number of factors, including the degree of product differentiation and the expected response of competitors, will affect this relationship; we also mentioned that additional considerations like the ease of actual and potential entry should be taken into account. The main conclusion of this analysis is that low levels of market share and concentration are a fairly reliable guide to the *absence* of market power; high levels are best seen as prima-facie evidence of market power that consideration of other factors can modify or refine. In what follows, we review the use of concentration measures by the US authorities and the CEC and discuss in more detail additional considerations that can be taken into account when measured concentration is large.

2.4.3.1 *Measures of concentration*

The US Merger Guidelines take as their measure of concentration the Herfindahl–Hirschman index (HHI). Because it is based on squared market shares, the HHI assumes that in a market with asymmetric firms competition will be weaker than when firms are equally sized. The Guidelines establish three classification thresholds. First, where the post-merger HHI is below 1,000, the merger will 'ordinarily' be approved. Secondly, a post-merger HHI between 1,000 and 1,800 means the market is 'moderately concentrated'. Within this region, an increase in the HHI of less than 100 points is a sufficient condition for the merger to be approved, whilst one of more than 100 points raises 'significant competitive concerns'. Thirdly, a post-merger HHI greater than 1,800 means the market is 'highly concentrated'. Within this region, an increase in HHI of less than 50 points is a sufficient condition for the merger to be approved; one of more than 50 points raises 'significant competitive concerns'; and one of more than 100 points is 'likely to create or enhance market power'.

Thus the US Guidelines lay down with reasonable precision the factors relevant to the assessment of a horizontal merger. In particular, the classification of HHI thresholds appears to give the authorities little discretion in the assessment process, although the Guidelines themselves state that 'market share and concentration data provide only the starting point for analyzing the competitive impact of a merger'. However, our discussion so far has implied that market definition will often be subject to a number of weaknesses. Relevant markets will often be imprecisely defined, and it would be inappropriate to attach too much weight to the apparent precision of concentration measures and concentration thresholds. It is interesting, therefore, to wonder how closely decisions by the US authorities to challenge mergers do in practice reflect the wording of the Guidelines. Evidence on this question is provided by Coate and McChesney (1992).

With a sample of 70 horizontal mergers investigated between 1982 and 1987, Coate and McChesney find that in many respects the Merger Guidelines are not applied as written. This is especially true of concentration, where, although low HHIs are indeed sufficient for a merger to be approved, high HHIs are far from sufficient for a merger to be challenged. For example, of the 49 mergers in their sample with post-merger HHIs above 1,800 and increases above 100, only 22 were challenged, whereas the Guidelines imply that all such mergers will be challenged in the absence of strong mitigating factors. Indeed, of the 13 mergers with post-merger HHIs greater than 3,000 and increases above 1,000, only 6 were challenged. This evidence suggests that the US anti-trust authorities have used concentration measures mainly to identify the absence of potential market power; as a screening mechanism, in other words, rather than a decision rule. This practice is consistent with the theoretical analysis presented in section 5.2, provided that the additional factors used to reach decisions on mergers with high measures of concentration have been applied systematically. However, the fact that only 6 of the 13 most concentrative mergers were challenged may indicate that even the role of concentration in constituting prima-facie evidence of market power has been rather weak.

The CEC uses the market share of the merging parties as its indicator of concentration. This reflects the view that the Merger Regulation (until the recent decision on *Nestlé/Perrier*) does not explicitly allow for the possibility of oligopolistic dominance. Like the US authorities, the CEC has applied its measures of concentration in a very flexible and discretionary way; we discuss this more fully in Chapter 3.

2.4.3.2 *Entry and contestability*

The first additional factor which is taken into account by the US and European anti-trust authorities to assess whether high concentration may lead to the exercise of market power is the strength of entry and potential competition. The US Merger Guidelines define entry to be 'easy' if it would be: timely (implying committed entry within two years of a price increase); likely (implying a sufficiently high expected profitability of entry); and sufficient (to return prices to pre-merger levels). Note that sufficiency is not defined in terms of returning prices to competitive levels, just to pre-merger levels. Basing entry analysis on this definition, therefore, might lead to market power being underestimated in just the same way as it might have been under the definition of a market given in former versions of the Guidelines, where the pre-merger prices rather than competitive prices were the baseline (see section 2.4.2.2). The Guidelines state that where entry is easy, the merger 'raises no antitrust concern and ordinarily requires no further analysis'. Conversely, non-easy entry is a necessary condition for a firm to be able to exercise market power.

In practice, it seems that the assessment of entry has been particularly important. A multivariate analysis performed by Coate and McChesney (1992) reveals that the magnitude of entry barriers has been far more important than concentration in explaining merger decisions.

Unfortunately, existing theories offer little guidance to assess the definition of ease of entry used by the DOJ. Schmalensee (1987b, p. 57) offers the conjecture that actual cases where entry is 'easy', as defined by the DOJ, are very rare indeed. He argues that, since planning and executing entry in many industries can take well over two years, a test period longer than two years may be appropriate. An issue he does not consider, but which may be of importance, is that the effect of a given entry lag on the behaviour of incumbent firms may vary greatly according to the nature of the product in question. For perishable consumer goods, even a short entry lag may allow incumbents to exploit significant market power; for durables or investment goods, buyers may be able to defer purchases if they anticipate that new entry is likely to materialize in the future. In the aerospace industry, for example, entry lags are typically long (of the order of five to ten years). But prices are often determined several years ahead, so that it can take a long time for an announced price rise to come into effect; and in the meantime buyers have the opportunity to investigate alternative sources of future supply, and if necessary, to defer equipment purchases to take advantage of them. What this suggests is that, since the importance of entry lags varies from industry to industry, there may be benefits in surveys of customers to determine their importance, alongside more straightforward information about elasticities of demand.

Barriers to entry can be defined as the level of pure profits that can be maintained in an industry without attracting new entry. In principle, one can distinguish natural from strategic barriers to entry. Natural barriers arise from scale and scope economies (which may imply sunk costs) or from superior knowledge (accumulated over time). Strategic barriers are set up by incumbents to deter potential entrants, and a variety of strategies have been identified theoretically

– including the maintenance of excess capacity, excessive investments in advertising to accumulate goodwill, brand proliferation, product choices and pre-emptive patenting. There is also some empirical evidence from surveys that firms are using these strategies. Yet it is very hard, for any of these kinds of entry barrier, to undertake reliable diagnosis and measurement based on the observable behaviour of firms. In the absence of reliable procedures of diagnosis, merger control based on analysis of entry barriers may be unduly swayed by rumour and guesswork.

Recent work in industrial organization nevertheless provides some encouragement. For instance, Geroski (1991) presents a model for estimating the height of entry barriers into a given market. He applies this model to 95 three-digit UK Minimum List Heading industries in 1983 and 1984. This approach seems to be potentially very useful for merger policy. However, its usefulness is limited by the data available. If a relevant market happens to coincide with a UK three-digit industry classification, then the approach is clearly helpful. Where the data does not conform to the defined product and geographical market, the approach is of more limited use.

Among other factors used to assess dominance, the US and EC anti-trust authorities also consider the effects of a merger on the likelihood of tacit and express collusion. A merger may enable collusion by facilitating coordinated interaction between the firms involved to raise prices. In an approach that clearly springs from recent game-theoretic literature, the DOJ examines the extent to which post-merger market conditions are conducive to reaching terms of coordination between firms, detecting deviations from those terms, and punishing such deviations. According to Coate and McChesney (1992), these considerations have had a significant influence on merger decisions. But here again, even if economic theory offers some guidance as to the factors that facilitate collusion, it is hard to devise appropriate empirical tests for their presence. This problem is not just one of testing a theory, but runs up against a deeper obstacle, which is the vulnerability of all tests for the presence of collusive behaviour to the knowledge by firms that they are being used. As soon as firms learned that a particular test was being applied, it would be simple and virtually costless for them to change the nature of their collusion to escape that test. Perhaps the most that can be said is that merger control is unlikely ever to be able to do much to detect actual tacit collusion – but that it may and should make substantial progress in understanding the objective market circumstances that make tacit collusion easier to sustain.

2.4.3.3   *Efficiency considerations*

Interestingly, early merger decisions in the United States included an 'efficiency offence' rather than an 'efficiency defence'. For instance, in the *Brown Shoe* case,[17] the court treated potential efficiency benefits of the merger as a rationale for blocking it (Salop (1987)). A potential efficiency offence can also be found in the CEC decision on *AT&T/NCR* (see Chapter 3).

Recent versions of the US Guidelines do, however, explicitly allow for efficiency considerations. According to the 1992 Guidelines, the Department of Justice considers possible internal efficiency gains (cost savings) that could be realized only through merger (and not, for example, simply through expansion of plant capacity). It also emphasizes efficiencies resulting from technical rationalization: for instance, those associated with economies of scale, better integration of production facilities, plant specialization or lower transport costs. It is rather more sceptical about claimed efficiencies resulting from reduction in general selling, administrative and overhead expenses, on the ground that those are harder to demonstrate. The Guidelines also explicitly recognize a possible trade-off between allocative and productive efficiency in stating that expected net efficiencies must be the greater, the more significant is the potential for the exercise of market power.

Whether the CEC Merger Regulation allows for some form of efficiency defence is still somewhat debatable. According to Jacquemin (1990), the wording of the Regulation excludes any such defence; it provides for 'the development of technical and economic progress provided that it is to consumers' advantage and does not form an obstacle to competition'. This wording is somewhat odd, since it suggests that the efficiency defence can be used only when there is no conflict between efficiency and competition; that is, when an efficiency defence is unnecessary. Yet according to Siragusa and Subiotto (1991), this interpretation is so far untested.[18] As indicated in Chapter 3, efficiency arguments have been used very few times so far – and then somewhat inconclusively. For instance, in the

Aerospatiale/Alenia/de Havilland case they were dismissed on the grounds that the alleged benefits were small, and not that they were irrelevant.

2.4.4   *Assessment methods: overview*

We have discussed at some length a number of practical methods by which competition authorities can and do attempt to assess the likely impact of a proposed merger on the potential for the exercise of market power. We have evaluated the actual methods used by the US federal authorities and the European Commission and have identified a number of biases and shortcomings in these procedures, as well as areas in which there is considerable uncertainty about what it is feasible and appropriate for them to do. One conclusion that must emerge from this discussion is that the margin of uncertainty surrounding merger analysis is bound to remain substantial. Competition authorities must therefore take into account the probability that in their evaluation of merger proposals they will make many mistakes. Improved procedures can help to reduce the likelihood of mistakes, but cannot eliminate them. And improved procedures may themselves incur costs, such as the delay they impose on the implementation of merger proposals, as well as the direct costs of implementing more complex forms of investigation.

It is sometimes tempting to seek refuge in the view that merger control is necessarily a quick and dirty process, and not to worry unduly about trying to improve it so long as its basic philosophy appears sound. That is not our view. It is possible to think carefully about those improvements to procedure that are worth making, and those that are not. But before we can do so we need to develop a clearer sense of the costs that merger control imposes, so that we can trade off the benefits of procedural improvements against any increases in those costs. This is the topic of the last section of this chapter.

2.5   The implementation of procedures

The design of a competition policy includes at least three components: a framework for analysis, a set of procedures that allows decisions to be based on this analysis, and an institutional framework within which such a set of procedures can be credibly implemented. The first of these three components, namely the framework of analysis, has been discussed in sections 2.2 to 2.4. The objective of the present section is to provide some insight into the design of decision procedures, on the assumption that the institutional framework allows the authorities to commit themselves credibly to these procedures. Difficulties of commitment, and the larger bargaining problem between firms and the authorities (of which commitment is only one aspect) will be discussed in Chapters 4 to 7.

There is a common perception, supported by our survey of firms (reported in Chapter 4), that delays in the process of investigation and decision are highly undesirable from the perspective of potential merging partners, and that the Merger Task Force has handled cases with impressive speed. In addition, from the coming into force of the Merger Regulation, it was taken for granted that effective merger investigations would require more plentiful resources than had previously been available to the competition services within the Commission. Accordingly, the distribution of resources within the Competition Directorate has been somewhat tilted in favour of the Merger Task Force.

In what follows, we shall consider how to weigh the relative merits of the speed and the reliability of investigation procedures. Before doing so, we briefly discuss what level of resources a competition agency should command.

2.5.1 *The resources of a competition agency*

The most important observation to make concerning the resources of a competition agency is that these constitute a very small fraction of the potential costs of overall competition policy. An investigation into a merger case may occupy no more than three or four rapporteurs, and there is little evidence that increasing this number would result in significantly better analysis. More importantly, significant resources in the merging firms may be required to find and analyze information, respond to questions and anticipate the reactions of the merger authorities; a large multinational firm responding to a 'second request' for information from the US

Department of Justice might easily need to use the services of around 150 paralegal staff worldwide.[19] But if, as seems reasonable, a significant proportion of this information is what the firm would itself have needed to obtain and process before deciding whether to undertake a merger, then the incremental costs of a request for information may be relatively small. Much the most important cost of a merger investigation is the delay it imposes on the managerial changes than can be implemented in the merging firms: even if the benefits of a merger are likely to amount to no more than 2% of turnover, postponing these for three months for an investigation would cost ECU 25 million for the smallest transactions covered by the EC's merger regulation. It follows that resources spent enabling the agency to undertake investigations quickly with no loss of analytical quality could yield net gains of at least ECU 8 million per month of investigation time saved; such a sum can buy quite a few person-hours of time.

2.5.2   *The speed of investigation*

A more difficult judgment concerns the degree to which reductions in the quality of analysis can be tolerated in order to speed up investigations. There are two types of risk when the quality of analysis is reduced: first, that undesirable mergers will be wrongly allowed, and secondly, that desirable mergers will be wrongly prevented. In Appendix 2.1 at the end of this chapter we develop a simple algebraic model to explore the trade-off between these two types of risk. First of all, we consider the possibility that faster investigations simply reduce the accuracy with which mergers are classified. If the accuracy with which desirable mergers are approved and undesirable mergers are blocked deteriorates to the same extent, the conclusion is (to us at least) very striking: for plausible values of the parameters it takes a deterioration in the accuracy of merger analysis of *less than one percentage point* to offset increases in speed of investigation of the order of a month or so. The intuition behind this result is rather simple: the costs of a month's delay are related to the failure of the benefits of a good merger to be realized during that delay (and are therefore, at plausible real discount rates, less than a percentage point of the total discounted benefits of the merger); they may therefore be offset by a deterioration of less than a percentage point in the probability of classifying the merger correctly, failure to do so incurring a cost equal to the whole discounted benefit of the merger (analogous remarks apply to bad mergers). Even if it is assumed that faster procedures do not reduce the probability of correctly classifying good mergers but merely increase the risk that bad mergers will be rushed through, gains of a month or so in investigation time can still be offset by deteriorations in accuracy of a few percentage points.

The model in this form is unnecessarily simplistic, and we go on to extend it in a number of ways, in particular to take account of the possibility that the characteristics of merger proposals put forward for review are not independent of the process of scrutiny, but will themselves vary according to the rigour of the investigation firms expect to undergo. The results serve to strengthen our conclusion, namely that improvements in the accuracy of procedures of the order of a few percentage points are well worth achieving if they extend the process of merger control by no more than a month or two. This conclusion contrasts very strongly with the common tendency of firms to argue that it would be intolerable for merger control procedures to take any longer than they currently do, and that therefore any reforms that might slightly lengthen the process should be ruled out of court as impractical (we have received this reaction in some quarters in response to our call for greater use of consumer surveys, for example). In our view, such arguments reflect a failure of many firms to be convinced of the need for merger control at all, rather than an objective appreciation of how the job of merger control can best be performed.[20]

Nevertheless, it is clearly essential to examine the operation of the Merger Regulation from the point of view of firms as well as from the point of view of the competition authorities. Such a perspective can tell us two things: first, what firms perceive to be the strengths and weaknesses of the existing procedure, and secondly, what effect the presence of the Merger Regulation has on the behaviour and the business strategies of these firms. This task will be undertaken in Chapter 4. First, however, we must examine the decisions of the CEC since the coming into force of the Regulation in the light of our discussions of the general principles of merger analysis. This is the task of Chapter 3.

Appendix 2.1   Speed versus accuracy in merger control: a simple model

Let there be two types of merger, those with positive social value V and those with negative social value $-W$. For the time being, let us assume that the population of mergers is exogenous so that good and bad mergers occur respectively in proportions q and $(1-q)$; but the agency can identify mergers as belonging to either category only with a certain probability. The accuracy of the procedure is such that good mergers are approved with probability p_1 and bad mergers with probability p_2; we shall assume optimistically that $p_1 > p_2$. Then the overall proportion p of mergers approved is:

$$p = qp_1 + (1-q)p_2 \tag{A2.1}$$

so that in the case where p is equal to the overall proportion q of good mergers in the population, $p_2 = (1-p_1)q/(1-q)$. Then the overall welfare change S brought about by the merger process is

$$S = DVqp_1 - DW(1-q)p_2 \tag{A2.2}$$

where D is the discount factor over the period taken by the investigation (equal to $1/(1+r)^n$ where n is the number of months taken by the investigation and r is the monthly interest rate). And the contribution C of the competition agency is the difference between S and what would have occurred without intervention:

$$C = W(1-q)(1-Dp_2) - Vq(1-Dp_1) \tag{A2.3}$$

namely, the value of bad mergers prevented less the value of good mergers prevented, appropriately adjusted for the costs of delay. We can explore the consequences of choosing n (the number of months of investigation), or equivalently of choosing D (the discount factor) so as to maximize S. Let us begin by assuming that V, W and q (namely, the parameters of the population of mergers under consideration) are unaffected by D, so that the only result of a change in D is to change the two probabilities p_1 and p_2. Then the appropriate first-order conditions are:

$$p_1Vq - p_2W(1-q) + DVq\frac{\mathrm{d}p_1}{\mathrm{d}D} - DW(1-q)\frac{\mathrm{d}p_2}{\mathrm{d}D} = 0$$

$$\tag{A2.4}$$

where the first two terms show the direct effect of delay in postponing the gains from good mergers and the losses from bad mergers, while the last two terms offset these with the impact of delay on the probabilities of approval of good and bad mergers respectively.

For practical purposes it will be useful to use

$$p_1 Vq - p_2 W(1 - q) + DVq \frac{\delta p_1}{\delta D} - DW(1 - q) \frac{\delta p_2}{\delta D} = 0 \quad \text{(A2.5)}$$

which is a discrete approximation to (A2.4) for small δD, to tell us what change in the probabilities of correct classification would just offset the effect of a change in the length of investigation. For simplicity we need to make assumptions about how p_1 and p_2 would change together, so let us consider three cases:

$$\frac{\delta p_1}{\delta D} = \frac{-\delta p_2}{\delta D} \qquad \text{(A2.6a)}$$

$$\frac{\delta p_1}{\delta D} = 0 \qquad \text{(A2.6b)}$$

$$p_2 = \frac{(1 - p_1)q}{(1 - q)} \qquad \text{(A2.6c)}$$

These correspond respectively to the case where speeding up investigations reduces the probability that a good merger is approved and increases the probability that a bad merger is approved by exactly the same number of percentage points; the case where speeding up the process leaves unchanged the probability of approval of good mergers but tends to rush bad mergers through with higher probability; and the case where the change in p_1 and the change in p_2 exactly offset each other so that the overall probability of approval of mergers is equal to the true proportion of good mergers in the population.[21] Then, writing $W = wV$ to indicate that the cost of bad mergers is w times the benefit of good mergers, we have under the three cases:

$$\frac{\delta p_2}{\delta D} = \frac{-\delta p_1}{\delta D} = \frac{[p_1 q - p_2 w(1 - q)]}{D[w + q(1 - w)]} \qquad \text{(A2.7a)}$$

$$\frac{\delta p_2}{\delta D} = \frac{[p_1 q - p_2 w(1 - q)]}{Dw(1 - q)} \qquad \text{(A2.7b)}$$

$$\frac{\delta p_2}{\delta D} = \frac{[q - p_2(1 + w)(1 - q)]}{D(1 + w)(1 - q)} \qquad \text{(A2.7c)}$$

Let us take some illustrative values to see what kinds of magnitude are in question: the monthly interest rate is 1% ($r = 0.01$); good mergers are approved with a probability 0.95; bad mergers are approved with a probability 0.45; the total proportion of good mergers is 0.9; the present discounted value of a good merger is the same as the discounted social cost of a bad merger (so $w = 1$).

Then we can consider the consequences of reducing the time for investigation from four months to three months, and use equations (A2.7) to tell us what worsening of the probability of correctly classifying mergers would just offset the benefits of reduced delay. At a monthly rate of interest of 1% we can use the approximation that a reduction of 1 in the value of n is roughly equal to a one percentage point increase in the value of D. Then the value of $\delta p_2/\delta D$ can be interpreted as the number of percentage points by which the probability of approval of a bad merger would have to rise to offset the benefits of each month of reduced delay. Letting p', p'' and p''' respectively be the values of $\delta p_2/\delta D$ determined by (A2.7), gives us:

$$p' = 0.84 \qquad \text{(A2.8a)}$$

$$p'' = 8.4 \qquad \text{(A2.8b)}$$

$$p''' = 4.2 \qquad \text{(A2.8c)}$$

Equations (A2.8) make clear that the costs of reducing the probability of correctly classifying good mergers are much more serious than the costs of raising the probability of incorrectly approving bad mergers, simply because there are (by assumption) nine good mergers for every one bad. That is why, if the probability of correctly classifying good mergers falls by as many percentage points as that of correctly classifying bad ones, the fall that offsets the benefits of greater speed is so small (a mere 0.84 percentage points). Even with no deterioration in the process for good mergers, a rise in the approval rate for bad mergers from 0.45 to 0.55 would be enough to outweigh the gains from reduced delay.

Notice that no assumption has been made about the absolute magnitudes of gains and losses from mergers; the value of V cancels out in equation (A2.5), and the trade-off remains the same regardless of these absolute magnitudes. The results are nevertheless sensitive to assumptions about the benefits of good mergers relative to the costs of bad mergers, or about the relative frequency of the two types in the population of cases under consideration.

The model just presented is too simple in a number of respects. Perhaps the most important one is the assumption that the population of mergers under scrutiny is independent of the investigation process. In reality we have every reason to expect that the quality of mergers proposed by firms will depend partly on the nature of merger control. One way in which this might occur is by making q vary with D. Then in place of equation (A2.5) the appropriate first-order conditions are:

$$p_1 Vq - p_2 W(1 - q) + DVq \frac{dp_1}{dD} - DW(1 - q) \frac{dp_2}{dD}$$

$$+ DVp_1 \frac{dq}{dD} + DWp_2 \frac{dq}{dD} = 0 \qquad \text{(A2.9)}$$

where the two new terms represent, respectively, the gains forgone from those good mergers that would have been approved but which will not now be undertaken, and the losses due to the bad mergers which escape the screening procedure and which would not otherwise have been proposed. Let us set the third and fourth terms of (A2.9) to zero in order to focus on the question 'how much deterioration in the quality of mergers proposed would be enough *on its own* to offset any advantages from a faster procedure?' Then the equivalent of equations (A2.7) is:

$$\frac{\delta q}{\delta D} = \frac{-[p_1 q - p_2 w(1 - q)]}{Dp_1 + wDp_2} \qquad \text{(A2.10)}$$

and in the numerical example:

$$q' = -0.60 \qquad \text{(A2.11)}$$

which tells us that a deterioration of a mere 0.60 percentage points in the proportion of good mergers under investigation is enough to offset the benefits of a one-month reduction in investigation time.

Perhaps a more realistic way to model the dependence of the quality of mergers on the investigation procedure is to suppose that the magnitude of the costs and benefits of mergers may vary. The most intuitive way to think of this is as making W alone dependent on D; the nature of good mergers may be little affected by the procedure of investigation, but firms proposing anti-competitive mergers may well tailor their proposals to the nature of the scrutiny they expect to receive. More specifically, the faster the procedure the more costly the merger they can risk proposing. Making w endogenous instead of q yields in place of equation (A2.10):

$$\frac{\delta w}{\delta D} = \frac{[p_1 q - p_1 w(1 - q)]}{D(1 - q)p_2} \tag{A2.12}$$

which in the numerical example yields:

$$w' = 18.7 \tag{A2.13}$$

showing that an increase of 18.7% in the average costs of a bad merger is sufficient to outweigh the reduction of one month in investigation time. Note that this apparently greater change (compared to a value of a mere 0.60% for q') is due to the fact that only the costs of bad mergers are affected; changes in q by contrast involve changes in the expected benefit from good mergers, which are by assumption much more numerous than bad mergers.

To a first approximation one can consider these different effects as additive. So, for example, a 10% increase in the average costs of a bad merger and a 5% increase in the probability that bad mergers are approved would together more than outweigh a month's reduction in investigation time.

The model is intended not to answer definitively the question 'how long should merger investigations take?' but rather to illustrate the kinds of factor that should be taken into account in attempting to answer such a question. The reasoning can be applied to investigations in several stages: at a first screening stage, the fact that most mergers are likely to be good ones (that is, q will be a high value) suggests a considerable value of speed. At a subsequent stage mergers chosen for further investigation are more likely to be bad ones, so that the value of speed is correspondingly diminished. The assumptions in the numerical example are fairly conservative (in particular a 1% real monthly interest rate certainly overstates the costs of delay), but even so the message is clear: it takes a rather small deterioration in the quality of investigation to outweigh increases in speed of the order of a month or two.

We have stressed the importance of taking seriously the idea that firms may consciously adapt their business strategies to the perceived nature of the merger control regime. Even though it is costly to firms to have mergers blocked, they may be prepared to take a calculated risk of such an outcome in return for the perceived private benefits of those mergers that are approved. It was suggested above that a firm proposing a merger that is socially harmful (but is not known to be so for certain by the agency) may vary the character of the proposal according to what it believes it might get away with. For example, suppose that the expected benefit B to a firm from proposing a merger with social cost W is given by:

$$B = X(W)Dp_1 - (1 - p_1)Y \qquad (A2.14)$$

where $X(W)$ is the private benefit from the merger if approved, which is an increasing function of its social cost, and Y is the cost to the firm of a merger refusal in terms of time, trouble, legal fees and goodwill. Then we can suppose that both p_2 and D might in principle vary with W; a more damaging merger might provoke both a longer investigation and a reduced probability of clearance. Then the firm's choice of W would aim to maximize B, yielding the first-order conditions:

$$\frac{dX}{dW}Dp_1 + X(W)\left(D\frac{dp_1}{dW} + p_1\frac{dD}{dW}\right) + Y\frac{dp_1}{dW} = 0 \quad (A2.15)$$

which says that the direct gain to the firm from a more socially costly merger will be offset by the cost of a reduced probability of

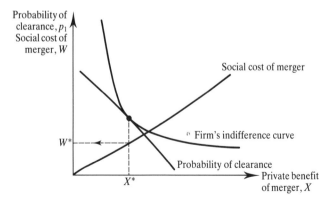

Figure A2.1   The social cost of merger, as determined by the firm's optimal choice of the private benefit of merger.

clearance (a cost proportional to the discounted benefits forgone), a lengthened investigation and an increased expected cost of refusal. Figure A2.1 shows how, in the case where the main effect of a more damaging proposal is to reduce the probability of clearance, a firm might typically choose some intermediate value of W: the convexity of its indifference curve reflects the fact that the expected benefit to the firm is the product of the probability of clearance and the benefit of an approved proposal.

Notes

1. In *Hoffmann-La Roche* the Court explicitly rejected the claim that 'an abuse would imply that the economic power conferred by a dominant position was the means by which the abuse was realised'. The case concerned loyalty discounts, and it is arguable that their presence may have implied the exercise of market power whether the Court recognized this or not. However, one of the reproaches the Court levied against loyalty discounts was that they tend to diminish the buyer's 'choice of sources of supply', which is a structural argument and may not (at least if the market is contestable) imply the presence of market power.

2. It is also useful to note that, ignoring income effects, the own-price elasticity of demand for a product is equal in absolute value to the sum of the cross-price elasticities of demand for competing products with respect to the price of the product concerned (see Henderson and Quandt (1980), pp. 30–1). The intuition is that, when consumers reduce their demand for a product in response to a price rise, they will substitute into other products (in the absence of income effects). The result is useful because it is sometimes easier in practice to obtain evidence on the cross-price elasticities with respect to a number of key potential substitutes than to obtain evidence on the own-price product demand elasticity directly.

3. A third factor that may be significant is whether or not there are buyers who enjoy significant market power on their side. The most that can be said is that strong buyer power may mitigate some of the effects of the market power of sellers; but neither economic theory nor empirical studies have so far offered any very convincing account of how significant a phenomenon this will be.

4. There is a much simpler special case when products are homogeneous and firms take competitors' output levels (rather than prices) as given – the Cournot case. Here the market power enjoyed by a firm is simply proportional to its market share (that is, the own-price firm elasticity is inversely proportional to the market share). Unfortunately, the relevance of this case to real markets in which products are differen-

tiated is very limited. For instance, in the absence of cost differences across firms their market shares will be symmetrical: this means that a merger between any two firms will give the merged parties no larger a market share than that enjoyed by the remaining firms after the merger. This gives us no guidance for the analysis of mergers which grant firms control over specific kinds of product that are not produced by their competitors.

5. Even where pre-merger demand elasticities can be estimated, there may be biases associated with extrapolating these to the post-merger situation. For instance, in the *Artificial Sweetener* case (*United States* v. *Archer-Daniels-Midland Co.*), it was ruled that the elasticity of demand for artificial sweeteners would significantly increase at higher levels of prices than those currently observed, because such products would then compete with sugar. Estimating the potential market power of the proposed merger on the basis of the current elasticity would thus overestimate the extent to which the merged entity could actually raise its price.

6. This follows simply from noting that if:

$$(p_i - c_i)/p_i = ks_i$$

where s_i is the market share of firm i and k is the constant of proportionality, then multiplying both sides by s_i and summing across firms yields the average price–cost margin on the left-hand side and k times the HHI on the right-hand side. Noting that s_i for a monopolist is equal to one, k is then the monopolist's margin for the market in question (say 5%), and therefore is equal to the reciprocal of the elasticity of market demand (that is, the elasticity of demand for all the products in the market taken together). We indicated in section 2.2.3 that proportionality of market power to market share would obtain in extremely unrealistic circumstances (homogeneous goods and Cournot conjectures, for instance). Nevertheless, the argument here can be generalized to take into account somewhat more general functional relationships of market power to market share.

7. *Brown Shoe Company* v. *United States*, 370 US 294 (1962).

8. This upper limit is a weighted sum of competitors' market shares, where the weights are the expected changes in competitors' output in response to the merger. The weights are themselves a function of cost and demand parameters.

9. The criterion of Farrell and Shapiro will also exclude any mergers that are not privately profitable but are socially desirable. These may well be less frequent, and might call for a public policy to give positive encouragement to mergers, a drastic departure from common practice (at least in the EC and the United States, though some countries such as Spain provide fiscal incentives to that effect). Concern to encourage merger activity might nevertheless be a more pressing issue when there are international spillover effects from merger activity, an issue that is tackled in detail in Chapter 6 below.

10. Going back to Meeks (1977). See Ravenscraft and Scherer (1987) for the US and Hughes (1992) for a survey of the UK evidence. See also Vermaelen (1992) and Haspeslagh and Jemison (1991).
11. Clearly it will not always be necessary for a firm to spend as much, especially if it has a prior advantage over others (such as the ear of a minister) in the race to secure the monopoly position. Risk-averse firms will also typically spend less than the expected value of the rents it confers.
12. It is true that there are circumstances in which too high a probability of bankruptcy can diminish the incentive for managers to work hard and well in the interests of the firm. But these circumstances arise only because managers hope for some rents from continuing to be employed by the firm.
13. A more detailed version of this argument is found in Seabright (1990). Even if prices can be changed rapidly in response to entry, there may still be some scope for limit pricing behaviour because of the signals it sends to potential competitors about the profitability of the market.
14. *United States* v. *E.I. du Pont de Nemours & Co*, 351 US 377 (1956).
15. See, for instance, Froeb and Werden (1991, 1992).
16. See Froeb and Werden (1992) for an example where such an adjustment is made.
17. *Brown Shoe Company* v. *United States*, 370 US 294 (1962).
18. Brittan (1990) has done little to clarify matters by stating that efficiency is a relevant factor but is not a defence.
19. J. Ordover, personal communication.
20. More cynically, if firms believe that faster procedures would increase the overall probability of approval, they have an interest in exaggerating the costs to themselves of delay.
21. This corresponds loosely to a kind of rational expectations assumption on the part of the agency.

3

The merger decisions of the European Commission

3.1   Introduction

In this chapter we present an analysis and assessment of the reasoning presented by the European Commission in justification of its decisions under the Merger Regulation since September 1990. The purpose of doing so is not primarily to see whether the Commission's decisions were in fact the right ones to make in the circumstances. Too much of the information that would be needed to make that assessment reliably is not available to us, for unavoidable reasons (such as business confidentiality) as well as some avoidable ones (as we discuss below in Chapters 7 and 8). Instead, the purpose of this chapter is to infer from the Commission's published reasoning what in fact have been the procedures and criteria it has used in the assessment of merger proposals, and to evaluate these in the light of the arguments we have already developed in Chapter 2. To make this inference will require substantial examination of the detailed reasoning in a large number of cases[1], partly because a general tendency in the Commission's procedures cannot be revealed in single cases, and partly because (as will be seen) there has not always been consistency between the reasoning deployed in different cases. Nonetheless, even bearing in mind the limitations of this kind of inference, we conclude that the Commission's procedures are open to a number of criticisms:

1.   The definition of concentrative joint ventures is open to considerable manipulation, in that changes in the form of transac-

tions may be encouraged by the desire of firms to have their proposals reviewed under the Regulation instead of under procedures elsewhere.

2. The procedures used for market definition are frequently inconsistent; in particular supply substitution is sometimes taken into account at the market definition stage and sometimes at the stage of assessing dominance, with usually no clear rationale for the difference in treatment. Supply substitution is also sometimes counted twice. The failure to take supply substitution into account will probably tend on average to result in excessively narrow market definitions. Although it is not possible to point with confidence to particular cases in which this bias has made a difference to the market definition adopted, we indicate one or two instances where it could have been significant.

3. Both market definitions and some of the factors relevant to the assessment of dominance rely unnecessarily on qualitative assertions and hunches even when more quantitative evidence could have been made available. While we appreciate the limitations on the availability of quantitative evidence, we suggest a number of ways these limitations can be overcome consistently with maintaining a reasonably streamlined procedure.

4. Examination of cases confirms our conjecture that the Commission uses a sequential rather than a simultaneous procedure for product and geographic market definition, which as discussed in Chapter 2 will tend on average to lead to a further bias in favour of narrow markets.

5. The assessment of dominance has also displayed an unnecessarily unsystematic and arbitrary character, especially in estimating the strength of remaining competitors, potential entrants, and countervailing buyer power.

6. Claims about efficiencies have been treated inconsistently, in one case as a potential (if practically negligible) defence, and in others as a potential source of dominance.

7. Conditions ('remedies') attached to decisions have often done little to meet competition concerns, since they have relied on excessive optimism about the future development of competitive forces. They have also, and to an increasing degree, relied upon undertakings from the parties whose credibility may be in some doubt.

Overall, we conclude that the unnecessarily unsystematic character of the procedures as they appear from the cases reviewed makes it particularly difficult to judge whether the Commission's judgment in individual cases has been sound. This raises issues of transparency that are pursued in greater depth in Chapter 6. We also, if more tentatively, conjecture that the character of the procedures, especially with regard to remedies, is suggestive not so much of random variations as of the outcome of a process of negotiation in which firms and the Commission bargain over the outcome of a particular case. This implies the need to investigate in greater depth the nature of firms' reactions to the Regulation, and consequently sets the scene for our survey of firms which is presented in Chapter 4.

3.2   Definition of a concentration

The EC Merger Regulation applies to 'concentrations with a community dimension'. A concentration is defined as an acquisition of control which confers either sole control or concentrative joint control. Control in turn is defined as 'the possibility of exercising decisive influence on an undertaking' (XXI Report, p. 352). A concentration has a community dimension if (i) the aggregate worldwide turnover of all the parties taken together exceeds ECU 5 billion, (ii) the aggregate EC-wide turnover of at least two of the parties taken individually exceeds ECU 250 million and (iii) at least one of the undertakings does not achieve two-thirds of its EC-wide turnover within one and the same member state. In addition, Article 9 of the Regulation provides member states with the possibility of asking for referral of an acquisition with community dimension to their own jurisdiction if they fear the creation or strengthening of a dominant position in a distinct market within their territory. The decision whether or not to grant the referral rests with the Commission.

In what follows, we shall briefly discuss the significance of these thresholds and review the way in which the Commission has defined sole and joint control and has distinguished between concentrative and cooperative joint ventures.

3.2.1   *Strategic choice of jurisdiction*

One can ask whether the definition of a concentration with a community dimension is appropriate from the perspective of the allocation of power between the Commission and the member states. This issue is taken up in Chapter 6 and again in Chapter 8. For the time being, the significance of this definition arises mainly from the alternative jurisdictions that would apply to acquisitions which are not considered to be 'concentrations with a community dimension'. In principle, a joint acquisition of control which is considered to be cooperative rather than concentrative can be reviewed under Article 85/86 of the Treaty of Rome, if the proposed acquisition 'affects trade between the member states'. A concentration which does not have a community dimension will generally be reviewed by national anti-trust authorities provided they exist. To the extent that these alternative jurisdictions might apply different criteria and procedures, the design of acquisitions may take into account the jurisdiction under which the operations will fall. For instance, a (presumably large) minority partner can be added to increase the turnover of the undertakings concerned and thereby meet the size thresholds. The deal may also be structured as a concentrative rather than cooperative joint venture.

The prospect of alternative jurisdictions will presumably be a relatively minor consideration in the majority of deals where the commercial rationale can be expected to dominate. Still, these considerations may matter at the margin. A priori, one would also expect that investigation under the Merger Regulation will be preferred by the firms when the alternatives are a review either by the German authorities or by the Commission under Article 85/86. Indeed, the German anti-trust authorities have expressed concern from the outset that the Merger Regulation may be too lax. Reviews under Article 85/86 are thought to be less desirable for at least three reasons. First, procedures under Article 85/86 are open ended and tend to be lengthy. Secondly, their implementation is perceived to be rather more inflexible (see Rosenthal (1992)). Finally, rulings are valid for a fixed period of time[2] whereas decisions under the Merger Regulation have no time limit.

At the end of 1992, the Commission put forward some guidelines for the assessment of collaborative joint ventures and announced the implementation of an accelerated procedure for the treatment of these deals.[3] These initiatives do not address firms' anxieties about the time limits on exemptions, but should nonetheless reduce the relative benefit associated with a review under the Merger Guidelines.

Just as firms may react strategically to the choice of jurisdictions that face them, one can also expect the authorities in charge of these jurisdictions to respond to firms. This issue is discussed at some length in Chapters 4 and 5. For the time being, let us simply note that in response to firms, the Commission can choose the degree of flexibility that it will use, for instance in the assessment of joint control or in the distinction between concentrative and cooperative joint ventures. It is worth emphasizing the terms of the trade-off faced by the authorities: on the one hand, rigorous enforcement will lead firms to make potentially large adjustments to their deals in order to ensure that they fall under the preferred jurisdiction. On the other hand, lax enforcement will reduce this cost but might entail a loss of credibility for the agency. And unless enforcement were consistently lax it might also increase the uncertainty faced by firms.

3.2.2   *Sole control*

Let us first consider the evaluation of sole control where the alternative is not joint control with a well-identified partner. This issue arises in cases of acquisitions. In the absence of specific provisions for minority shareholders, a sufficient condition for the existence of sole control is the holding by one company of more than half of the share capital of another company. Even when one company acquired only a fraction more than half of the capital of another company, as when Magneti Marelli acquired control of 50.1% of the shares of CEAc, sole control was conferred. A majority is not, however, a necessary condition because sole control may also be conferred when the ownership of a minority shareholding gives the acquirer a 'relative majority'; that is, when the remaining shareholders cannot individually or collectively determine the commercial activities of the company.

The assessment of a relative majority is in principle a delicate matter; the degree of effective control associated with any holding is affected by the distribution of remaining shares as well as particular provisions of the articles of associations of the company and corporate laws. The cases handled by the Commission were, however, rather clear cut; after the acquisition in *Arjomari/Wiggins Teape* (25), for instance, Arjomari held 39% of the shares in Wiggins Teape. With the remainder of the shares held by 107,000 other shareholders, none of whom owns more than 4%, attributing sole control to Arjomari seems rather uncontroversial.

3.2.3   *Joint control*

Let us now consider the evaluation of control where the alternatives are either joint control by well-identified partners or sole control by one of them. This issue is important because it determines the companies whose turnover will determine whether the various size thresholds are met. For instance, in the case of *Varta/Bosch* (12), if the joint venture had been classified as one in which Varta had sole control (with 65% of the shares), it would not have fallen under the jurisdiction of the Merger Regulation (the worldwide turnover of Varta is less than ECU 5 billion). In the event, it is highly debatable whether German anti-trust authorities would, like the Commission, have cleared the deal. Officials from the Bundeskartellamt have indicated in our interviews that their assessment would probably have been different from that of the Commission. Similarly, the Commission has ruled that Lucas and Eaton exercised joint control over their joint ventures despite the fact that Lucas had a majority shareholding (in both joint ventures). If it had been considered that Lucas exercised sole control, the deal would have been reviewed by the Monopolies and Merger Commission (Lucas' worldwide turnover is under ECU 5 billion).

Joint control exists where the parent companies must agree on the decisions taken by the joint venture. A necessary condition for joint control is thus the existence of a *de facto* common veto over 'important' decisions. Where there is unequal participation, joint control can be created by rights or contracts.   Since it is very rare that capital participation is equal, the Commission has focused on the rights and contract details of each operation. In particular, the Commission examines control over the firm's strategic plan and the appointment, dismissal and remuneration of executives. The Commission has in general taken a common veto over both of these aspects of company organization to be sufficient to guarantee joint control (see for instance *Varta/Bosch* (12), *Aerospatiale/MBB* (17),

Elf/BC/CEPSA (98), *Apollinaris/Schweppes* (93) and *Conagra/Idea* (10)).

For instance, in *Varta/Bosch* (12), Varta has 65% and Bosch 35% of the shares in the joint venture. But the terms of the agreement stipulate that a 75% majority is required for approval of the budget plan and for the appointment or dismissal of directors, and that there is equal representation on the supervisory board. In examples like these, it seems clear that in principle neither party could take important decisions without the consent of the others. This sharing of power may entail a significant cost for Varta, which holds about two-thirds of the shares. Given that if Varta had been considered to exercise sole control, the deal would have been reviewed in Germany, it can be interpreted as the price that had to be paid to fall under the Merger Regulation.

Taking a common veto over the business plan and executives' terms of appointment as sufficient for joint control seems in principle a sound criterion, and the Commission has examined this in detail. In some cases, however, additional information on the content of the business plan would have been useful. Indeed, business plans vary a great deal across companies in terms of the horizon considered, the matters covered and the degree of details included. Such details could be specified more systematically in the decisions.

In some cases, the Commission decided there was joint control where the strategic plan and the terms of appointment were not both subject to common veto. For instance, in *Sanofi/Sterling Drug* (72), the Commission concluded that the OTC drugs business was jointly controlled, even though Sterling Drug has a 70% interest and five out of eight board members, and Sanofi has no veto right; the existence of extensive provisions for settling potential disputes was taken as sufficient evidence for granting joint control. Similar concerns arise in *Lucas/Eaton* (149), *Ingersoll Rand/Dresser* (121) and *Saab/Ericsson Space* (178); in all of these cases it was imaginable that one firm would be capable of exerting sole control, and more detail of the business plans would be particularly informative.

When there are more than two parents, the Commission has also ruled that there was joint control even though some of the parents did not exercise a power of veto. For instance in *Avesta/British Steel/NCC/Axel Johnson* (239), annual operating budgets and business plans require the prior written consent of British Steel, NCC and at least one of Axel Johnson and AGA. These last two partners do not therefore individually have a veto power. An analogous situation arises in *Philips/Thomson/Sagem* (293), where Thomson and Sagem do not individually have a power of veto, whilst Philips does.

This raises a broader issue, which is that the Commission can only base its rulings on observable and verifiable agreements. Nothing prevents shareholders from concluding a secret agreement through which sole control is delegated to one of them, even though written agreements and articles of incorporations suggest joint control. The party giving up its control right may do so simply because there are some strategic benefits associated with delegation (see Vickers (1985)), or as part of a more complex agreement involving side payments or control over other firms. Such agreements are of course not enforceable (in court) and suppose a degree of tacit (or explicit but secret) collusion between partners. However, when the partners are involved in several markets or firms at the same time, the scope for stable collusive agreements is greatly enhanced (see Bernheim and Winston (1990)).

The relevance of secret agreements is illustrated by the case of *Mediobanca/Generali* (159). In this instance, Mediobanca increased its shareholding in Generali from 5.98% to 12.84%. Given that Generali owns 87% of the shares and in the absence of any relevant special agreement, the Commission had apparently sound reasons to declare that the transaction did not enable Mediobanca, alone or with others, to exercise control over Generali. Accordingly, on 19 December 1991, the operation was declared not to fall under the Merger Regulation. The ruling mentioned, however, an agreement between Mediobanca and Euralux, the second largest shareholder in Generali (4.77%), not to sell shares to anyone else, but said that there was no agreement for a joint exercise of voting powers.

The Commission's decision has been challenged by three minority shareholders (Zunis Holding SA, Finanz srl and Massinvest SA) of Generali who claim that there was a secret agreement between Generali, Mediobanca and Lazard Frères (the owners of Euralux). According to these minority shareholders, the agreement enables Mediobanca and Euralux to gain joint control over Generali. They claim that the Commission was misled as to the nature of this agreement and to the extent of Mediobanca's control and influence. In particular, reference is made to a steering committee through which Mediobanca and Euralux had exercised considerable influence over Generali's management even before the increase in sharehold-ing. These parties requested the Commission to re-open the pro-ceedings of the case, but the Commission refused on 31 July 1992. In the first direct challenge to the Commission over the Merger Regulation, the minority shareholders have appealed to the Court of Justice against the refusal to re-open proceedings, questioning the Commission's understanding of the concepts of control in Article 3 of the Regulation.

On the whole, it seems that the possibility of stable and secret agreements through which control is delegated should not be lightly dismissed. These can be avoided only by raising the cost of delegation for both partners; for instance, mandatory agreements on the allocations of dividends could be specified, to ensure that it is not in the interest of the party to represent the operation as involving joint control when it actually has sole control.

3.2.4   *Concentrative and cooperative joint ventures*

In principle, a joint venture is considered to be concentrative if (i) the joint venture performs on a lasting basis all the functions of an autonomous economic entity and (ii) the joint venture does not lead to the coordination of the competitive behaviour of the parties among themselves or with the joint venture.

By contrast, a joint venture is considered to be cooperative if it has as its object or effect the coordination of the competitive behaviour of undertakings which remain independent. Given that a joint venture is by definition controlled by the parents, it would seem that it is only the parents that can be considered to be independent of each other. This suggests that a joint venture can be deemed cooperative only when it leads the parents to coordinate their behaviour.

It is worth noticing at the outset that the definitions in the Regulation of cooperative and concentrative joint ventures are not exhaustive: in particular, nothing is said about joint ventures which involve the coordination of behaviour between entities which cannot be considered to be fully independent. Yet, through the concept of 'industrial leadership' described below, the Commission *has pro-gressively filled the gap* between the two definitions by stating that a joint venture which is not independent from one of the parent cannot be said to be cooperative and *hence* is concentrative.

There are therefore now two alternative ways of being considered a concentrative joint venture: one is to show that the joint venture meets the positive conditions stated in the Regulation for being considered concentrative; the other is to show that the joint venture does not meet the conditions for being cooperative. The Commission has therefore taken the view that a joint venture which cannot be said to be cooperative will be concentrative, even though the Regulation does not imply this. We first review the positive approach.

3.2.4.1 *Concentrative joint ventures: the positive approach*

According to this first approach, the Commission has to establish that the joint venture is autonomous and that there is no coordination between the joint venture and the parents and between the parents.

In *Varta/Bosch* (12) and *Ericsson/Kolbe* (133), the Commission specified three conditions which jointly guarantee the features of autonomy in all functions: (i) the joint venture should be an independent supplier and buyer in the market, (ii) the human and material resources of the joint venture should be of such a nature and quantity as to ensure its long-term existence and independence and (iii) the joint venture should exercise its own commercial policy. The first of these conditions remains fairly general and in this respect it is not particularly helpful;[4] the notion of autonomy of the joint venture is also potentially in conflict with the notion of control that the parents are supposed to have over the joint venture. Possibly for this reason, the Commission has not often referred to conditions of autonomy in its decisions.

Rather, the coordination of competitive behaviour of the parties among themselves or with the joint venture is the central feature of the decisions and is a difficult one for the Commission to assess. Indeed, it is not the absence of coordination which determines whether the joint venture is concentrative; the establishment of a joint venture by its very nature requires a certain degree of understanding and coordination between the parents that the Commission considers legitimate. It is only coordination over and above what is deemed necessary for the operation of the joint venture which could imply that the joint venture is cooperative. Hence, the Commission has to assess the degree of coordination, without a clear benchmark as to what is deemed necessary. In addition, the coordination must be evaluated in terms of probable future developments rather than with reference to the legal provisions of some binding agreement.

The main discriminating factor which has been used to assess coordination is the position of the parents in the market of the joint venture. When parents remain active or potential competitors in the market of the joint venture, the Merger Regulation does not apply. Conversely, when both parents completely and permanently withdraw from the market of the joint venture, the joint venture is considered to be concentrative. What matters then is the evaluation of exit by the parents from the relevant market and, where exit is only partial, whether it leads to coordination between parent and joint venture. So market definition and the evaluation of coordination are intimately linked. The following issues arise in the evaluation of withdrawal.

(i) Exit and re-entry   In general, it is fairly easy to check whether parents have withdrawn from the market in which the joint venture operates. It is also, however, important to assess whether parents would have an incentive and the ability to re-enter. This is more difficult. For instance, in *Draeger/IBM/Hmp* (101) the parents withdrew from the joint venture's market but have the means to re-enter. The Commission judged that re-entry was unlikely because of costs and risks, but left those unspecified. However in *Herba/IRR* (188), the Commission considered that re-entry was realistic after the expiry of a no-competition clause. Accordingly, this case was treated as cooperative.

(ii) Market definition   The importance of market definition in assessing exit by the parents is illustrated by the case of *ABC/GDE/Canal+/WH Smith TV* (100). This joint venture was considered not to be cooperative because Pay-TV (provided by Canal+) and free access TV (provided by WH Smith TV) were distinct product markets. This judgment was motivated by the observation of different product characteristics (related to programmes and advertising). The shortcomings of an approach to market definition based solely on product characteristics have been discussed in Chapter 2 and will be illustrated in section 3.3. For

present purposes, we note that the classification of the joint venture in this case hinges on a market definition which may seem disputable.

(iii) Scope of activity   The extent of the withdrawal by parents also depends on the scope of activity which is considered; for instance, in *Lucas/Eaton* (149), Lucas distributes 15% of the joint venture's sales in an independent market. This was not considered to be a significant impediment by the Commission.

(iv) Neighbouring markets   The Commission also considered joint ventures in which parents operate in markets 'neighbouring' that of the joint venture. The concern here is that spillover effects between markets may enable the coordination of behaviour. The Commission did not define what is meant by neighbouring markets: for instance, in *Lucas/Eaton* (149), the possibility of spillovers between car brakes (Lucas) and heavy-duty breaking systems (the joint venture) was examined but was found to be irrelevant because of 'different conditions of competition' and technological difference. This suggests that these products do not belong to the same anti-trust market, and that technological spillovers are unlikely. It would be useful to clarify the content of the term 'neighbouring' markets.[5]

On the whole, the Commission appears to have shown considerable flexibility in the assessment of potential coordination. According to some commentators (see Hawk (1991, chapter 17)), the degree of flexibility shown by the Commission has also increased over time. We would only note the risk that flexibility can sometimes be achieved at the price of both consistency and credibility.

3.2.4.2 *Concentrative joint ventures and industrial leadership*

In cases where one parent stays in the same market as the joint venture, it is difficult to argue that the joint venture is concentrative in a positive sense: there is clearly coordination of behaviour between the joint venture and the parent that stays in the market. In such cases, the Commission has developed the concept of industrial leadership:[6] it is argued that provided the parent which remains in the market has the main responsibility for the joint venture (it acts as an industrial leader) the parent and the joint venture cannot be considered independent. As a consequence, the joint venture cannot be said to be cooperative and *hence* it is concentrative.

As mentioned above, the possibility of establishing the concentrative nature of a joint venture by establishing that it does not fulfil a sufficient condition for being cooperative does not actually follow from the Regulation. At the same time, the application of Article 85 may not be appropriate in such cases because of the ownership links between the entities. The Commission has thus filled the gap by extending the scope for joint ventures to be considered concentrative. The concept of industrial leadership is still an odd one, to the extent that it explicitly refers to the fact that one parent exerts more influence than the other in the joint venture, even though (by construction) they exercise joint control. There might thus be a conflict between the concepts of joint control and that of industrial leadership by one parent.

The case where the concept of industrial leadership was introduced was *Thomson/Pilkington* (86). Thomson took a 49.99% stake in Pilkington Optronics, a subsidiary of Pilkington. The parents had joint control over PO since they possessed equal stakes in the JV and each nominated half of the board of directors of PO. However, Thomson had the main responsibility for the market behaviour of the JV since it appointed its chief executive officer.

Under the terms of the agreement, Pilkington is to withdraw completely from the market of the JV whereas Thomson 'will remain in the same *field of activity* as the joint venture' (emphasis added). In particular, Thomson will focus sales of optronics on France with PO focusing its sales of the same product on the UK. The Commission considers that since Thomson has the main responsibility for the market behaviour of the JV, the firms will operate as one economic unit. Accordingly, Thomson and the JV cannot be considered independent units which coordinate their behaviour, and the JV cannot be said to be cooperative.[7]

The concept of industrial leadership was used in a number of other cases, including *Air France/Sabena* (157) (a joint venture between Air France and the Belgian Government), *Northern Telecom/Matra* (249), *Fortis/la Caixa* (254), *Ericsson/Kolbe* (133) and *Linde/Fiat* (256). In *Ericsson/Kolbe*, Ericsson remained on a market served by the JV, that for digital transmission technology. The conflict between industrial leadership and joint control is particularly apparent in this case; indeed, it is stated that 'Ericsson will assume the overall responsibility for' the JV.

The Commission argued in this case that the competitive relationship between Ericsson and the joint venture would remain unchanged (paragraph 12 of the decision). For the Commission argued that Ericsson would stay in the same market as the joint venture and assume overall industrial responsibility for it. But it argued at the same time that the two entities would still compete. This ignored the fact that Ericsson has both the incentive and the capacity to collude with the joint venture. The Commission appeared to be trying to establish that the joint venture was not cooperative on the grounds *both* that the entities were not independent *and* that they would not coordinate;[8] but clearly lack of independence implies some coordination.

Finally, it is worth noticing that in those cases where the concept of industrial leadership was applied, the Commission considered, in the assessment of dominance, the joint market share of the parent taken as the industrial leader and of the joint venture.[9] This seems appropriate and is consistent with the idea that a concentrative joint venture is one in which there is full coordination between the industrial leader and the joint venture.

3.2.5 *Assessment of jurisdiction: some conclusions*

The main conclusions to emerge from the analysis above are the following:

1. There is some scope for tailoring deals in such a way as to fall under a preferred jurisdiction. The Commission seems to have responded by increasing its flexibility in the assessment of control and the evaluation of joint ventures to accommodate firms.[10]
2. So far, the identification of sole control in cases of acquisitions has been fairly straightforward, even though the matter may in principle be delicate.
3. The distinction between sole and joint control when partners are well identified has sometimes been based on unclear grounds: in a number of cases, common veto powers were not required. The matters in which joint control is exercised could usefully be made more precise (and verifiable).
4. The possibility of stable and secret agreements through which control is delegated should not be lightly dismissed. These can only be avoided by raising the cost of delegation for both

partners: for instance, mandatory agreements on the allocations of dividends could be specified.

5. The Commission has not applied strict criteria in the assessment of potential coordination between a joint venture and its parents or between the parents. The withdrawal of parents is favoured by fairly narrow definitions of some product and geographic markets. These definitions have sometimes not been substantiated. It has been claimed (and not by ourselves) that the flexibility of the Commission has been increasing over time.

6. The Commission has developed the concept of industrial leadership according to which a joint venture which is not cooperative is concentrative. This is an interpretation of the Regulation which is quite favourable to firms.

Overall, it is hard not to be struck by the efforts the Commission has made to find a case for treating transactions under the Merger Regulation if at all possible. Given the desire of firms to avoid falling under the slower Article 85 procedures, such efforts are understandable, but they seem like a second-best solution to the problem, which should be met by ensuring greater parity of treatment. Furthermore, the concept of industrial leadership, while ostensibly a matter that affects purely whether transactions fall under the Regulation or under Article 85, is to some extent in tension with the attribution of joint control, a matter that (as we have shown) may affect the choice of jurisdiction between the Commission and member states and not just between different units within the Commission. It would not be in the interests either of the Commission's reputation for consistency or of its relations with member states for it to be seen to be trying too hard to have its cake and eat it in matters of jurisdiction, even if that is what firms by and large prefer.

3.3   Defining the relevant market

As we indicated in section 2.2.2, a relevant anti-trust market is defined as the narrowest market in which a given degree of market power could be exercised. The assessment of a candidate market entails, in principle, the estimation of the own-price firm elasticity of demand faced by a hypothetical monopolist in that market. This own-price firm elasticity of demand is determined both by consumers' willingness to switch to alternative products at given prices of those products (demand substitution in our terminology) and by the reaction of competitors outside the candidate market (supply substitution in our terminology) who can either change their own pricing policy or enter the market in the short term by changing their product range. Ignoring income effects, the own-price elasticity of product demand (the reaction of consumers) can be assessed directly or through the sum of the cross-price elasticities of demand between the product considered and all the other products.

Two important issues that emerged from our discussion of market definition in Chapter 2 were: the manner in which it takes into account supply substitution, and whether the tests for product and geographic market definition are performed simultaneously or in sequence. Fishwick and Denison (1992) argue that the European practice under Article 85/86 tends to focus on demand-side substitution; we consider below whether this is also true of the analysis of mergers. As far as the procedure for product and geographic market definition is concerned, the CEC clearly states that estimation occurs in sequence and not simultaneously. On page 356 of the XXIst Report on Competition Policy (1992) the wording is as follows: 'The appraisal of concentrations includes generally three steps of analysis: the determination of the relevant product market, the determination of the relevant geographic market and the assessment of the compatibility of the merger with the common market.' This approach appears to be borne out in most of the decisions we have examined. We shall review product and geographic market definition procedures in turn.

3.3.1 *Product market definition*

The CEC defines a relevant market as 'those products which are regarded as interchangeable or substitutable by the consumer, by reason of the products' characteristics, their prices and their intended use'. It has distinguished 'two grounds on which separate relevant product markets were established' (XXIst Report, p. 357). These are 'lack of sufficient substitutability between the products concerned' and 'existence of different conditions of competition albeit the products themselves being fully interchangeable or even identical'. We discuss in turn several aspects of the Commission's approach, starting with the content given to these various terms.

3.3.1.1 *Conditions of competition*

The CEC does not specify exactly what is meant by 'conditions of competition', but clues may be gained from examining the *Magneti Marelli/CEAc* (43) and *Varta/Bosch* (12) cases.

A distinction was made in *Magneti Marelli/CEAc* and in *Varta/Bosch* between the original equipment (OE) market for starter batteries for the initial equipment of new vehicles and the replacement market for starter batteries for the equipment of used cars. The distinction was made on the basis of different 'conditions of competition', which arose because supply to the OE market requires high technical capacity, intense R&D, 100% reliability of the products, just-in-time delivery and supply certification granted by the car manufacturers. Supply to the replacement market, on the other hand, implies strong seasonal fluctuations in demand for a larger number of battery types. As to the nature of the product, replacement batteries can be used in some cars of different producers, otherwise OE batteries cannot. Hence a hypothetical monopoly supplier of the OE market could raise prices without encouraging suppliers on the replacement market to switch production into OE batteries. If this is the case, then different 'conditions of competition' mean here a weak response by existing producers of replacement batteries, or equivalently low supply substitution.

'Conditions of competition' might also refer here to seasonal fluctuations in demand. Seasonal fluctuations might, however, increase the probability that suppliers of replacement batteries would respond aggressively to a price increase by OE producers. Indeed, the demand for OE batteries is likely to peak in the summer, when the demand for new cars is highest, whilst demand for replacement batteries will peak in the winter. Hence the seasonal fluctuations offset each other, so that a producer of replacement batteries would have an incentive to enter into the OE market to smooth out production.

These two cases illustrate that the term 'conditions of competition' *refers to some consideration of supply substitution.* They also indicate that the Commission did not systematically define markets solely in terms of demand substitution. It seems that different conditions of competition meant in one case a probable aggressive response by competitors; it is not clear what the Commission meant by emphasizing fluctuations in demand but this could imply that a weak response could be expected from competitors outside the relevant market. In any event, it might be a useful clarification to define 'conditions of competition' in terms of competitors' responses, and to analyze different market characteristics in terms of their impact on these responses. In our opinion, it would also be useful to acknowledge explicitly the use of supply substitution as well as demand substitution in market definition.

3.3.1.2 *Demand substitution versus supply substitution*

As we have already discussed, the relevant market is the narrowest market in which significant market power can be exercised. This market power is associated with the elasticity that the dominant firm would face and this elasticity is in turn determined by the possibility that consumers might switch to competing products outside the relevant market, as well as by the reaction of the firms supplying these products.

In a number of cases, the Commission has defined markets by focusing on demand substitution, without explicit reference to 'different conditions of competition'. In such cases, some products are excluded from the relevant market but are considered again in the assessment of dominance. This practice is valid if the relevant market is determined only in terms of demand substitution, but it is inconsistent when the Commission considers both demand and supply substitution, as it does in some other cases; indeed, when the market is defined taking both demand and supply substitution into account, the assessment of dominance is solely concerned with the possibility that the merging parties could exercise the potential market power which (by construction) exists in the relevant market. That implies that products outside the relevant market are *irrelevant* to the assessment of dominance. If considering these products is deemed to be important, it means that the market has not been appropriately defined in the first place.

For instance, in *Courtaulds/SNIA* (113) and *Metallgesell-schaft/Safic Alcan* (146), some products are excluded from the relevant market but considered later. In the *appraisal* section of the *Sanofi/Sterling Drug* (72) case, it is stated that there 'is some degree of substitution from alternative products not included in the oper-ational market definition given above'. This approach is appropriate if indeed the markets are defined solely in terms of demand substitution, but not otherwise. The fact that the Commission switches from one approach to the other without warning is confusing.

The risks of an approach based solely on demand substitution are also well illustrated by the market definition in *Pepsi Co/Kas* (298). In this case, the Commission observed that there might be low demand substitution between different flavours of carbonated soft drinks, but a high supply substitution (switching from the production of one flavour to the other is easy in the short term). Nevertheless, the Commission decided that specific flavours were distinct markets, a particularly narrow definition. In the assessment stage, the Commission then had to consider that the market share of Pepsi Co in the lemon market substantially overstates anti-competitive effects because of supply substitution; indeed, the Commission was trying to assess dominance in a market where there is little potential market power to start with.

However, the Commission has sometimes used supply substitution in a way which is very close to the approach that we recommend in section 2.2.2. For instance, in *Lucas/Eaton* (149) the Commission states in paragraph 21 that supply substitution from producers of commercial brakes is unlikely within a short period of time (one year) in the market for heavy-duty brakes; quite appropriately (and in line with the procedure that we recommend in Chapter 2), the Commission then considers potential competition from producers of commercial brakes in the assessment of dominance.

3.3.1.3 *Product characteristics and substitutability*

The principal method used by the Commission to infer substitutability is the observation of product characteristics. The mere observation that particular products have different characteristics does not imply any particular degree of substitutability or cross-price elasticity between them. For any pair of characteristics, there will be some degree of substitutability; and the choice of relevant characteristics may sometimes be difficult. Several cases illustrate the shortcomings of the approach.

First, the lack of substitute products is sometimes defined as a product characteristic, which could be confusing; for instance, in *La Redoute/Empire* (80) and *Otto/Grattan* (70) the product market is defined as catalogue mail order because of certain product 'characteristics', one of which is that some people have no alternative to home shopping. If people have no alternative to home shopping, this is an indication of low demand elasticity, and could be recognized directly as such.

Goods with different characteristics may not be substitutable, but this is not always true. For example, in the *Courtaulds/SNIA* (113) case it was stated in paragraph 14 that product characteristics indicate a distinct product market for acetate yarn. But later on, in paragraph 26, it is stated that in the event of a 'significant' price increase for 'acetate yarn, it could be expected that purchasers would at least to some extent switch to other yarns, despite their different characteristics'. Again, in the *Metallgesellschaft/Safic Alcan* (146) case, in paragraph 13 natural rubber was not considered 'substitutable' with synthetic rubber because of different product characteristics. But in paragraph 26 it was stated that demand for natural rubber can 'at least partially be satisfied ... by synthetic rubber'. What this case illustrates is not necessarily that the Commission is acting in an inconsistent manner (though it may be), but rather that there are strong practical limitations to a non-quantitative approach to market definition. These limitations arise from the fact that there will always exist some substitutability between products: the question is whether a given degree of substitutability is enough to restrain market power.

A recent example of the limitations of a non-quantitative approach is provided by the case of *British Airways/TAT* (259). The problem was to determine which bundles of routes constituted the relevant market, and in particular whether Gatwick and Heathrow should be considered in the same market for the Paris–London and Lyons–London routes. Several factors affect the amount of sub-stitutability between the airports. These include the access facilities to London (which point to a joint market) and the possibilities for connection (which point to different markets). The Commission simply observed that 'a certain degree of substitutability ... can be considered to exist'. This, in itself, is not very informative.

The difficulty in selecting the appropriate characteristics is illus-trated in the case of *ABC/Generale des Eaux/Canal+/WH Smith TV* (110) where it was stated that the 'value of Pay-TV to the consumer can only be determined in relation to the alternative viewing possibilities of free access channels'. But of course other forms of entertainment and leisure activity are also substitution possibilities.

It might have been useful in this instance to ask consumers what their demand response would be to a given increase in the price of Pay-TV or at least to enquire about alternative substitutes.

These three cases illustrate that observation of product characteristics may not always give a good idea of demand substitution. This is because it is difficult, without having a great deal of information about consumer preferences, to know which characteristics are important, and in what proportion.

3.3.1.4 *Consumer surveys*

In the case of *Tetra Pak/Alfa-Laval* (68), the Commission sought more systematic information regarding anticipated behaviour by market participants. This is the only instance where the Commission sent detailed questionnaires to a large number of customers (dairies) situated throughout the Community, as well as to the principal competitors of Alfa-Laval and Tetra Pak, and to Alfa-Laval and Tetra Pak themselves. Respondents were asked to state whether, following a given rise in the price of aseptic packaging machines, they would switch demand (or expect demand to be switched) from aseptic packaging machines to non-aseptic packaging machines. Over 75% of respondents considered that a price increase of greater than 20% would be necessary to lead them to switch demand, indicating fairly clearly that the products were not in the same market. In this instance it could be presumed from observation of the products' characteristics that the products were not in the same market (aseptically packaged milk lasts six times longer than non-aseptically packaged milk, meaning that distribution networks must be much faster for non-aseptically packaged products). Nevertheless, the questionnaires provided strong confirmation of the market distinction.

In a number of cases, it seems that results from questionnaires could usefully have supported some assertion by the Commission. For example, in *Renault/Volvo* (4) it is stated that certain goods are 'not normally considered by customers as substitutable'. Extra quantification may be useful here and elsewhere. It is also probable that use of questionnaires would enable greater consistency of treatment across firms, even if market definition did not follow the results of the surveys to the letter.

3.3.2   *Geographic market definition*

The CEC defines the geographic market as 'the area where the undertakings concerned are involved in the supply and demand of products or services, in which the conditions of competition are sufficiently homogeneous and which can be distinguished from neighbouring areas because conditions of competition are appreciably different in those areas' (XXIst Report, p. 358). This assessment of geographic markets has used a variety of factors including the existence of barriers to trade and imports, the possibility of transferability of demand and purchasing policies, and factors like 'substantial differences in prices' and 'significant differences in undertakings' market shares or market presence in neighbouring areas'. Here again, supply substitution has been considered in some cases but ignored in others (as in the definition of product markets). A number of comments are appropriate.

3.3.2.1 *National preferences*

National preferences are repeatedly mentioned as a factor affecting the definition of geographic markets. This is appropriate to the extent that it refers either to the unwillingness of customers to buy a product from a foreign country simply because it is produced abroad, or to the existence of barriers erected by national governments against foreign products. It is inappropriate and should be considered under product market definition when it refers to the fact that customers have tastes that lead them to prefer the characteristics of some items which happen to be produced domestically. So, for example, it is not clear why the Commission considered 'national buyer preferences' in the *Renault/Volvo* (4) buses case under the 'geographic market' heading. Whether the Commission referred to a bias in favour of nationally produced items or to some characteristics of domestic production when it used the term 'national buyer preferences' is unclear.

3.3.2.2 *The distinction between geographic and product market*

The question of differences in tastes across national markets arises in the *Magneti Marelli/CEAc* (42) case. Here the Commission defined the geographic market for replacement starter batteries to be France, on the basis of the fact that the same batteries are sold at different prices in France from those abroad. The Commission attributed this price differential to, among other things, consumer preferences for well-known brands (it was not specified whether or not these brands were national). A minority of the Advisory Committee on Concentrations disputed the Commission's analysis, arguing that preferences were not nation-specific and the power of buyers strong - thus suggesting that the geographic market was larger than France. The existence of differential pricing suggests that the products are in different overall relevant markets, and if we could be sure that the batteries in France and abroad were identical in all respects except for production location then there would be good grounds for believing that the geographic markets were distinct. However, the Commission's claim that there are strong preferences for brands in France implies that batteries are heterogeneous in non-locational characteristics, that there is low cross-price demand elasticity between brands and non-brands, and perhaps between different brands; and therefore that the batteries are in different product markets. The difference in opinion between Commission and Advisory Committee might have been easier to resolve had there been a sharper distinction between the concepts of geographic and product markets.

3.3.2.3 *Consumer surveys*

As with product markets, the Commission did not generally use detailed questionnaires in order to assess the scope of the geographic market. One exception is the case of *Solvay-Laporte/Interox* (197), where the parties held a view as to the scope of the geographic market which differed from that stated in a Commission decision of 1984. Therefore the Commission conducted a survey of major producers and users of hydrogen peroxide. From the case report, it can be inferred that this questionnaire asked about market shares in different countries, prices in different countries and the importance of imports in each country. Given that these variables are all proxies for the primary variables of transport and production costs, it might have been simpler just to ask respondents the primary question directly: namely, if the price of hydrogen peroxide were permanently increased by 5% only within the UK, to what extent within a year would buyers (be expected to) shift their demand from hydrogen peroxide produced at home to that produced abroad? The Commission would then estimate whether this demand shift would be sufficient to render the original price increase unprofitable. Given that the Commission asked only for data on secondary variables, it is perhaps not surprising that the results of the survey were inconclusive.

3.3.2.4 *Consistency across cases*

Elsewhere in its analysis of geographic markets, the CEC concentrated on the height of trade barriers and the size of inter-country price differentials. These, combined with transport costs, would be the factors one would expect to be most important in determining the scope of the geographic market when cross-border mergers are involved.

However, the Commission has not always been consistent in applying these criteria. With reference to the *Eridania/ISI* (62) case, the CEC states in the XXIst Report (1992) that from the 'demand side, the Italian market (for sugar) seemed to be a market open to imports because prices in Italy were higher than in neighbouring countries' (p. 359). This wording is odd and seems to be in contradiction with other decisions. For instance, in its outline of the concept of geographic market, the Commission indicates that price differences between two regions are a sign of *heterogeneous* conditions of competition since they point towards the existence of barriers to entry. Heterogeneous conditions of competition in turn denote different geographical markets. This principle was applied for instance in *Varta/Bosch* (12). In this case, the Commission observed that 'the manufacturers are able to charge in Germany and Spain for the same types of batteries different prices to those which they charge in the other member states'. This fact, amongst others, helped to establish that there were 'appreciably different conditions of competition in the various member states' and therefore that 'the replacement markets for starter batteries in Germany and Spain are ... considered as national markets'. In the *Eridania/ISI* case, price differences are taken rather surprisingly as a sign of low entry barriers.

3.3.2.5 *Supply substitution and geographic markets*

Our argument that product market definitions will tend to be unduly narrow when supply substitution is not taken into account applies equally to geographic markets. The Commission has considered supply substitution in some cases and not in others. For instance, in *Lucas/Eaton* (149), the Commission considered only demand substitution and ruled that the relevant market for heavy-duty brakes was the European Community; one can reasonably wonder whether the relevant geographic market should not have included the United States in this case. (Indeed, it is stated in the description of the operation that the main clients of the joint venture will be located in the United States and Europe, and it is also reported that Lucas has significant sales in the US.) By contrast, in *Otto/Grattan* (70), the Commission ruled that the relevant market for mail order was the UK. In this case, the decision referred in some detail to the barriers that would make short-term reactions by competitors outside the UK unlikely. In other cases, the Commission ignored supply substitution in market definition but considered it later. For instance, in *Elf/BC/CEPSA* (98), the Commission decided that Spain was the relevant geographic market. However, imports from the rest of the Community were considered as a significant factor in the assessment of dominance. In some specific market segments, the Commission even considered increases in imports to be 'imminent', partly as a consequence of trade liberalization undertaken in the context of the internal market programme. Clearly, if imports were considered imminent, supply substitution from the rest of the Community should have been taken into account in the definition of markets.

3.3.3   *Market definition: some conclusions*

A number of conclusions emerge from our analysis of market definition:

1. Supply substitution has been considered in some cases and neglected in others. A consistent approach should be adopted. As indicated in section 2.2.2, we would strongly favour an approach based on both demand and supply substitution.
2. The shortcomings of an approach to market definition based solely on the observation of product characteristics are somewhat striking, for both product and geographic markets. Alternative approaches which directly estimate elasticities from past observations or anticipated behaviour (surveys) could usually

be implemented at reasonable cost. These would not be necessary for cases that clearly raise no competition concerns even on the narrowest plausible market definitions; but for cases where the market definition might matter it makes sense to use more quantitative evidence.

3. Some terms, like conditions of competition and substitutability, have been used in a way that is confusing, if not contradictory. A more precise definition, for instance in a set of published guidelines, would be useful.

4. The definition of geographic markets has interpreted price differences across countries somewhat inconsistently. This matter could also be usefully cleared up in published guidelines.

5. Finally, product and geographic markets have been defined sequentially, rather than simultaneously; this introduces a tendency towards excessively narrow market definition.

3.4   Assessing dominance

As indicated in Chapter 2, the assessment of potential dominance by the Commission uses the market position of the merged firm, the strength of remaining competition, buyer power and potential competition. We examine below the role of each factor in the decisions taken by the Commission.

3.4.1   *Market position*

The Commission takes the market share of the merging parties as its measure of concentration. This reflects the fact that the Merger Regulation does not explicitly allow for the possibility of oligopolistic behaviour, as market share measures do not allow for firm interactions. Several aspects of the use of market shares by the CEC can be singled out.

3.4.1.1   *Market shares as necessary conditions*

In evaluating the significance of market shares the Commission examines the trends of market shares, the time period over which high market shares have been held and the 'market context' (for

Table 3.1 Market shares and decisions (in descending order of market share).

Case (with details)	Post-merger market share	Pre-merger market shares	Decision	Reason(s) why merger approved
Air France/Sabena [Brussels–Lyons; pre-remedy] (157)	100%	50% and 50%	6.1b	See post-remedy entry below.
Tetra Pak/Alfa-Laval (68)	90%	90% and 0%	6.1c 8.2 without cond.	No increase in market share.
Alcatel/Telettra [microwaves] (42)	83%	18% and 65%	6.1c 8.2 with cond.	Strong buyer power; potential competition.
Courtaulds/SNIA [W. Europe] (113)	65%	32%, 10% and 23%	6.1b	Strong actual and potential competition.
Aerospatiale/Alenia/de Havilland [40–59 seats] (53)	64%	45% and 19%	6.1c 8.3	Merger blocked because: high market shares; weak actual and potential competition.
Magneti Marelli/CEAc [pre-remedy] (43)	60%	40% and 20%	6.1c 8.2 with cond.	See post-remedy entry below.
Renault/Volvo [trucks] (4)	54.3%	46.4% and 7.9%	6.1b	Strong actual competition.
Air France/Sabena [Brussels–Lyons; post-remedy] (157)	50%	50% and 50%	6.1b	Possible actual & potential competition.

ABB/BREL [diesel units in EC] (221)	50%	15% and 35% [estimate]	6.1b	Strong actual competition.
Nestlé/Perrier [pre-remedy] (190)	47.5%	15.6% and 31.9%	6.1c 8.2 with cond.	See post-remedy entry below.
Varta/Bosch (12)	44%	22% and 22% [estimate]	6.1c 8.2 with cond.	Actual competition.
Du Pont/ICI [pre-remedy] (214)	43%	?	6.1c with cond.	See post-remedy entry below.
Magneti Marelli/CEAc [post-remedy] (43)	40%	40% and 20%	6.1c 8.2 with cond.	No increase in market share.
Du Pont/ICI [post-remedy] (214)	38%	?	6.1c with cond.	Actual competition?
Nestlé/Perrier [post-remedy] (190)	36.8%	15.6% and 31.9%	6.1c 8.2 with cond.	Actual competition?
Digital/Kienzle (57)	26%	22% and 4%	6.1b	Strong actual competition; fast market growth.
Alcatel/AEG Kabel (165)	25%	12% and 13%	6.1b	Strong buyer power.

example, the rate of growth of the market). Low market shares (normally below 25%) generally lead to approval. As we indicated in Chapter 2, such a benchmark is reasonable and the great majority of cases which come before the Commission are cleared under this rule.

The CEC states in its XXIst Report that 'high market shares can be an indication of the existence of a dominant position' and that 'current market shares normally, but not necessarily, reflect future competitive strength'. Table 3.1 lists decisions in which there were substantial (over 25%) market shares, and indicates whether the case was approved within a month of notification (Article 6.1b); whether it raised serious doubts (Article 6.1c) and was subsequently approved subject to remedies (Article 8.2 with cond.) or approved without remedies (Article 8.2 without cond.); or whether it was blocked (Article 8.3). The table is highly incomplete, however, because of the difficulty of obtaining market share data from the case reports.

Table 3.1 illustrates that many cases have not been blocked despite having high post-merger market shares and substantial increases in market share. Notable examples include *Alcatel/Telettra* (42), *Varta/Bosch* (12), *Du Pont/ICI* (214), *Nestlé/Perrier* (190), *Courtaulds/SNIA* (113), *Renault/Volvo* (14) and *ABB/Brel* (221). The last three of these cases were approved within a month of notification. In addition, one case with high market share figures, *Aerospatiale/Alenia/de Havilland* (53), was blocked. This analysis clearly indicates that the Commission has taken factors other than market share into consideration. Interestingly, however, a large number of mergers have been allowed, not so much because entry was easy, but rather because actual competition was considered strong.

The fact that market shares were not considered to provide a reliable guide to potential market power can presumably be associated with the observation presented earlier that the practice of market definition by the CEC is biased in favour of excessively narrow markets. This arises both because product and geographic markets are determined sequentially and because market definition sometimes focuses only on demand substitution in circumstances where aggressive competitor response might be important. When markets are excessively narrow, there is little market power that can be exercised to start with and the link between market share and market power is weak. As discussed in section 2.2.2, the assessment of dominance through market shares and concentration indices then becomes rather uninformative.

3.4.1.2 *Market shares and actual competition*

The most common reason why a merger with high market share was nevertheless approved was because of strong actual competition. It indicates that the Commission was not satisfied with market shares. This is partly because the definitions of markets were excessively narrow but in some cases because market shares were viewed by the Commission as poor indicators of market power. It might also suggest that taking into account the distribution of competitors' market shares in a more systematic manner could be useful. It would be desirable in any case to ensure greater consistency across cases; in the current situation, arguments regarding the strength of actual competition are purely a matter of judgment and could be open to abuse. This is illustrated by a number of cases.

In *Renault/Volvo* (4) a 54% post-merger share in the market for trucks was not taken as an indication of dominance because there is effective competition from Mercedes, which supplies 18% of the market. This is an illustration of why market share may not be a good measure of the strength of remaining competition: market share measures do not distinguish the competitive strength of a market with many little sellers from one with a few big sellers. The Commission assumed here that Mercedes would provide strong competition.

Varta/Bosch (12) was another case in which a high market share was combated by actual competition. As we discuss in section 3.6.2 on remedies, a dominant position was avoided by Fiat and Deta/Mareg each ending up with 10% of the market. An important consideration here was that Fiat's access to a distribution network for a brand name meant that the 'competitive potential of the new entity will be more important than the current market shares achieved through the market share might indicate'.

One case in which market shares were taken as a sign of dominance was *Aerospatiale/Alenia (ATR)/de Havilland (DHC)* (53). This merger would have led to the new entity supplying 64% of the 40–59 seat regional turbo-prop aircraft market. This would have entailed DHC being eliminated as ATR's strongest competitor. Fokker, the next-strongest competitor, does not have a very long order back-log;[11] and the remaining competition is weak. Thus it was not so much the market share *per se* which indicated dominance, as the fact that the characteristics of the aircraft supply market mean that strong competition can be provided only by large firms.

3.4.1.3   *Collective dominance*

As we have indicated, the EC Merger Regulation neither explicitly allows for nor rules out the possibility of collusion as a source of dominant position: it states only that a merger will be prohibited if effective competition is significantly impeded. However, the wording of the Regulation itself is restricted by the previous decisions of the European Court of Justice (ECJ). The definition of dominant position in the Merger Regulation, for example, follows that given by the ECJ for the application of Article 86. Soon after the Regulation came into force Sir Leon Brittan, the then Competition Commissioner, began indicating that the CEC would use it to control oligopolistic dominance, since he regarded the possibility of effective competition being impeded by collective firm behaviour as being a very real one (Linklaters & Paines (1992), p. 9). Thus the Commission was seeking a test case where it could establish its *de facto* ability to control collective dominance. Although the possibility of oligopolistic behaviour was raised in *Alcatel/AEG Kabel* (165) and *Thorn EMI/Virgin Music* (202), the Commission did not find such a test case until February 1992 with the arrival of *Nestlé/Perrier* (190).

In *Alcatel/AEG Kabel*, the Bundeskartellamt made an Article 9 request for referral on the basis that the merger would create a situation of oligopolistic dominance because three suppliers would together hold more than 50% of the relevant market. In German competition law there is a presumption that three or fewer enterprises having the highest market shares are presumed each to be market-dominating if together they have a market share of at least 50% (see Heidenhain (1991)). In EC law there is no such presumption, so the Commission would have to demonstrate that effective competition between the members of the oligopoly could not be expected on structural grounds. In the event, the Commission found that counter-vailing buyer power was strong enough for the merger not to create a dominant position, so the merger was approved (without referral to the Bundeskartellamt).

In *Thorn EMI/Virgin* the market share of the new entity was less than 25% in most of the relevant markets affected. This, combined with the presence of other strong players on the market, meant that there was not a dominant position for the merged entity. However, the post-merger five-firm concentration ratio on the market for recorded music is 83%. This, together with the fact that the market shares appear to be stable over time, led the Commission to state that there could be 'a situation of collective dominance'. It then considered the likelihood that the acquisition would create or strengthen a dominant position amongst the five major record companies taken together. This meant assessing the likelihood of effective competition between the five companies. The Commission found that a number of cooperative agreements exist in the industry involving the five major companies and that 'the scope for price competition seems to be limited'. As part of its examination the Commission carried out a 'number of inquiries in order to evaluate the market behaviour of the main participants in the market'. These inquiries did not produce any evidence that 'the market is performing in an anti-competitive manner', and thus the merger was approved despite the high and stable market concentration, entry barriers, absence of price competition and the existence of cooperative agreements. It is regrettable that the Commission did not give details of their inquiries in the case report. The importance of this case from a competition policy standpoint is that it was the first instance of the Commission's investigating the possibility of interactions between firms.

The oligopoly test case for the CEC appeared in July 1992 in the form of the contested takeover bid of the French bottled water group Source Perrier by the Swiss foods group Nestlé. This high-profile case gave the Commission the opportunity to establish as a precedent its ability to control collective as well as single-firm dominance. The economic details of this case are discussed in section 3.6.4 on remedies below, but the key question was whether post-merger relations between Nestlé–Perrier and BSN would be cooperative or competitive. The Commission found that Nestlé and BSN would become jointly dominant in the French market for bottled water. The Commission argued from the standpoint of its duty under Article 3(f) of the EEC Treaty to maintain effective competition. Since the Merger Regulation does not in so many words restrict the concept of a dominant position to that of only one firm, the Commission must apply the Regulation to dominance shared by more than one firm, since otherwise effective competition will be impeded. A minority of the Advisory Committee took the view that the Regulation does not apply at all to collective dominance. Another minority stated that it only applies where there are structural links between the firms involved.

Table 3.2 Lower-bound estimates of Herfindahl–Hirschman indices (in descending order of post-merger HHI).

Case [with details]	Post-merger HHI	Change in HHI	US category	CEC decision
Air France/Sabena [Brussels–Lyons; pre-remedy] (157)	10,000	5,000	Market power	6.1b
Tetra Pak/Alfa–Laval (68)	8,100	0	Approval	6.1c 8.2 without cond.
Alcatel/Telettra [microwaves] (42)	6,890	2,340	Market power	6.1c 8.2 with cond.
Alcatel/Telettra [line transmission] (42)	6,560	3,280	Market power	6.1c 8.2 with cond.
Aerospatiale/Alenia/de Havilland [60 seats] (53)	6,350	0	Approval	6.1c 8.3
Aerospatiale/Alenia/de Havilland [40 seats] (53)	4,740	1,530	Market power	6.1c 8.3
Courtaulds/SNIA [W. Europe] (113)	4,730	2,570	Market power	6.1b
Aerospatiale/Alenia/de Havilland [40-59 seats] (53)	4,680	1,710	Market power	6.1c 8.3

Magneti Marelli/CEAc [pre-remedy] (43)	4,000	1,600	Market power	6.1c / 8.2 with cond.
Renault/Volvo [trucks] (4)	3,730	730	Market power	6.1b
Aerospatiale/Alenia/de Havilland [20-70 seats] (53)	3,090	1,220	Market power	6.1c / 8.3
Aerospatiale/Alenia/de Havilland [20-39 seats] (53)	2,910	100	Market power	6.1c / 8.3
Nestlé/Perrier [pre-remedy] (190)	2,660	1,000	Market power	6.1c / 8.2 with cond.
Air France/Sabena [Brussels–Lyons; post-remedy] (157)	2,500	0	Approval	6.1b
ABB/BREL [diesel units in EC] (221)	2,500	1,050	Market power	6.1b
Magneti Marelli/CEAc [post-remedy] (43)	2,400	0	Approval	6.1c / 8.2 with cond.
Digital/Kienzle (57)	2,360	180	Market power	6.1b
Nestlé/Perrier [post-remedy] (190)	2,310	640	Market power	6.1c / 8.2 with cond.

Table 3.2 *(cont.)*

Case [with details]	Post-merger HHI	Change in HHI	US category	CEC decision
Varta/Bosch [pre-remedy] (12)	2,300	970	Market power	6.1c 8.2 with cond.
Varta/Bosch [post-remedy] (12)	2,140	810	Market power	6.1c 8.2 with cond.
Courtaulds/SNIA [World] (113)	2,040	120	Market power	6.1b
Du Pont/ICI [pre-remedy] (214)	1,850			6.1c with cond.
Du Pont/ICI [post-remedy] (214)	1,440			6.1c with cond.
Thorn EMI/Virgin [recording] (202)	1,380	190	Significant competitive concerns	6.1b
Mannesmann/VDO (164)	1,360	60	Approval	6.1b
Alcatel/AEG Kabel (165)	1,250	310	Significant competitive concerns	6.1b
Digital/Philips (129)	850	240	Approval	6.1b
Thorn EMI/Virgin [publishing] (202)	700	160	Approval	6.1b

In consequence of the joint dominant market position, the Commission concluded that Nestlé should dispose of a number of lesser brands to a single purchaser. The effectiveness of this remedy depends to a very large extent on whether a significant third force will be created.

3.4.1.4 *Market shares and Herfindahl–Hirschman indices*

Table 3.2 (pp. 108–10) reports lower-bound estimates of the Herfindahl–Hirschman index for those cases which came before the CEC and for which sufficient data was available. The same comments about incompleteness that were made with reference to Table 3.1 also apply here. Table 3.2 shows that on its own definition of the relevant market the CEC was more lenient in approving mergers than would be implied by the thresholds cited in the US Guidelines. However, as indicated above, the Commission's procedures for market definition may be somewhat biased in favour of narrow markets, relative to the US practice. In addition, the Federal Trade Commission is in practice considerably more lenient in applying the concentration rules than is indicated by the Guidelines. When comparing figures, it must also be remembered that the philosophy of anti-trust in the United States places great emphasis on the danger of oligopoly whilst the European Commission's outlook has been to emphasize the position of single firms. Thus the HHI, which is an index of oligopolistic strength, is not a fair basis of comparison. Nevertheless, it is probably fair to say that a merger resulting in a high measure of concentration is more likely to be blocked in the United States than in the EC.

3.4.2   *Buyer power*

Buyer power was central in the Commission's decisions in at least three cases (*Alcatel/Telettra* (42), *Viag/Continental Can* (81) and *Alcatel/AEG Kabel* (165)).

We would expect that buyer power is much more effective in restraining market power when the buyer has several sources of supply and thus has the opportunity to play off suppliers against one another. An example of this point was the case of *Viag/Continental Can*, where 60% of market sales went to five buyers. The buyers have a dual/triple sourcing policy so that they can 'easily play off one supplier against another'. Consequently buyer power was important in combating high concentration.

In this light the reliance placed on buyer power in *Alcatel/Telettra*, where the merged entity has a market share greater than 80% (a larger figure than that of *Aerospatiale/Alenia/de Havilland*) and the rest of the market is fragmented, seems excessive. The source of the strong buyer power is Telefonica, the national telecommunications systems purchaser. Telefonica buys 100% of public switches sold in Spain, 90% of the transmission equipment and 60% of the microwave equipment. A remedy removed ownership links between Telefonica and Telettra (see below in the section on remedies). Telefonica was seen as being independent of the merged entity, and as being capable of switching purchases in the near future to alternative suppliers should Alcatel–Telettra raise prices. The likelihood of such switching taking place depends on both the incentives facing Telefonica and the availability of alternative suppliers. As we discuss in section 3.6.1 on remedies, there are transaction cost benefits for Telefonica from not switching. This also implies that the existence of pro-competitive forces in *Alcatel/Telettra* relies on keen new entrants.

3.4.3 *Entry and potential competition*

We turn now to the role of potential competition in the Commission's decisions. As we would expect from our discussion in section 2.3.3, entry was a particularly important factor in those cases where market shares were high, namely in the cases of *Alcatel/Telettra* (42), *Courtaulds/SNIA* (113), *Aerospatiale/Alenia/de Havilland* (53) and *Air France/Sabena* (157). The Commission regards 'strong evidence of a high probability of strong and quick market entry' as a sufficient condition for a market position to be non-dominant. Whilst it is not specified what 'quick' means, these are the same criteria as those of the US Guidelines, namely likelihood, timeliness and effectiveness.

3.4.3.1 *Entry lags*

Surprisingly, the Commission assessed entry lags explicitly in only two cases. In *Aerospatiale/Alenia (ATR)/de Havilland (DHC)*, the

Commission estimated that the entry lag was six to seven years because of the process of marketing research (two to three years) and R&D, production and delivery (another four years). In addition, there are sunk costs of designing, testing and gaining regulatory approval. Hence potential competition is weak, giving a firm with strong market position the chance to exercise market power.

The only other case in which the Commission explicitly estimated the entry lag was *Lucas/Eaton* (149), in which the time necessary to permit design and retooling work was put at two years. Despite this lag, the Commission stated that the threat of entry 'will to a certain extent constrain the competitive behaviour of existing manufacturers'. It will be recalled that two years is the threshold for entry to be 'easy' under the Department of Justice's definition. The Commission did not attempt to estimate the other two necessary conditions for entry to be easy under the US definition: likelihood and sufficiency of entry.

3.4.3.2 Entry barriers

A number of entry barriers were explicitly considered by the Commission, including transport costs, brand awareness and regulatory barriers.

Regulatory impediments were considered in *Alcatel/Telettra*, but only to a limited extent. As mentioned in section 3.6.1, entry (by AT&T and Ericsson) was 'essential' in combating the high market share of the merged entity. Potential imports by Siemens were also important. AT&T has no sales of microwave equipment in Spain at present, though since 1988 its line transmission sales in Spain have grown strongly; the firm thinks it can expand sales in the Spanish market. Ericsson produces mainly public switching and digital transmission equipment. It has only limited production of microwave equipment but regards entry barriers as being low because no product adaptation is necessary. Siemens has only a 'marginal position' in the transmission markets in Spain, with a 9% market share. It considers that the two important entry barriers are the vertical integration of Telefonica with suppliers and the fact that the Public Procurement Directive, according to which national purchasers must consider all possible domestic or foreign suppliers, will not be effective in Spain until 1996. The remedy broke the vertical ownership links with Alcatel–Telettra, though there are transaction cost reasons why

Telefonica may wish to limit the number of suppliers (see section 3.6.1 on remedies). With regard to public procurement, Telefonica has assured the CEC that it will technically approve new suppliers and will arrange for contacts to be made with new suppliers, be they domestic or foreign, where possible. However, given that there is no guarantee that foreign suppliers will be considered until 1996, more analysis was needed here of the likely entry lag as well as the profitability of entering a market with entry barriers. Given the small current market positions of the potential entrants and the very strong market position of the incumbent firm, more analysis was also needed of the sufficiency of entry in restraining the market power of Alcatel–Telettra.

In *Courtaulds/SNIA*, potential competition from yarn imports produced in the United States and the Far East were essential in combating high market shares. The Commission estimated the likelihood of entry by considering the costs of transport (5% plus a 10% EC tariff) and setting these against lower extra-EC energy and labour costs. On the basis of this calculation the Commission concluded that any attempt by the merged entity to raise prices would tend to pull in imports.

In *Alcatel/AEG Kabel* (165) entry barriers were apparently not considered at all. Given that the relevant market was that for telecommunications cables, there would surely be some sunk costs of investment. The analysis of potential competition is also incomplete in *TNT/Canada Post et al.* (102), where it was stated only that entry barriers were 'considerable'. Given that the proposed joint venture has high market share, entry barriers were an important factor here and should have received detailed attention.

In *Nestlé/Perrier* (190) the Commission indicated that brand awareness and transport costs were entry barriers. However, the Commission also observed that most of the 32.3% of the French market for bottled water that is not controlled by Nestlé–Perrier or BSN is accounted for by the own-brand sales of supermarkets. Although transport costs were supposed to be high, in the last five years there have been 15 attempts at entry into the French mineral water market (Linklaters & Paines (1992)). According to the Commission, a price increase by Nestlé or BSN would very probably, therefore, trigger more entry attempts. It is not clear, however, whether these fifteen attempts were successful. Some of them are bound to have failed, otherwise market shares would be more dispersed than they currently are. So barriers to entry may have been significant after all. In any event, it would seem that a more careful analysis of previous entry attempts could have yielded interesting insights.

3.4.4 *Assessing dominance: some conclusions*

Seven main conclusions emerge from our analysis of the Commission assessment of dominance:

1. A post-merger market share of less than 25% is sufficient for a deal to be cleared, and normally within a month of notification. In the light of our discussion in section 2.2.3, this appears sensible. In addition, and also sensibly, where market share did not much increase the merger was cleared.
2. Currently market shares do not appear to be treated as very informative indicators of market power. Market shares do not provide a reliable signal to prospective merging parties; they do not even give a particularly good indication of whether a case will require remedies. The lack of confidence that the Commission has displayed regarding the significance of market share may be associated with the observation made earlier that the definition of markets is biased towards excessively narrow markets. In those circumstances, indicators of market power lose some of their significance.
3. Market shares have been qualified in many different ways. The Commission has used a variety of additional factors associated with the structure of supply in the relevant market. At present, the additional considerations which are invoked may appear sometimes arbitrary.
4. The 'strength of remaining competitors' is most often used to complement market share information. It would help for such considerations to be invoked somewhat more systematically.
5. The Commission is now prepared to investigate the possibility of interactions between firms. Yet the procedure to evaluate oligopolistic interactions is not systematic (as revealed for instance in *Du Pont/ICI* (214)).
6. The Commission seems to place a good deal of faith in buyer power even when buyers face few alternative suppliers.

7. The Commission has relied heavily on entry possibilities in several cases. Yet the analysis of entry has been sketchy, for example estimating entry lag in only two cases. More systematic attention to the timeliness, likelihood and sufficiency of entry would be useful.

3.5   Efficiency: defence or offence?

As we discussed in section 2.4.3.3, it is not entirely clear whether the EC Merger Regulation allows for efficiency considerations. Efficiency has nevertheless been mentioned in a number of cases, sometimes as an offence and once as a possible defence, only to be dismissed as negligible in the case in question.

In *AT&T/NCR* (50) possible synergies were considered under the 'Conglomerate Aspects' heading. The Commission asked whether AT&T's technical and marketing know-how could be used to 'enhance the position of NCR in the workstation market'. One mechanism through which this might occur is through a 'potential complementarity' between technical know-how and the marketing of workstations, which could give rise to 'synergies' through the possible development of 'more advanced communication features at a lower cost'. However, for 'the moment such a complementarity cannot be foreseen as there are no precise indications of concrete technical developments or possible marketing strategies'. Nevertheless, the Commission does not rule out the possibility that 'potential advantages flowing from synergies may create or strengthen a dominant position'.

Thus in this case the Commission regarded cost savings as a negative factor which could lead to the creation or strengthening of a dominant market position. Similar concerns arise in *Dräger/IBM/HMP* (101), *Pan Am/Delta* (130) and *Sextant/BGT-VDO* (290). In those cases, the Commission seems to imply that the competitive advantage that the joint ventures might obtain is itself a matter of concern (see Jenny (1992)). There is of course sometimes a trade-off between productive and allocative efficiency, and this should be recognized; it is another matter, however, to state that improvements in productive efficiency are undesirable because they lead to allocative inefficiencies. Carried to its logical conclusion, such an argument would imply that, if only privately profitable mergers are proposed, none should be allowed. A less critical interpretation of the Commission's decision here ties in with a point made in the discussion of dominance: namely, that the Commission appears to regard the existence of small and medium-sized firms as a good thing in itself. Thus cost savings which force out small and medium-sized firms may be seen as undesirable. This decision is nevertheless slightly disturbing, and could send to other firms contemplating merger the perverse signal that cost savings are a bad thing, and will make the merger less likely to be approved.

In *Aerospatiale/Alenia/de Havilland* the parties themselves put forward an estimate of cost savings amounting to 0.5% of combined turnover. These cost savings would be realized through synergies in marketing and product support, and through rationalizing parts procurement. The European Commission regarded these cost savings as 'negligible', and they were irrelevant to the final decision. The question arises whether the Commission, in its position of limited information, would have been able to detect whether more substantial claims about cost savings were realistic or not. Of course, if the firms' lawyers had been reading the *AT&T/NCR* case report, they might have concluded that they would be better off not claiming large cost savings.

3.6   Remedies

In several cases, the merger proposal brought by the firms to the Merger Task Force was unacceptable in its original form. In these instances, the firms had the choice of either aborting the proposal altogether or endeavouring to alter the proposal in some way in order to make it acceptable to the Commission. The second route involves bilateral bargaining between the firms and the Commission, in order to arrive at an appropriate remedy. The purpose of this section is to assess what criteria the Commission used in judging whether or not a given remedy is likely to be effective in combating market dominance, and whether in fact the remedies agreed upon are likely to be effective.

Remedies are typically incorporated into merger proposals in one of two legal forms. First, a given merger proposal can be accepted in its existing form subject to modification as allowed for under Article 8.2 of the Merger Regulation. In this instance the Commission attaches to the decision conditions and obligations intended to ensure that the remedy is in fact undertaken. Up to 6 October 1992 the decisions taken under Article 8.2 with conditions were *Varta/Bosch* (12), *Alcatel/Telettra* (42), *Magneti Marelli/CEAc* (43), *Accor/ Wagons-Lits* (126), *Nestlé/Perrier* (190) and *Du Pont/ICI* (214). Secondly, the merger proposal itself can be altered during negotiation between the firms and the Commission. This means that the merger can be cleared within a month of notification under Article 6.1b. Decisions of this kind include *Fiat/Ford* (9), *TNT/Canada Post et al.* (102), *Courtaulds/SNIA* (113), *Air France/Sabena* (157) and *BA/TAT* (259).

Remedies usually take the form of horizontal or vertical de-integration or divestment, with the aim of stimulating actual or potential competition. The de-integration is complete in some cases and only partial in others. We consider these various types of remedies cases and subsequently discuss the process through which remedies are negotiated and their enforcement.

3.6.1 *Vertical linkages*

There were two cases in which the remedy involved vertical de-integration. The first was that of *Alcatel/Telettra* (42), in which Telefonica, the Spanish telecommunications equipment monopsonist, sold its 5% minority holding in Telettra, Spain's largest supplier of telecommunications equipment, to Alcatel, the second largest supplier of this equipment in Spain, when Alcatel and Telettra merged (and held a market share of more than 80%).

In this industry, transaction costs of changing suppliers mean that the optimal length of contracts between Telefonica and its suppliers is one to two years. In paragraph 9 of the case report, the Commission states that 'for public switching ... it is generally not considered feasible to have more than two or three suppliers because of the high cost and technical complexity of this type of equipment. For transmission equipment ... it is usual to have [three to five] suppliers'. Thus there are good reasons why Telefonica might prefer to have a small number of suppliers. Transaction costs are also such that incumbent suppliers have a strong advantage. That also implies that to the extent that Telefonica's managers are not maximizing profits (because of ineffective corporate control, for instance), the potential for collusion and the sharing of rents between Telefonica and a few privileged suppliers should be taken seriously.

The potential for collusion cannot be dismissed lightly – in particular because Telefonica's managers can choose whether or not to license buyers. The Public Procurement Directive, according to which national purchasers must consider all possible domestic or foreign suppliers, will not be implemented in Spain until 1996. Telefonica has indicated to the Commission that it will be happy to approve new suppliers. It is unclear whether this should be interpreted as a commitment to do so.

Whether Telefonica will indeed share rents with some privileged suppliers thus depends very much on the effectiveness of the control which is exercised on Telefonica's managers by the Spanish government. Evidence on the relative effectiveness of corporate and government control is not entirely clear cut (see Pestieau and Tulkens (1992)), so that a priori the status of Telefonica as a state-owned firm might not necessarily make matters worse. However, this discussion suggests that the appropriate remedies should probably have considered issues of corporate control.

It is clear that in principle, the severance of a formal link between the buyer and the privileged incumbent supplier can only help in reducing the scope for collusion. However, the significance of the formal link which has been removed between Telefonica and Telettra is questionable; given that the holding concerned is rather small (5%) and given the fact that Telettra is Fiat-controlled, Telefonica might have enjoyed very little effective control over Telettra in the first place.

The second remedy involving vertical de-integration was that used in the case of *TNT/Canada Post, DBP Postdienst, La Poste, PTT Post and Sweden Post* (102). This operation concerned a joint venture between the private transport services firm, TNT, and five national postal administrations. Under the terms of the original proposal, the joint venture would have had exclusive access to the national postal outlets for a period of five years. This exclusive access would have foreclosed entry to the national postal outlets by competitors of TNT. In addition, the joint venture was to have had the rights to subcontract certain services to the five postal authorities, raising the possibility of cross-subsidization and privileged contract conditions for the joint venture. These factors, combined with the fact that entry barriers are 'considerable', led the Commission to conclude that the joint venture 'might lead to a dominant position' in the market for international express delivery services.

Three remedies were agreed upon. First, the exclusive access period was reduced from five to two years, two years being judged necessary as a transfer period. Second, there was an unspecified reduced 'scope' of the exclusive access. Third, equal treatment in subcontracting was promised by the parties. The extent of foreclosure has thus been significantly reduced even though it is hard to assess it precisely because the nature of the agreement relating to the scope of the joint venture has not been made public. It is not entirely clear what the benefits of this foreclosure may be: postal agencies provide retail facilities on their network and it would seem that (in the absence of unlikely capacity constraints) they could act as distributors for a number of competing courier companies. The transaction costs which may justify the foreclosure have not been detailed in the decision. Still, two years is a relatively short period of time and from this perspective the remedies have greatly improved matters over the original agreement. The joint venture as it stands probably cannot do much harm, even though the rationale for foreclosure is not entirely clear.

3.6.2 *Horizontal links*

The first type of horizontal remedy concerns the removal of ownership links with an actual competitor. These occur in *Varta/Bosch* (12), *Accor/Wagons-Lits* (126), *Magneti Marelli/CEAc* (43) and *Courtaulds/SNIA* (113). This last case differs from the others to the extent that a divestiture was proposed by Courtaulds in the first instance; indeed, the merger would presumably have been approved without any remedies, since, although only four firms supply the acetate yarn market, there is strong competition from Hoechst, which has 42% of the world market. Nevertheless, as part of the merger proposal, Courtaulds undertook to dispose of its minority interest (12%) in, and one representative on the board of directors of, the third-ranking competitor INACSA. The Commission did not investigate the degree of effective control conferred upon Courtaulds by this holding, and approved the merger under Article 6.1b. We discuss the other three cases next.

(i) Varta/Bosch The remedies in *Varta/Bosch* involved two changes of ownership which led to increases in actual competition. The proposal of the joint venture was unacceptable in its original form to the Commission since, amongst other things, it would have created a 44% market share in Germany with a 25% lead over the next competitors. Then two 'factual changes' occurred. First, Fiat acquired CEAc (through Magneti Marelli/CEAc) with a market share in Germany between 2% and 5%. Through CEAc, Fiat acquired Sonnenschein, which has a 5–10% market share in Germany. So Fiat's market share in Germany increased from 1% to 10%. These acquisitions gave Fiat both possession of a brand name in a market where consumers prefer brands and access to a distribution network within Germany. This, combined with the financial strength of Fiat, led the Commission to conjecture that Fiat would provide 'strong competition' on the German market – in particular that the competition would be stronger than a 10% market share might be expected to confer.

The second factual change was that Varta undertook to cut its cooperative links with the Deta/Mareg group of companies. Accordingly Varta will 'within an agreed period' terminate Deta/Mareg's rights to use Varta's (intellectual) property rights and will end any overlapping of supervisory and management boards between itself and Deta/Mareg. The Commission expects Deta/Mareg to become an 'independent competitor with a 10% market share'.

Both remedies involve conjectures about the strength of future competition. Fiat's and Deta/Mareg's 10% market share each are expected to be able to combat the joint venture's 44% market share with a large (more than 25%) lead.[12]

(ii) Magneti Marelli/CEAc The original proposal in the Magneti Marelli/CEAc operation would have given the new entity 60% of the French market in replacement batteries, since CEAc has a 40% share and Fiat, of which Magneti Marelli is a subsidiary, had a majority shareholding in CFEC, which is France's second biggest battery producer, with a 20% market share. In order to avoid creating a dominant position, Fiat agreed to reduce its majority shareholding in CFEC to 10% and to reduce its supervisory board membership to one. Thus the aim of this remedy was to remove ownership links between CEAc and CFEC. But the split was only partial, since Fiat still owns 10% of CFEC. With dispersed share

ownership and cosy relations with fellow block shareholders, Fiat could still have considerable influence on business affairs at CFEC. But the Commission apparently did not examine how much effective control over CFEC will remain with Fiat after the implementation of the remedies. The question arises as to why the Commission did not insist that Fiat divest itself of all of its ownership interests. Surely, this would have been a more secure way of preventing collusion between CFEC and CEAc than leaving some (unspecified) degree of effective control in Fiat's hands.

It is also worth noting that whereas in Alcatel–Telettra an ownership stake of 5% was implicitly judged sufficient to give Telefonica significant control over Telettra (else the remedy was pointless), in Magneti Marelli/CEAc an ownership stake of 10% was judged insufficient to give Fiat significant control over CFEC. Of course a direct comparison is not necessarily valid here, given that each operation had its own characteristics. But the observation does illustrate the importance of estimating the degree of effective control conferred upon a firm by a given ownership stake. Such estimation requires consideration of national corporate control laws and customs, as well as of the dispersion of ownership. These consider-ations, to the extent that they were part of the decision, should be made explicit.

The rather light treatment of Fiat's capacity for exercising control via horizontal links in this case is also interesting in the light of the Commission's decision in *IFINT/EXOR* (187). This was a hostile bid by the Agnelli family company (which controls Fiat) for the company that, in concert with two others, controlled just over 49% of the shares of Source Perrier; the bid was part of a prolonged battle for control in which Nestlé was eventually victorious. But before the bid failed, the Commission cleared the deal with an Article 6.1b decision, in spite of concerns about links between the Agnelli group and BSN, the second largest producer of mineral water on the French market. The Agnelli group owned 5.8% of BSN and a member of the Agnelli family was a member of both the management and the strategic boards of BSN. The Commission was content to note that the relevant companies in the Agnelli group 'have undertaken not to participate in any discussion of the management and strategic boards of BSN relating to the activities of the latter in the mineral water sector, and not to exchange with BSN any information capable of influencing the competitive behaviour of these companies in the mineral water sector'. Given the virtual impossibility of monitoring or enforcing this undertaking, as well as the fact that it would not have been difficult to require the Agnelli group to dispose of its interest in and seats on the boards of BSN, this 'remedy' seems to us to have been carrying the notion of scout's honour a little far.

(iii) Accor/Wagons-Lits   In the case of the contested takeover bid by Accor of Wagons-Lits, the Commission found that the new entity would enjoy a market share of 89% on the market for motorway catering and 69% on that for light meals. Further, the new entity would be 18 times larger than its nearest competitor as regards light meals, would enjoy financial strength out of all proportion to that of its competitors, and would be protected by very high barriers to entry. Rejecting a series of objections put forward by the parties to this reasoning, the Commission required Accor to sell all of Wagons-Lits' French motorway catering activities. Thus a likely case of single-firm dominance was forestalled by obliging Accor to dispose outright of Wagons-Lits' entire interest in the market concerned. This remedy is clear and likely to be very effective.

3.6.3   *Facilitating entry*

Three cases have involved remedies which in one way or another facilitated entry into the relevant market. In *Fiat/Ford* (9), Fiat agreed to terminate its exclusive distribution network, removing an entry barrier into the Italian market. In consequence the Commission predicted that competitors were 'likely' to move into the Italian market if prices were raised.

In *Air France/Sabena* (157) a package of remedies was agreed upon in order to prevent the parties from assuming a dominant position on certain routes within France, between France and Belgium, and between France and Africa. The original proposal would have given the parties a total monopoly on the Brussels–Lyon, Brussels–Nice and Brussels–Paris routes. Air France, Sabena and the governments of France and Belgium agreed with the Commission to undertake the following package of remedies. First, one of the two companies will withdraw from the Brussels–Nice and Brussels–Lyons routes to allow at least one rival airline into the market (if indeed a competitor requests service on these routes); they also commit themselves not to increase frequencies after entry has taken place. Second, rival EC carriers will be allowed to enter in competition (in 'reasonable conditions') with the Air France–Sabena shuttle service planned between Brussels and Paris; Air France and Sabena will not oppose slot allocations to competitors as long they provide a number of flights no greater than that of Air France/Sabena.[13] Third, a certain proportion of takeoff and landing slots will be kept available for rival companies at Brussels airport. Fourth, Air France and Sabena will abandon certain flights to Africa (typically one a week), if a competing airline is prepared to serve the routes. These remedies thus involve the facilitation of entry by competing airlines on designed routes. The Commission has said it is 'very likely' that a willing carrier will come forward, although it was not known at the time of the decision whether certain carriers had already expressed an interest (Hill and Betts (1992)). At the time of writing, entry (by SAS) has occurred on the Brussels–Lyons route. One can wonder about potential market power in the Brussels–Paris route, given that even in the best scenario the market share of Air France–Sabena will remain above 50%. Nevertheless, the analysis in this case is unusually detailed and thorough, for instance in the specification of the conditions in which competing airlines could operate ('reasonable conditions').

Similar competition concerns arose in *BA/TAT* (159), an airlines case whose decision came eight weeks after that of *Air France/Sabena*. The terms of the initial proposal led the Commission to judge that 'the position of BA and TAT as a result of the transaction may significantly impede competition' on the Gatwick–Paris and Gatwick–Lyons routes. The major source of this dominant position was an entry barrier caused by an absence of new slots, combined with a near total monopoly over the routes by BA–TAT. The entry barrier is particularly high on the route to Paris, since the high density of traffic and the existing extensive services offered by BA and TAT mean that 'a new entrant needs to compete with a sufficient number of return flights reasonably spread throughout the day'. Traffic between London and Lyons is currently modest but 'a considerable potential for expansion is foreseen'. If and when the demand for flights between Gatwick and Lyons increases, the 'problem of availability of slots could constitute a major barrier to entry'.

In order to meet the Commission's concern, BA entered into a commitment which opens up to some degree the allocation of slots to new entrants. The terms of the commitment were as follows. In the event that a carrier wishing to start or increase services on the Gatwick–Paris route does not obtain the necessary slots from the airport coordinator, BA will make up to 12 slots available in order to enable the operation of six additional daily return flights spread out through the day.[14] The parallel offering is made for Gatwick–Lyons, where up to four slots will be made available (two return flights, one in the morning and one in the afternoon). The Commission judged that 'the commitments *eliminate* the problem of market entry' (emphasis added) and thus approved the merger under Article 6.1b.

That the commitment will eliminate the problem of entry is something of an overstatement; the strength of competition which would result from entry in the best possible scenario was not analyzed by the Commission. Even assuming the most favourable outcome in which there were constant average capacities and load factors across companies, BA–TAT would still control half of the market (the same as Air France–Sabena on the Brussels–Paris route). In addition, further entry will still be determined by the number of slots that will be available and the allocation of slots is somewhat biased in favour of incumbents. The conditions under which potential competitors could operate also seem rather less favourable than those specified in *Air France/Sabena* where 'reasonable' conditions of competition were assessed and specified in great detail. On the whole, the remedies put forward in this case, even if they are directed to the right problems, still appear somewhat weak. Air France has now challenged this decision in the Court of First Instance. At the time of writing, no decision has been taken by the Court and it is not clear what the outcome of this procedure is likely to be.

3.6.4 *Additional competition*

The remedies in the cases of *Nestlé/Perrier* and *Du Pont/ICI* marked a new direction in the Commission's regulatory approach. For in both cases the remedy necessitated the creation from a divested part of one of the party's production activities of a new 'third force' to compete with the merged entity. In both cases the agreements stipulate that the assets are to be sold by a set undisclosed deadline to a single buyer. It is not up to the Commission to choose the buyer: the terms of the sale and initially the identity of the buyer are matters to be agreed upon between potential buyers and the merging parties. The sale will then go ahead subject to approval by the Commission of the identity of the buyer (in *Du Pont/ICI* the buyer will have to operate in the same market as the divestor). We consider each case in turn.

(i) Nestlé/Perrier   In February 1992, Nestlé notified the Commission of its intention to acquire Perrier. The takeover would have left Nestlé–Perrier with 48% of the French market for mineral water, with the next-largest market supplier being BSN with a 20% share. In an attempt to pre-empt competition concerns and possibly to avoid full investigation by the Commission, Nestlé agreed in the lead-up to the bid with BSN to sell to BSN one of Perrier's bottled water brands – Volvic – if the bid succeeded. This would reduce the market share of Nestlé/Perrier to 36.8% and increase BSN's share to 30.9%, leaving others with a total of 32.3%. It appears that much of this residual market was accounted for by own-brand sales by supermarkets (Linklaters & Paines (1992), p. 9). Whilst this compromise might have mitigated the competition concerns about Nestlé's market position alone, from the point of view of collusive behaviour the Volvic sale does not obviously improve the situation since the market positions of Nestlé–Perrier and BSN became more symmetric without their combined share falling at all.

The Commission, sensitive from the beginning to the possibility of joint dominance, decided to open a full investigation into the merger. There appeared to be little danger of single-firm dominance by either Nestlé or BSN. But the Commission decided that the merger would give Nestlé and BSN a position of collective dominance. Nevertheless, rather than blocking the takeover outright, the Commission negotiated a remedy with Nestlé and Perrier. Under the terms of the remedy Nestlé has to dispose of eight of its lesser brands (including Vichy, Saint Yorre, Thonon and Pierval) to a single approved buyer who must not sell them on to BSN or back to Nestlé–Perrier within ten years. The brands – which have to be sold by a set undisclosed deadline – represent 20% of French mineral water capacity. Nestlé is to keep those brands it most wants, including Contrexeville and Perrier itself (de Jonquieres and Hill (1992)). The sale of Volvic to BSN is to be delayed until after the other remedies have been implemented. In addition, the remedy specifies that Nestlé must not provide data on sales volumes which is less than one year old to any trade association or other body which might make the information available to competitors.

Thus the primary aim of the remedy is to maintain competition in the French market for mineral water. The effectiveness of this remedy depends on how strong the competition will be from the new 'third force' and in particular whether it will prevent collusion between Nestlé–Perrier and BSN. With regard to collusion, Nestlé–Perrier has after the remedies a 37% market share and BSN 31%, so it is not clear that duopoly behaviour is much less likely than before. Indeed, as noted above, it may be more likely, given that the market shares of the two companies are now more equal. The prohibition on Nestlé's providing sales information which might reach competitors is an attempt to prevent collusion between Nestlé, BSN and the new third force. This is unlikely to make a great deal of difference, however, given that sales information may not be needed to sustain collusion, and also that there appear to be well-established informal information flows between Nestlé and BSN arising from their history of close relations. A few months before the merger BSN played a pivotal role in helping Nestlé to defeat a rival bid for Perrier by the Italian Agnelli family. This was the initial reason why Nestlé agreed to sell Volvic, Perrier's second largest brand, to BSN.

One can also be fairly sceptical regarding the strength of the new competitor. Nestlé–Perrier can choose whom to sell the eight brands to; it has an incentive to choose a firm which provides as weak competition as possible. In addition, the buyer with the highest willingness to pay will presumably be that one that intends to maintain a fair degree of collusion with Nestlé–Perrier and BSN. In a sense, Nestlé–Perrier should be able to sell ex ante some of the future monopoly rents that the Commission is trying to prevent in the first place. Given these incentive constraints, it is quite possible that the buyer will not be a strong competitor. In addition, it is not clear whether the Commission will have much control over any break-up of the newly formed third force.

It is not only outside observers who have expressed dissatisfaction with the Commission's decision in *Nestlé–Perrier*. Representatives of the Perrier workforce have brought an action in the European

Court of First Instance (Hampton (1992)). They challenge the Commission decision on two grounds. First, that the Commission has infringed the procedural rights of employee representatives of the companies concerned by the merger and has failed to respect fundamental social rights recognized by Community law, including the Social Charter. Second, that the Commission has failed to maintain effective competition in France and has introduced the concept of oligopolistic dominance without legal basis. Interim measures were refused by the Court of First Instance, which nevertheless conceded that the claim for review was admissible. At the time of writing, it is unclear what will become of the Perrier workforce's claim for judicial review.

(ii) Du Pont/ICI   The original deal in *Du Pont/ICI* was an asset swap in which ICI gained Du Pont's acrylic business plus some cash and Du Pont gained ICI's nylon interests. This would have resulted in Du Pont having 43% of the nylon carpet fiber market. In consequence of this high market share the Merger Task Force recommended that the deal should be blocked. The competitors of ICI and Du Pont also complained about the deal. However, the European Commission approved the merger subject to Du Pont implementing a package of remedies. There is some evidence to suggest that the Merger Task Force was sceptical of this decision, although this is only a matter of conjecture (Jackson and de Jonquieres (1992)). According to this package, Du Pont must: (i) transfer a quarter of ICI's annual nylon carpet fiber capacity to a single as-yet-unnamed competitor which must be a fibers manufacturer; (ii) sell an entire R&D facility, including technical personnel, to the same competitor – the competitor will 'share' a factory with Du Pont; (iii) manufacture under contract to the competitor for at least five years; and (iv) give the competitor exclusive rights to ICI's 'Timberelle' trademark, which is carried on 80% of ICI's carpet fiber production. The remedies will reduce Du Pont's market share from 43% to 38%.

The remedy imposed in this case suffers from the weakness mentioned above, in that letting one of the merging partners dispose of assets may be inadequate given the incentives faced by both the buyer and the seller. The dependence of the new competitor on Du Pont's handover policy will probably be such that it will be weaker than ICI was in the past. The effect of the remedy on Du Pont's market share is not very large either.

3.6.5   *Implementation and monitoring*

We have already argued that a number of remedies rely on a great deal of confidence regarding the development of pro-competitive forces. In many cases, the remedies are based on conjectures that may or may not turn out to be validated. In this context some process of formal monitoring could be useful, if only to ensure that the experience of previous remedies can be drawn on for the future.

In addition, certain important remedies (for instance, in *Air France/Sabena* and *BA/TAT*) have been negotiated in the context of decisions under Article 6.1b, that is during the one-month investigation period.[15] However (according to Article 8), it is doubtful whether the Commission is legally entitled to imposed remedies in the context of such decisions. It remains to be seen whether the Commission has the ability to enforce these remedies in court.[16]

Even when remedies can be enforced, monitoring is appropriate. For instance, in *Varta/Bosch*, it is perfectly possible that the new competition will provide effective competition, especially if Fiat expands its foothold in the German market for replacement batteries. But it is by no means certain: the joint venture remains in a strong market position with an established brand. Given that the remedies do not clearly remove the possibility that a dominant position will be created, there is a case for establishing a reporting requirement whereby as a condition of the remedy the merging parties would be required to re-submit in the future at certain intervals information of the kind asked for on the Notification Form. This information would include details of Starterbatterie's prices and costs, and would enable the Commission to assess whether Fiat and Deta/Mareg are in fact strong competitors. Such a reporting requirement could valuably be made part of all remedy deals agreed under Article 8.2 With Conditions.

Close monitoring might also be useful in cases involving disposal of assets. As mentioned above, the incumbent is in a strong position. The scope for manipulation is also greater, the more complex is the deal. From this perspective, given the complexity of the deal involved, Du Pont is in a particularly strong position to make the new competitor as dependent as possible on Du Pont, and therefore to make the competition weak. Given that the new competitor is as yet unknown but must be a fibers manufacturer, there is no guarantee that the firm will have the financial strength or the management capacities needed to compete with Du Pont in the future. The outcome could be usefully monitored.

3.6.6   *Strategies of Negotiation*

One cannot help noticing that the frequency of remedies has increased over time, and also that some are now openly being challenged (*BA/TAT, BA/DAN AIR* and *Nestlé/Perrier*). Many factors could explain these new trends (if they are confirmed), including a change in the average characteristics of mergers. It is also possible, however, to interpret them in the context of the larger bargaining problem that arises between firms and the Commission. This matter will be discussed in Chapter 5. For the time being, let us simply note that the evidence is also consistent with the idea that companies are expecting the Commission to be ready to negotiate on many issues, and anticipate in difficult cases that a deal involving remedies is likely to be struck. The nature of the remedies that have been agreed upon and the increased occurrence of open challenges also suggest that the Commission may have been in a weak bargaining position. This interpretation will actually be supported by the results of our survey, presented in Chapter 4.

From this perspective, it might also be useful to note that the only case that was blocked was an early one, for which no remedy had been proposed by the firms. Since then, there have been several cases where the merger proposal in its original form might have given rise to an equally strong position of dominance (*Air France/Sabena* or *Nestlé/Perrier*, for example), but where a remedy was negotiated which allowed the merger eventually to be approved.

3.6.7   *Remedies: some conclusions*

A number of conclusions stand out from this analysis of remedies:

1. A number of remedies rely on conjectures regarding the strength of pro-competitive forces which are not well substantiated in the decisions. Often the effects of the remedies are evaluated only in the most optimistic scenario.
2. The effectiveness of remedies sometimes depends heavily on the behaviour of the merging partners, in particular in the disposal

of assets. They do not have adequate incentives to dispose of assets in such a way as to maximize the strength of countervailing competition. A close (and formal) monitoring by the Commission could be useful.

3. In some cases, remedies still leave the merging parties with substantial potential for the exercise of market power (in terms of the source of market power initially identified by the Commission). In such cases, remedies appear somewhat cosmetic.

4. Sometimes weak remedies have been imposed where there were clear and more effective alternatives.

5. Cases where clear-cut and convincingly substantiated remedies are imposed are not very numerous. One cannot help entertaining the thought that remedies are often negotiated under pressure and that the merging partners enjoy significant bargaining power.

6. The Commission has been negotiating remedies in the context of decisions taken after one month. These remedies may not be enforceable given that the Commission is not entitled legally to negotiate remedies in the context of these decisions.

3.7   Concluding remarks

Our review of the Commision's decisions suggests a number of ways in which the analysis undertaken by the Commission could be tightened. In particular, the current procedures introduce a bias in market definition in favour of excessively narrow markets. In this context, the analysis of dominance cannot rely on systematic indicators like market shares or concentration indices; an appreciation of the strength of competition then relies on additional considerations which are difficult to substantiate for the Commission and hard to evaluate for an outsider. By removing the biases in favour of narrow markets, which would entail the consideration of supply substitution and a simultaneous definition of geographic and product markets, a more systematic and verifiable analysis of dominance could be undertaken. Similarly, the analysis of entry could be tightened by relying on more systematic measurement of lag times and simple estimates of cost structures, like an allocation between fixed, variable and sunk components.

The Commission also seems to have been extremely flexible in the imposition of remedies, the appreciation of joint control and the evaluation of potential coordination between joint ventures and their parents. In such matters, the Commission has often not made a convincing case for its assessment (even though a systematic analysis was feasible). These omissions raise doubts about the procedures, and one cannot help thinking that some of the decisions are the results of negotiations between the firms and the Commission, in which firms enjoy substantial negotiating power. This issue will be further discussed in Chapter 4, where our conjecture is confirmed by the responses of firms to our survey, and in Chapter 7, where we analyze institutional details.

Apart from the evidence of surveys and our (unattributable) discussions with the Commission's own staff, our conjectures about the negotiating process are of course hard to substantiate. One other possible source of evidence may be of relevance, and that is evidence about the internal consistency of the written decisions. While reading a number of case reports we have had the impression that the analysis in the early sections appeared, both substantially and rhetorically, to be leading in a direction rather different from that which appeared in the final decision. One possible explanation for this impression is that the decisions concerned were hastily rewritten fairly late in the investigation process. If such an interpretation were correct, it would support our conjecture that some rather hasty negotiations have taken place in the course of which some firms have been able to strike relatively favourable deals. When we have put this interpretation to some Commission officials and legal representatives of firms, it has not provoked great disagreement. But our own assurances on this point may not by themselves constitute very compelling evidence.

In order to provide some more objective evidence about the internal consistency of the reports concerned, we conducted an experiment to see whether a larger group of trained economists would share our impression of the case reports. We presented a sample of seven case reports, from which we excised the concluding sections and any other evidence suggesting what decision had actually been taken, to two separate groups of graduate students in economics (one in Brussels and one in Cambridge). These graduate students were not previously aware of the results of any decisions under the Merger Regulation (fortunately graduate students in economics rarely read newspapers). We asked the students to predict, *on the basis of internal evidence alone*, what the decision of the Commission had been in those seven cases. Note that we did not ask them what the decision should have been; we encouraged them to use rhetorical as well as logical evidence to predict what decisions the writers of the early sections of the case reports had been intending to lead up to. We told our subjects that decisions could take three forms: approval, blocking, or approval subject to conditions.

The cases we used and the results of the experiments are presented in Table 3.3. Our prior expectation was that the cases of *Varta/Bosch*, *Magneti/Marelli* and *Alcatel/Telettra* had conclusions which did not flow naturally from the exposition of the cases.

Table 3.3 Experimental survey of the predictability of the decision.

Case	Number of students predicting the case was:		
	Blocked	Approved	Approved with cond.
Alcatel/Telettra	3	13	3
BA/TAT	8	10	1
Courtaulds/SNIA	0	17	2
La Redoute/Empire	0	18	1
Magneti/Marelli	14	4	0
Metall./SAFIC	3	16	0
Varta/Bosch	19	0	0

First, let us notice that three of the four cases that we considered a priori internally consistent (*BA/TAT, Courtaulds/SNIA, La Redoute/Empire, Metall./SAFIC*) were identified by a strong majority of the students, who all thought the deals had been approved. The *BA/TAT* decision is less clear cut; a significant minority of students predicted the deal had been rejected. The prediction of a negative decision by the students can of course result either from the fact that the reasoning in the case is conducive to a negative decision, or simply because the reasoning is unconvincing.[17] It may be that in the case of *BA/TAT* the latter interpretation is valid, and a debriefing after the experiments gives support to this interpretation.

The results of the experiment suggest, against our expectation, that the *Alcatel/Telettra* decision is well supported by the case. Our intuition was however strongly confirmed in the cases of *Magneti/Marelli* and especially *Varta/Bosch* (where students unanimously predicted that the deal had been blocked).

This experiment provides only a suggestive indication that certain cases may indeed have been turned around fairly late in the process through a process of negotiation in which firms had strong bargaining power. It is only a hint that the problems of capture that we discuss in Chapters 5 to 7 may indeed have been present.

Notes

1. We nevertheless cite in the text only a minority of the decisions taken, since most decisions do not raise issues of particular significance. However, we have reviewed all cases published by 21 September 1992, as well as important decisions up until mid-March 1993. We have drawn also on widely available sources like industry studies, official publications by Eurostat, the OECD, national anti-trust authorities and the financial press, as well as on interviews with officials of the Merger Task Force and national anti-trust authorities, lawyers and financial commentators.
2. The duration is determined on a case-by-case basis and usually lasts from 5 to 15 years.
3. CEC Press Release IP(92) 1009.
4. More details about the definition of functional autonomy can be found in *Nestlé/Baxter/Salvia* (58) where all the joint ventures created by Baxter and Nestlé were found to lack autonomy. The factors that were cited relate mostly to intellectual property rights and are fairly specific to the pharmaceutical and nutrition industries.
5. This concept appears in German competition law, where it denotes markets which include products for which strong supply substitutability is expected.
6. Before the concept of industrial leadership was established, coordination between the parent and the joint venture was sometimes ignored. For instance, in *Apollinaris/Schweppes* (93), coordination between the joint venture and the parents was not considered even though one of the parents continued to operate in the same market as the joint venture.
7. It seems inappropriate that the concept of industrial leadership was established in this case; indeed, in the definition of markets, the Commission stated that the relevant markets were national. Accordingly, since the JV operated only in the UK and Thomson operated only in France, the Commission could have argued that the parents had completely withdrawn from the market of the JV; nevertheless, the autonomy of the JV (which is necessary to establish its concentrative character) might have been difficult to justify.
8. A similar point can be made in *Linde/Fiat* (256).
9. Except in *Thomson/Pilkington* (86) because of geographic market definition.

10. There is also some scope for the Commission to structure its inquiries to ensure that deals are not referred to member states under Article 9. According to Linklater and Paines (1992), the case of *Mannesmann/Hoesch* (222) was pursued in phase II, partly to frustrate the German request for a referral. If correct, this interpretation would suggest that the Commission can indeed show a great deal of flexibility.

11. In principle, a long order backlog is, however, an indication that a company is unlikely to be an aggressive competitor, because it is unable to increase supply. This argument could usefully have been qualified.

12. The Commission, in its statement of objections (paragraph 32), refers to a lead larger than 25%. But in paragraph 58, it refers to a lead of 25%. As far as we can make out, the largest competitors are Fiat and Deta/Mareg, so that the lead is 34%.

13. The French and Belgian governments, in their respective undertakings, do not, however, make any reference to this provision.

14. The undertaking by BA specifies, however, that it is not required to provide a slot within one and a half hours of another similar slot already held by a carrier (BA?) for use on the route. If BA has currently the best slots in terms of timing, the entrant might be at a disadvantage.

15. It has been suggested to us in interviews with Task Force rapporteurs that for this reason the Commission originally sought to limit the remedies that could be negotiated with respect to Article 6.1b decisions – that is, during the one-month period – to clear any irreversible structural remedies that were already in place at the time of the decision. However, this intention has given way before strong pressure from the merging parties, so that 6.1b decisions are now negotiated on the basis of undertakings for the future.

16. It is by no means certain how enforceable even the formal remedies under Article 8 will turn out to be. For example, those that require asset divestiture by an agreed deadline could in future be challenged if market conditions have worsened for the seller in the meantime.

17. Interestingly five of the six British subjects in the experiments predicted a negative decision in the *BA/TAT* case. Students in Brussels were convinced.

4

The reactions of firms

4.1   Introduction

Previous chapters have examined the direct impact of the Merger Regulation on the economy by considering how a merger authority might in principle analyze the proposals presented to it by firms, and by reviewing how the European Commission (advised by the officials of the Merger Task Force) has in fact done so in the more than two years since the Regulation came into force. These are its most visible effects, the things that the Commission has done. But the Regulation, like all regulation, may have less visible effects, less visible because they are embodied in what other parties have done, and sometimes even in what other parties have not done, because of their awareness of the Regulation's presence on the European scene. In this chapter we look at the procedure it has put in place through the eyes of those most directly affected by it: actual and potential merging parties.

In the heyday of technocratic optimism about state intervention in the economy, it was natural to view merger control as a simple exercise in benign surgery, a removal from an otherwise potentially healthy economy of those mergers that diminished competition without yielding adequate countervailing benefits. Such optimism has long since been discredited. In Chapter 2 we introduced the idea that the surgery is not simple: in practice any authority faces a degree of uncertainty as to which mergers are the unhealthy ones. In Chapters 4 to 7 we discuss two even more fundamental problems.

In Chapters 6 and 7 we suggest that we cannot even take it for granted that the surgery is benign; regulators may not always be acting straightforwardly in the wider interests of society at large, but may be 'captured' by special interests. First, however, we draw attention to the fact that the economy can hardly be likened to a patient, immobile on the operating table. When a regulatory authority threatens intervention in the actions of independent agents in a decentralized economy, the agents react. They will typically react to diminish the threat to themselves represented by the intervention. In the process, unless their own interests are closely allied to those the regulatory process is intended to serve, agents' reactions to protect themselves will often tend to diminish the regulation's effectiveness. And if their interests *were* so closely allied it is unlikely the agents would have been appropriate targets for regulation in the first place.

The presence of merger control typically has indirect effects of four main kinds on the economy. These effects may consist, first, of mergers that would otherwise be attractive to firms, but that they do not even try to undertake because of fear that they will not be approved or because of the costs of seeking regulatory approval.[1] Secondly, some transactions may take place in a form different from that which they would have taken in the absence of regulation; we have discussed some of the incentives for this (particularly with regard to issues of control and cooperation in joint ventures) in Chapter 3. Thirdly, firms may engage in activities outside the merger process itself to seek to influence the regulatory outcome in their favour: lobbying, publicity and influence-gathering (what Krueger (1974) calls 'rent-seeking' activities). And finally, they may behave differently towards third parties (their clients, competitors or suppliers) because of the criteria they expect the authorities to use in assessing the proposal: a 5% rule based on pre-merger prices may encourage collusion to raise the benchmark price level; a failing firm defence may encourage predation to weaken the takeover target; influential customers may be favourably treated to encourage them not to oppose the deal; an aggressive campaign to gain market share may be postponed so as not to trigger concerns about dominance.[2]

It is one thing to say in theory what are the potential indirect effects of merger control; it is quite another to demonstrate how important they are empirically. In the nature of things it is very hard to know what firms would have done in the absence of the Merger

Regulation. It is not even always clear what is the appropriate standard of comparison: do we want to know whether the Regulation imposes indirect costs compared to a system in which mergers are not regulated at all, or simply compared to the partial system of national merger control which was in operation prior to 1990? In principle we want to do both, but it is not always clear which comparison is illuminated by any particular piece of evidence.

The solution we have adopted is twofold. First, we have sent questionnaires to firms and their legal advisers, both to get their general opinions about the new system and to discover how, if at all, their own strategic planning is affected by its presence; the results of this survey are reported in this chapter. Secondly, we have analyzed the merger control procedure in the light of our information from both firms and officials, in order to see what kinds of strategic incentive it establishes for firms to modify their behaviour as part of the bargaining process involved in negotiating clearance of a merger transaction; we discuss this analysis in Chapters 5 to 7.

4.2   Responses to our surveys

We sought to find out how firms view the operation of the Merger Regulation in two main ways. First we sent a questionnaire to firms involved in cases during the first two years of operation of the Regulation; secondly, we wrote (and in some cases spoke) to representatives of a number of the main law firms involved in advising companies about European mergers.

4.2.1   *The survey of firms*

A total of 198 questionnaires were sent to firms; we received completed questionnaires from 59, a respectable but not a remarkable response rate for a mail survey. Table 4.1 shows the breakdown of these replies by country of origin, and the percentage breakdown is compared against the equivalent figures for the cases notified to the MTF during this period: 24 of the 59 firms were in services (41%, almost exactly the same proportion as for the MTF caseload as a whole); 26 cases (46%) involved a party outside the EC, somewhat more than the MTF average of 26%; 26 were parties to concentrative joint ventures with a Community dimension, and 15 to acquisitions of majority ownership (46% and 25% respectively, as against MTF proportions of 44% and 43%). Overall, apart from a degree of overrepresentation of UK firms (in spite of the fact that our questionnaires were posted from a French address), our sample does not seem to have been unrepresentative to any important extent.

Table 4.1 The survey respondents.

Country	Number of replies	Percentage	MTF percentage
Benelux	4	7	6
France	11	19	19
Germany	11	19	15
UK	15	25	17
Other EC	1	2	16
Sweden	5	8	6
Switzerland	5	8	4
USA	5	8	11
Rest of world	0	0	6
Anonymous respondent	2	3	

Sources: Own data, MTF

The questions fell into two categories, the answers to which are given in Tables 4.2 and 4.3:

1. Those asking for details of the procedure as perceived by the firm concerned.
2. Those asking for the firm's opinion of the usefulness of the procedure or the helpfulness of the MTF's staff.

A number of conclusions stand out from the results shown in Tables 4.2 and 4.3. First of all, firms appear to have been favourably impressed by the operation of the Merger Regulation, even though it represents for them an interruption in the commercial timetable of a business transaction, and in some cases a substantial amount of work. The great majority of them believe the officials of the MTF are both willing to listen and capable of understanding the situation faced by businesses; not quite so many but still a majority believe the information requirements of the procedure are reasonable and that the process itself has struck about the right balance between speed and attention to detail. It is possible that this reaction is

Table 4.2 The procedure.

	Question	Answers	
1	Was this your first experience of dealing with DG-IV?	Yes: 24	No: 35
2	Did you contact DG-IV before agreeing the broad outlines of the deal with your partner?	Yes: 12	No: 47
3	Did you and your partner hold separate or joint discussions with DG-IV?	Separate: 9 Both: 3 Partner held no discussions: 4	Joint: 43
4	Did you obtain professional advice from: (a) a law firm? (b) a public relations firm? (c) an economic consultant? (d) a professional lobbyist? (e) all of the above? (f) none of the above?	Yes: 49 Yes: 9 Yes: 8 Yes: 5 Yes: 3 Yes: 9	No: 10 No: 50 No: 51 No: 54 No: 56 No: 50
5	Did your preliminary discussions with DG-IV result in significant modifications to the agreement with your partner company?	Major modifications: 5 Minor modifications: 15 No modifications: 39	
6	How many person-days were required to collect information for and to complete the Notification Form?	Average: 45.0 Minimum: 2.0 Maximum: 720	
7	How many meetings did you hold with officials from the MTF after Notification?	Average: 2.5	
8	How many weeks elapsed between your first contact with the MTF and Notification?	Average: 6.5	
9	How many weeks elapsed between Notification and the Commission's informing you of its decision?	Average: 6.5	
10	Did you receive support from any of the following (4 missing replies): (a) politicians? (b) officials from member states? (c) trade unions? (d) professional/commercial bodies? (e) press and broadcasting media? (f) all of the above? (g) none of the above?	Yes: 9 Yes: 13 Yes: 4 Yes: 6 Yes: 5 Yes: 1 Yes: 35	No: 46 No: 42 No: 51 No: 49 No: 50 No: 54 No: 20

Table 4.3 The opinions of firms.

	Question	Answers
1	Was the information required on the Notification Form relevant to the economic evaluation of the deal?	Yes, all relevant: 1 Yes, mostly: 36 Yes, somewhat: 16 No, mostly irrelevant: 5 No answer: 1
2	Did you find the officials of the MTF willing to listen to your point of view?	Yes, all the time: 22 Yes, mostly: 29 No, not much: 3 No, not at all: 0 No answer: 5
3	Did you think they appreciated adequately the commercial and industrial realities, and the organizational constraints faced by your company?	Yes, completely: 9 Yes, adequately: 35 No, inadequately: 10 No, not at all: 0 No answer: 3
4	Overall, do you think the procedures are: (a) insufficiently detailed? (b) too detailed? (c) about right?	 Yes: 1 Yes: 26 Yes: 29 No answer: 3

influenced by the expectations generated by dealing either with national competition authorities or with the somewhat slower procedures elsewhere in DG-IV (a majority had previous experience of contact with DG-IV, and in a few cases slow and bureaucratic responses elsewhere were contrasted unfavourably with those of the MTF). Nevertheless, overall it represents a substantial vote of approval for the new system.

Secondly, and no doubt relatedly, the evidence about the direct costs of the procedure for firms does not suggest these are very large: 45 person-days is not a great investment to make in collecting and presenting the data required on the Notification Form, especially since much of this information ought to be evaluated by competent management as part of the assessment of the transaction in any event. An average of 2.5 meetings with the MTF is not very demanding either, and the speed with which the procedure is brought to a conclusion suggests the overall direct costs it imposes on the participants are a negligible proportion of the value of the transactions concerned.[3] They are certainly negligible compared to the benefits of significantly improved accuracy in the classification of merger proposals; this trade-off was explored in Chapter 2.

Thirdly, the importance of the pre-notification procedure emerges very strikingly from these results. The average length of time spent in contact with the MTF prior to Notification (over six weeks) is slightly greater than that taken on average by the formal procedure itself; nearly a quarter of firms began discussions prior to agreeing even the broad outlines of the transaction with their partner. Furthermore, a lot of the changes imposed on deals are negotiated informally. Twenty firms (over a third of the sample) reported being required to undertake modifications to their transactions as a result of discussions with the MTF. Yet all but three of these modifications took place prior to a 6.1b decision (that is, unconditional clearance of the deal). This suggests a very considerable concern on the part of the MTF to avoid allowing competition concerns to delay clearance of a transaction, a concern which may be part of the explanation for the speed of the procedure but which also risks (as we discuss in Chapter 5) laying itself open to manipulation by firms seeking to negotiate unnecessarily anti-competitive deals.

Fourthly, there seems to be substantial variation between firms in their approach to employing professional advice, and engaging in lobbying, as part of the process of seeking approval for a transaction. Most respondents had engaged a law firm, but a substantial minority (17%) had not.[4] Only 15% or less had engaged other advisers, but three had employed the whole spectrum from economic consultants to public relations advisers and professional lobbyists. Over a third had received support from one or more of the groups referred to in question 10, with 9 supported by politicians, 13 by officials from member states and smaller numbers from trade unions, professional bodies and the press and media. Exactly what such support consisted in is unclear. But evidently some firms are extremely aware of the merger control process as one in which pressures from various interest groups can have an impact; others seem to be much less aware, but it seems likely that the growing sophistication of lobbying at the European level will lead to a continuing increase in the proportion of the former.

Tables 4.2 and 4.3 provoke the natural question of whether there was any systematic variation, both in the preparedness of firms for the procedure and in their opinions about it after the event. Let us first consider factors explaining the tendency of firms to seek support for their case from politicians and other individuals and organizations. Equation (4.1) below reports the results of a simple probit equation designed to investigate variations in replies to question 10: the dependent variable (LOBBY) is a simple dummy variable that takes the value 1 if the firm reported receiving support from one of the listed sources, and zero if it did not (figures in parentheses are asymptotic t-statistics):[5]

$$\text{LOBBY} = 0.40 + 0.26\,\text{JV} + 0.42\,\text{MAJCH} - 0.37\,\text{GR}\ 0.15\,\text{EX}$$
$$\quad\ (4.2)\quad\ (2.01)\quad\ \ (1.88)\quad\quad (-2.39)\quad (-1.19)$$

$$(4.1)$$

What this reveals is that firms engaged in joint ventures (JV) were more likely than others to have sought such support; this is a strong corroboration of our conjectures in Chapter 3 that the jurisdictional ambiguities raised by the definition of concentrative joint ventures provide a strong incentive for bargaining and negotiation. Firms whose deals were sufficiently problematic to need the negotiation of major changes (MAJCH) were more likely than others to have sought support (the coefficient on minor changes was insignificant). This also supports our views about the nature of the bargaining underlying the imposition of remedies. Interestingly, German firms (GR) were much less likely than others to have done so, and firms involved in deals which had at least one partner from outside the European Community (EX) were also somewhat less likely to have done so. The first three coefficients are (asymptotically) significant at 10%, and those for joint ventures and German nationality at 5%.

Equation (4.2) reports our analysis of the opinions of firms: were certain kinds of firm more prone to approve, and others to disapprove, of the procedure? To answer this we have constructed a composite index (a 'dissatisfaction index') by adding up points for each of the answers to questions 1 through 4 in Table 4.3. Thus the first answer to question 1 scores 1 point, the second answer scores 2 points and so on. Answer (c) to question 4 scores 1 point, while either of the other two scores 2 points. Missing answers are given the appropriate mean value, and the total score should represent a rough guide to the overall degree of satisfaction or dissatisfaction of the respondent firm (higher scores indicate less satisfaction). Somewhat to our surprise, the factors that one might have expected to influence firms in their replies proved insignificant. The length of time required to fill in the Notification Form, the number of interviews with the MTF, and whether discussions with the MTF resulted in modifications to the deal, are all unrelated to the level of the dissatisfaction index; the length of time taken to be informed of the decision is the only such factor even weakly statistically significant (at just over 10%). The insignificance of modifications in explaining dissatisfaction may be less surprising than it at first appears, since they almost all resulted in speedy clearance; any resentment felt by firms at the enforced changes may have been offset by relief that the procedure enabled them to be negotiated quickly. Alternatively, this could indicate that firms felt they had achieved most of what they wanted, and that the modifications were relatively slight compared to what they might have been.

Equation (4.2) reports some variables which are statistically significant or nearly so:

$$\text{DISSAT} = 7.45 - 1.34\,\text{GR} + 0.80\,\text{SERV} - 0.76\,\text{EX} + 0.08\,\text{TIME}$$
$$\phantom{\text{DISSAT} = }(14.8)\quad(-2.36)\quad(1.76)\qquad(-1.72)\quad(1.66)$$

$$R^2 = 0.12 \tag{4.2}$$

where, as before, GR indicates the respondent was a German firm and EX indicates that the deal involved a non-EC partner; SERV indicates the respondent was a service sector firm and TIME measures the time of the investigation in weeks (as reported by the respondent).

It is difficult to draw firm conclusions from a relatively small sample, particularly since the fit of the equation is not at all good. By and large, firms involved in transactions outside the EC seem to be happier than others, perhaps out of relief that the EC has a unified procedure for external transactions. Those in service industries are less happy, perhaps because they felt the investigation criteria less appropriate to their own spheres of activity (an interpretation which receives some support from the comments we report below). The time taken for the investigation is also weakly related to the level of dissatisfaction; all three of these variables, however, are statistically significant at only around 10%. By far the strongest statistical association in the data is that German firms are much happier with the system than others. Rather than postulate irreducible cultural differences in attitudes to bureaucracy, we would prefer to interpret this as reflecting the expectations formed by the pre-existing system of national merger control regulation. German firms, we suggest, find the EC system preferable to that of the Bundeskartellamt; whether this is because of the relative strictness with which the BKA and the European Commission treat potentially anti-competitive transactions, or because of other features of the two systems, is a matter on which our findings are silent.

In addition to their responses to the systematic questions, firms were invited to give their own opinions and comments at various points in the questionnaire. Many of these comments were amplifications of firms' opinions about the appropriateness of the procedure: thus some firms said that the procedure was excessively burdensome, especially in its informational requirements, for the average merger which evidently did not raise competition concerns; others commented favourably on the streamlined nature of the procedure and expressed appreciation of the flexibility of the MTF staff (for instance, in showing willingness to waive some of the information requirements, and in being willing to devote significant time to pre-notification discussion). Other comments were directed more to the general character of the procedure. A number of firms criticized what they described as the lack of a clear philosophy which made the operation of the Regulation less than transparent. One claimed this was because the policy was made too much on a case-by-case basis; another because the MTF was subject to excessive political pressure. Others commented on the distortions induced by the desire to be treated under the Regulation rather than under the more cumbersome Article 85 and 86 procedures. A couple of respondents said they had been influenced in deciding the form of a joint venture by the desire for it to count as concentrative, and thought this an undesirable distortion of business decision-making. One firm said that there was an excessively narrow focus on competition concerns to the exclusion of other legitimate criteria; another was concerned that this might become a serious problem if the turnover thresholds were reduced in the future.

In a few cases the written comments were significantly more critical than could have been expected from the responses to the main questions. One firm (in a service industry) was severely critical of the way in which analysis was performed of its own market, holding most of the MTF's procedures (and the bulk of the information required in the questionnaire) inappropriate to the activity concerned. Another added that the amount of information required was 'extraordinary'. One firm was scathing about 'poor economic analysis' and an 'excessively narrow definition of the market'; and in spite of writing that it had found MTF officials mostly willing to listen to its point of view, added that 'there was no evidence that our views were taken into account even when the Task Force were demonstrably wrong on points of fact rather than opinion; on opinion officials early on made up their minds ... to some extent dialogue was useless'. Another firm was critical of the fact that the helpfulness of the MTF was insufficient given the significant influence on the outcome of pressures from elsewhere in DG-IV and in the Commission more generally.

Interpreting these comments requires some care. There is a particularly striking discrepancy between the repeated criticisms of the procedure as unnecessarily time-consuming, and the (in our view) very small reported costs that the procedure in fact imposes on the firms concerned. This suggests to us a degree of irritation among senior executives at having to go through the procedure at all (and therefore a failure to be convinced of the need for merger control) rather than a considered judgment that the procedure is an inappropriate means of implementing merger control as it stands. That said, there are clearly respects in which the notification requirements, as well as the procedures of analysis, can and will be modified as the MTF gains experience. A second point worthy of comment is that a great many firms clearly had little idea what to expect from the procedure; their comments often reflect considerable surprise (usually pleasant, occasionally not) at the way in which their case was received. This suggests there would be considerable benefits for firms from the publication of guidelines setting out the nature of the procedure and reducing the uncertainty it entails.

4.2.2   *The survey of law firms*

Our enquiries to law firms had two main purposes. First, we sought independent corroboration of the details given to us by firms about the procedure under the Regulation. Secondly, we wanted to find out about those transactions which had not proceeded as far as Notification: was the presence of the Regulation acting as any kind of hindrance or disincentive to firms' commercial decisions? Our enquiries were necessarily less systematic than those with firms, for two reasons. First, we did not write to all law firms, but to those where we had contacts or recommendations: the substantial amounts of work required of each firm made us believe a more personal approach was more likely to bear fruit. Secondly, firms which had handled substantial numbers of cases necessarily gave us information based on estimates of averages and overall impressions, so there is already a degree of generalization embodied in their replies. Nevertheless, two conclusions emerged very clearly from these enquiries. First, the general picture of the procedure yielded by the replies of firms in Table 4.2 is strongly corroborated. Our law firms had between them handled 30 notified cases (there was some overlap with our sample of firms, but we do not know how much - although we know it was not complete). Of these cases three were referred elsewhere than to the Merger Task Force. The time spent to fill in the Notification form was reported to be roughly 27 days on average, 2 meetings were held, 5 weeks elapsed prior to Notification and nearly 4 afterwards. Interestingly, 7 of the cases were reported as being subject to major modifications and 5 to minor ones, with 15 unmodified. Overall, apart from an even greater proportion of modified transactions, the general picture of the procedure yielded by the evidence of law firms matches that of our earlier sample fairly closely. The lawyers themselves spoke uniformly well of the MTF and the helpfulness and competence of its officials; with one exception they all thought the procedure unnecessarily detailed but did not feel sufficiently strongly about this to expand on the point in comments of their own.

The second important conclusion to emerge is that there is no evidence whatever of transactions having been blocked or hindered prior to the Notification stage. Between them the law firms had handled some 250 European transactions that had not proceeded as far as Notification;[6] of these about 55 had, however, gone as far as preliminary discussions with the MTF. They all reported that in no case had a deal been called off for fear that it would be unacceptable to the MTF. In most of the cases involving preliminary discussions, however, the law firms reported that their advice to clients had been significantly influenced by the need to present deals in a form acceptable to the MTF; in three cases a deal was changed as a result of consultations (presumably to ensure that it did not fall within the Regulation). Overall, it appears that when deals that have been discussed with the MTF are not consummated the reason has always been commercial (the failure of the parties to agree or an unexpected worsening of market conditions) rather than the discouraging presence of the Regulation; nearly a third of all non-notified deals were called off for such reasons.

In general, therefore, the evidence of law firms gives the convincing impression that the presence of the Merger Regulation may in a significant minority of cases influence the form taken by a commercial transaction, but it does not influence whether or not that transaction takes place. Note, however, that this does not imply that the presence of a merger control authority has no disincentive effect upon merger activity. It may be that the mere presence of such an authority discourages firms from contemplating the most obviously anti-competitive mergers in the first place[7] (indeed, it is clear that the anti-trust implications of any proposed deal are among the first enquiries that firms make of their lawyers); if such a deterrent effect is present it takes place before transactions ever proceed as far as even preliminary discussion with the MTF. It is also conceivable that the delays imposed on the commercial timetable may lead to an increase in the number of adverse external developments of the kind that can lead to the collapse of transactions for other reasons (though the evidence for this, it must be said, is at best slight).

In any case, both national authorities and DG-IV have had and used merger control powers before, so the passing of the Merger Regulation has not created a radically more restrictive climate for firms, and we would not expect any additional deterrent effect to be visible in our data. Indeed, the evidence of Chapter 3 suggests that the Regulation has if anything facilitated the passage of a number of transactions. On the evidence we have, therefore, the indirect costs of the Merger Regulation *compared to the system previously in place* seem primarily to consist in changes made to the form of transactions rather than in the changes in the prevalence of merger transactions overall.

This judgment is corroborated by the specific comments of lawyers on the procedure. Several have commented that, especially in its more recent decisions, the Commission has shown itself willing, in the words of one, 'to let the deal get done if at all possible'. This applies both to the form of deals and to their substance. On form, one lawyer noted (approvingly) 'the recent trend towards *sub silentio* rejection of the prescribed application of the [concentrative joint venture] concept' – the implication being that the Commission had leant over backwards to allow a deal to fall under the Regulation instead of under the Article 85 procedure which a more natural reading would have prescribed. Another told us that 'all the Commission needs is a plausible reason to count the deal as concentrative, and it can usually be relied upon to say yes'. Yet another said it was doubtful that recent press speculation[8] (since the change of Commissioner at the end of 1992) about a more lax future application of the Regulation had any foundation, since 'the application has already become fairly lax'. Whatever the truth in these substantive judgments, it is clear from the (admittedly not necessarily representative) law firms we sampled that many of them believe the keenness of the Commission to approve merger transactions has given firms and their legal advisers considerable bargaining power, which they have every intention of using to the full. The implications of this bargaining power will be discussed more fully in Chapter 5.

Notes

1. Though attractive to firms, these mergers will sometimes be undesirable for society as a whole, and their discouragement will additionally save the authorities the time and trouble of investigating them.
2. One interpretation of the agreement to transfer the Volvic brand from Nestlé to BSN prior to the notification of the *Nestlé/Perrier* case was that it was designed to lessen the risk that Nestlé would be regarded as dominant. A more cynical interpretation is that it was designed to reduce the asymmetry in size between the two companies in order to facilitate collusion. The former, though not the latter, would be an instance of a regulatory distortion. The two explanations are not, of course, mutually exclusive.
3. If anything, our data suggests firms have tended to exaggerate upwards some of the costs: for instance, it is clear that a number of firms have reported stage 1 procedures as taking five or six weeks even though they are strictly limited to a month.
4. Many of these are firms with their own legal department, but such a department will not usually possess the degree of specialist expertise about European competition law that could be expected from a law firm with a Brussels office.
5. The equation reported was estimated by Ordinary Least Squares, but Maximum Likelihood Estimation made no appreciable difference to the significance of the coefficients.

6. These figures make no allowance for double counting of the same transaction where more than one firm was involved; we had no means to do this given that we did not (for obvious reasons) ask law firms for the identities of clients.

7. However, Aaronson (1992) comments on evidence that companies in fact fail to take the presence of competition policy constraints systematically into account even though it would be in their best interests to do so. In addition to survey data, he cites some cases, such as that of the sugar industry: 'Would you expect a company with nearly half the market for a product to bid for the company with the other half? Tate and Lyle did just that in 1986. The bid was referred, the merger turned down. The bid was made again in 1991, was referred again and the merger was again turned down' (1992, p. 141).

8. This speculation has been particularly strong in France, where (due in part to the repercussions of the de Havilland case) the Regulation has been viewed, both in academic discussion (see Glais (1992)) and in the press, as a much more restrictive instrument than we have implied here. As an example of the latter, see the item in the monthly economic review *Enjeux-les Echos* headlined 'A Bruxelles, la concurrence change de mains et le dogme passe à la trappe', where the new Commissioner is described as not sharing the 'ultra-liberal credo' of his predecessor, and 'another sign of increased flexibility' is the declaration by Commissioner Bangemann that 'merger control should aid restructuring and there should be an end to theories and dogmas' (February 1993, pp. 7–8).

5

The bargaining game

5.1 The bargaining game

5.1.1 *The problem*

Two points stand out from the surveys to distinguish the implementation of the Regulation from the straightforward exercise of a predetermined procedure that was the implicit model discussed in Chapter 2. One is that many respondents are aware that the procedure grants a substantial exercise of discretion to the Commission (sometimes they record this with an element of surprise, like the firm that had expected 'a highly theoretical approach' and discovered the Merger Task Force to be 'much more pragmatic than expected'). The second is that some (including most of the law firms) realize that the Commission would usually prefer not to create difficulties for merger proposals, and will therefore tend to exercise its discretion in a direction favourable to the approval of a transaction where possible. This process is greatly facilitated by the medium of the pre-notification discussions, which give each side the opportunity to adapt its negotiating position to that of the other. This raises the question what the effect of this discretion (and the incentives to exercise it in different ways) is upon the overall outcome of the merger control process. In order to understand it, we shall need to consider both the objectives of the authorities and the nature of their actions in implementing merger control, in a more sophisticated fashion than the simple model at the end of Chapter 2 (where we simply assumed that the authorities sought to maximize social welfare subject to some information constraints). Unfortunately, however, it is far from straightforward to understand exactly how the exercise of discretion operates in merger control.

One of the first problems in understanding discretionary bargaining in merger control is that the breakdown of negotiations has a cost for both parties. For the firm, a merger that is forbidden imposes evident costs in terms of organizational disruption, time, legal fees and so forth. But for the agency, refusing a merger may be costly too:[1] not only will the firm and its sources of political support be angry, but the agency faces the threat of possible judicial challenge with the attendant direct and indirect costs of time, trouble and loss of credibility if the challenge is successful (the magnitude and significance of these costs will be influenced by the extent to which the agency responsible for investigation is also responsible for decision, a factor that will be of considerable importance for the discussion of independence and transparency in Chapter 6 below). In the absence of imperfections in the bargaining process, therefore, we should never expect to see any mergers refused; there would always exist some compromise that was no worse for either party and did not involve the costs of a refusal. Firms would not persist with proposals that were likely to be refused, and the authorities would not insist on refusing mergers to which alternative negotiated remedies were available. Yet we do see mergers refused (albeit only one so far under the European Regulation)[2]. Why?

It is important to stress that explaining merger refusals is just as much of a problem if we suppose competition policy to be based on a very restrictive approach to merger control as if we suppose it to be very lax: the strictness or otherwise of the policy would explain which party made the most compromises, but it would not affect the incentive for compromises to be reached. One reason this is important is that it is tempting, but misleading, to draw direct conclusions from the frequency of merger refusals about the nature of the underlying policy. We would emphasize that the smaller number of merger refusals by the EC authorities compared to those by the German, British or US authorities cannot be used to infer that EC merger control is less restrictive than that of the other jurisdictions;[3] by itself it could just as well indicate that the EC has been more successful in dissuading firms from putting forward anti-competitive proposals. Our survey results in Chapter 4 cast some doubt on this latter interpretation, it is true; but that has nothing to do with the frequency of refusals *per se*.

The problem of explaining refusals is rather like the well-known difficulty of explaining strikes, which are inefficient, since any outcome that results from a strike could in principle have been negotiated immediately without the costs of the strike itself. The usual way in which economists attempt to explain strikes is to introduce asymmetries of information about the costs to each party of various outcomes (including the costs of a strike); the willingness to undergo a strike is then a means by which the parties signal their 'toughness' to each other.

It is extremely difficult to model convincingly the bargaining process in the presence of two-sided asymmetries of information (see Fudenberg and Tirole (1991), ch. 10, especially pp. 421–8). The basic problem is that of too many equilibria (or, more colloquially, that 'many things can happen' if the parties expect them to). This arises for two reasons. First, many different models are plausible candidates for representing the bargaining process in any particular case, and the choice between them may depend on rather fine distinctions in the order of negotiations and the structure of information available to the parties, distinctions that are hard if not impossible to verify empirically. Secondly, even within a given model there often exist large numbers of equilibrium solutions, some of which have qualitatively different properties. So to use the theory of bargaining as a diagnostic tool (to explain the processes underlying the observed outcomes) is very difficult unless one has some additional means of selecting among the large number of competing explanations.

The strategy we shall adopt here is the following. We shall briefly describe one special case that has been extensively studied in bargaining theory. This has the advantage that under certain circumstances it predicts very precisely that refusals will never occur. This allows us to focus on relaxing various assumptions of the model to see whether and to what extent we can succeed in describing the essence of the EC procedure more accurately. This special case (Fudenberg and Tirole (1991), pp. 400–21) involves one party who has private information and the other who has the first-mover advantage (for instance, a seller of a durable good making offers to a buyer with uncertain valuation of the good). The interpretation of this in the context of merger control would be as follows. Firms have the first-mover advantage in that they make 'offers' to the agency (in the form of merger proposals); it is the agency whose reputation for toughness is principally in question and which therefore has the most significant private information. The merger control agency interacts repeatedly with the firm over the course of the investigation and has therefore an interest in acting toughly to send a signal of its unwillingness to be manipulated.[4] And unlike a strike, the refusal of a merger proposal is not a temporary breakdown that can be resolved by re-opening negotiations; unless overturned by judicial review, the refusal of a merger is a permanent decision. In most circumstances, therefore, the effective asymmetry of information will be one-sided: firms will test out the agency's toughness, but the question of how tough is the firm itself may be of lesser relevance, since the firm is less likely to have something to gain from demonstrating toughness that could offset the cost of refusal of its present proposal.

So a model in which one party has the first-mover advantage and the other has private information might seem a plausible first approximation to the bargaining process played out between firms and the Commission. Unfortunately, though, the most applicable version of the one-sided asymmetry bargaining model (one which has a finite bargaining horizon and strictly positive gains from trade) satisfies the conjecture made by Coase (1972). This conjecture has two components: first, that when offers can take place very quickly (alternatively, as the discount rate tends to zero), the bargaining process always tends to yield the efficient outcome;[5] and secondly, that the party with the private information extracts all the benefit from the transaction. In this context 'efficient' is interpreted to mean that negotiations never end in a blocked merger; a compromise proposal would always be preferable to both parties.[6] And the fact that the party with the private information (in this case the Commission) extracts all the benefit from the transaction here implies that the Commission would be able (by using its incentives to establish a reputation for tough bargaining) to implement a policy that fully reflected its own preferences for merger control; the fact that bargaining allowed an element of discretion would not deflect it from implementing the policy that it would otherwise have chosen. On the face of it, therefore, this model will have serious difficulty explaining two central facts about the procedure as we have documented it under the Regulation. First, firms sometimes make proposals which are nevertheless blocked (albeit only once so far). And secondly (as we have argued in Chapter 3 and as our survey respondents have suggested in section 4.2), the actual decisions taken have embodied a somewhat more lax policy than the one to which the Commission is apparently publicly committed; the discretionary element in the negotiation is one from which firms appear to have been able to extract some benefit.

In the light of the Coase conjecture, how should we therefore interpret the actual processes of bargaining under the Merger Regulation as they have taken place in the first two years? Three main interpretations suggest themselves. The *first* is that the model of purely discretionary bargaining under one-sided asymmetric information is in fact the wrong model; the bargaining is not purely discretionary, or the informational asymmetries are bilateral, or both. The remaining two interpretations both rest on the view that the Coase model is, roughly speaking, the right one, and that the single instance of a blocked merger to date has represented a kind of error that can be expected to be avoided in the future as the parties become more adept at negotiating.[7] However, they differ on their explanation for the apparent laxness of the policy. The *second* interpretation suggests that the Commission may not have been employing an optimal bargaining strategy throughout; in particular, it may have failed to realize fully the benefits that might have accrued from a more careful attention to developing a reputation for consistent application of its stated policy.[8] The *third* interpretation is that there is no reason to suppose that the Commission has not been optimizing; the error lies instead in supposing that the Commission's aims have been the same as we (the analytical economists) have assumed them to be. This last interpretation raises the possibility of a significant distinction between the actual aims of the Commission in merger policy and at any rate a straightforward reading of its stated aims, due to the fact that the analysis of mergers has had to face political constraints at the decision stage. We discuss this possibility more fully under the heading of regulatory capture in Chapter 6.

We shall argue that all three explanations of the apparent contradiction between the Coase conjecture and the recent experience of European merger control contain important elements of truth; and we shall examine these three explanations more fully in turn.

5.1.2 *Three solutions*

The first potential explanation is that the Coase model is the wrong model. This may be for two reasons. One is that firms do not have unlimited discretion to renegotiate their merger proposals once notified. Although before notification of a merger proposal firms commit themselves to nothing, notification itself is a substantial commitment to a form of transaction, a commitment that must be undertaken while there is still significant uncertainty about how the authorities will react. Making changes to the form of a transaction subsequent to notification is still possible, but it is not costless, and there are only certain kinds of modification that can be made before it becomes easier to tear up the whole proposal and start again.[9]

The second reason is that firms may, after all, have a substantial incentive to develop a reputation for not giving in easily to pressure from the Commission to alter their proposals. A reputation for toughness may serve them well not just in subsequent dealings under the Regulation, but in other negotiations with other regulators or even with their competitors. This reputational incentive acts to create a certain commitment potential in much the same way as do the costs of modifying a proposal. And the consequence may be that both parties (the Commission as well as firms) have to commit themselves to a negotiating position while there still remains uncertainty about what the other party will do (and while there is still therefore a probability that bilateral pre-commitment will lead to breakdown). For firms, renegotiation imposes costs to their reputation as well as their bank balance. Likewise, the authorities do not have complete freedom to rule as they wish;[10] the criteria chosen for the merger control process act as a kind of restraint in the sense that they determine the basis upon which the authorities wish to establish a reputation. By stating publicly that they intend to evaluate merger proposals according to certain criteria, the authorities effectively invite firms to interpret significant failure to do so as a sign of weakness, of willingness to settle at any price and consequently of openness to continual manipulation. It is by inviting such an adverse reaction that they hope to give themselves a strong enough incentive to stick to the criteria. If, therefore (and it is a big 'if'), the authorities are confident of their ability to establish such a reputation, they may choose their criteria as though these constituted a merger strategy to which they had the power to commit themselves (as Fudenberg and Tirole (1991), p. 373) put it, 'reputation effects allow (a player) to make whichever of the two commitments it prefers').

Perhaps the best model of the merger control procedure is one in which, first, the agency makes a statement of the general procedure it will operate after notification; there then follows a stage of uncommitted negotiation between the agency and the firm, succeeded by a commitment on the part of the firm to a particular proposal, which can be modified but only at a cost depending on the degree of modification. In the final stage there is negotiation within the limits set, first, by the costs of modifying proposals, and secondly, by the reputational costs to the agency of failing to abide by its stated procedure. If the agency succeeds in establishing a reputation, and if there nevertheless remains some uncertainty about whether particular mergers will be diagnosed correctly, then the model of the appendix to Chapter 2 may not be a bad first approximation to the situation. A more fully specified model would take the repeated nature of the whole procedure (namely, the fact that the agency interacts repeatedly not just with any given firm but with many different firms) more explicitly into account.

In the simplified approximation, firms take the risk of refusal to depend on the characteristics of the proposed transaction, and design merger proposals to trade off the private benefits of anti-competitive transactions against the risks of detection. Knowing that firms will behave this way, the agency determines its general procedures to maximize the benefits of merger control (including where appropriate the private benefits to the agency in terms of better relations with the firms and their sources of political support). The question then becomes a primarily empirical one as to which estimates of the costs and benefits best match those of the real cases with which the agency must deal.

However, it is important to note that, in the model just sketched, it does not make sense for the agency to try to commit itself to appraisal criteria unless it actually intends to follow them. If it does not propose to follow the announced criteria, but instead to accept proposals that fall outside them, then it might as well announce different criteria.[11] This in no way implies that the merger control authority should not seek to reassure firms that it wishes to minimize the risks of failing to reach agreement. But it does imply that the proper way to do this is to design merger appraisal criteria with the costs of disagreement fully taken into account rather than to display *ex post* a lack of commitment to its prior announcement. What this suggests is that this model will still not be adequate to explain any tendency for the Commission's decisions to be less stringent than the policy to which it is apparently committed.

The second possible explanation is that the Commission has not in fact struck the balance it might have wished between flexibility and reputation. In particular, it may have failed to realize the commitment value of rules of procedure (including guidelines setting out criteria for merger analysis). Other things being equal, it is important to have clear and transparent procedures that can be not only implemented but *seen* to be implemented. If distortions of the procedure are invisible to third parties they are costless for the reputation of the agency; if they are costless for the agency they increase the temptation of the firms to manipulate the bargaining process. Paradoxically, therefore, an agency with a commitment to objective analysis has an interest in increasing its own potential for embarrassment by making its procedures as transparent as possible, in order to signal to firms its unwillingness to be manipulated. Commitment to a procedure is not a tiresome constraint for a regulatory agency, but a valuable way of signalling that it means business to those firms that might otherwise be in some doubt.

It is sometimes argued that merger control is such an essentially discretionary matter that rules of procedure and analysis can only be misleading at best, damaging at worst. Implicit in this argument is a comparison with other forms of regulation where the scope for rules is much more evident. Environmental regulation, where compliance with rules about such matters as air and water quality can be monitored by simple chemical tests, provides some of the best examples, though there are significant national differences in the degree of discretion these involve. Furthermore, there are often incentives for third parties to discover and publish information about non-compliance – either affected individuals, organizations or pressure groups (as in the case of pollution), or the press (who can make a story more readily out of a clear breach of regulations than out of a complex case of regulatory capture).

By comparison merger regulation is certainly a more discretionary matter. But it does not follow that it cannot be in any way constrained by a commitment to exercise that discretion visibly in line with certain criteria rather than others. Criteria of appraisal, though never applicable by rote, are nevertheless more precise in some cases than in others: for instance, whether a given merger diminishes competition, while necessarily a matter for judgment and discretion, is still a somewhat more precise question than whether, all things considered, it is in the public interest. There are therefore some advantages to requiring agencies to make judgments according to more rather than less precise criteria, because they diminish the extent for manipulation of the procedure by firms desiring to obtain approval for anti-competitive proposals.

What this means in detail has been discussed in Chapter 2. Two themes in particular have emerged. First, that procedures that can be (at least approximately) replicated are preferable to those that cannot. So, for example, tests of product or geographic market definition that are backed by some quantitative survey evidence of the intentions of buyers are preferable to those that rely on the (albeit well-informed) hunches of case rapporteurs. Rough breakdowns of production costs into fixed, variable and sunk components are preferable to general statements about entry barriers being high or low. And secondly, it is desirable for the agency to publish as much of its analysis and reasoning in individual cases as possible (which has the additional advantage of enabling firms involved in future cases to anticipate the agency's procedure of analysis). This ensures the best incentives to perform this analysis as thoroughly and objectively as it can (given the constraints of resources and time), as well as to use it as the foundation for its decisions.

How this kind of transparency might be achieved in the context of European merger control is a question we shall consider in more detail in Chapter 6, which deals with issues of regulatory capture. But first we should introduce the idea that regulatory capture itself may underlie a third possible explanation for the apparent discrepancy between the Coase conjecture and the actual experience of European merger control. As we shall see in Chapter 6, the fact that government is not a single decision-maker, but a multiplicity of actors with overlapping but distinct interests and access to different sources of information, is not a tiresome complication but a central feature in the explanation of many aspects of political and economic life. One possible explanation for the apparent discrepancy noted between the merger policy to which the Commission is publicly committed and the implications of its actual decisions is that this is indeed a real discrepancy, due to the fact that the announced policy is the intention of one set of decision-makers and the decisions are the actions of another set. If so, the value of greater transparency of procedures will lie not just in enabling the Commission to signal its policy intentions more credibly to firms, but also in ensuring that both its intentions and its actions are more closely observable by those in whose ultimate interests they are espoused.

5.2 Conclusions

Overall, it seems to us that all three of these explanations contribute something towards a more realistic understanding of the bargaining processes underlying the Commission's application of the Merger Regulation since 1990. Firms do not have unlimited ability to renegotiate their business deals, and they must to some extent commit themselves to transactions while still uncertain about how their proposals will be received (in spite of the very significant benefits of the pre-notification process in reducing the risk of misunderstanding). There is also some reason to believe that the widespread perception (noted particularly among lawyers) that the Commission has showed itself somewhat keener to approve transactions than is consistent with the criteria of analysis to which it is apparently committed, is disappointing to at least some in the Commission itself, who would prefer to have been able to send more credible signals of their unwillingness to be manipulated by firms.

This is not to say that the speed and flexibility of the procedures in themselves are anything other than a very significant achievement for the Commission, and the appreciation expressed of them by the respondents to our surveys represents a significant vote of approval for the new system (which by no means all commentators expected originally to work as smoothly as it has done). But while bouquets are no doubt gratifying, the business of merger control is not only about pleasing the business community. The extent to which other interests may thereby risk being compromised is the subject of Chapter 6.

Notes

1. This is not necessarily to say that there are not costs of accepting doubtful mergers (these might be challenged – some have been, as we

discussed in Chapter 3). The point is not that accepting any proposal is less costly than refusing it, but rather that there will usually exist some negotiated proposal that is less costly to the agency than a refusal. In addition, and as we discuss more fully in Chapter 6, it is arguable that there are at present insufficiently powerful advocates for competition to make the relative private costs to the agency of clearance and refusal an adequate reflection of the true social costs.

2. This compares to eight blocked by the Secretary of State for Trade and Industry in the UK and four blocked in Germany by the Bundeskartellamt. The issues in bargaining we describe therefore apply to these cases as well.

3. It would in any case be necessary to control for different overall competitive conditions across the EC compared to those within member states.

4. A different model of reputation due to Fudenberg and Levine and cited in Fudenberg and Tirole (1991), theorem 9.1, further provides reasons for thinking that the merger control agency should be able to commit itself credibly to any appropriate strategy. Here a single, patient, long-run player faces a sequence of 'one-off' players, and as the discount rate converges to zero the long-run player can commit him- or herself to any strategy which would be open to the player if he or she had complete take-it-or-leave commitment power in a one-shot game. We can therefore think of the bargaining game that describes each case as being repeated many times with the same agency facing different firms. This tells us that, to the extent the model approximates reality, the agency should be able, due to reputation effects, to commit itself to any merger control policy it prefers; the within-period bargaining game then adds to this the conclusion that firms will never persist with proposals that are likely, under that policy, to be refused. The only reason they may initially put forward such proposals is that they are uncertain how the agency will react in a particular case.

   However, the assumption that firms themselves have no interest in cultivating a 'tough' reputation is clearly not true for the largest firms. Indeed, it will be recalled from Table 4.2 that a majority of respondents to our questionnaire had had previous experience of dealing with DG-IV. Nevertheless, it will be relatively rare even for these firms to come before the Merger Task Force with a problematic proposal, so as a first approximation it may not be too inaccurate to suppose that firms have less to gain from developing a reputation for 'tough' negotiating than does the Merger Task Force itself. The most likely exceptions are firms in highly regulated industries who interact repeatedly with other regulatory agencies (this may partly explain why Air France perceives an interest in challenging the Commission's decision in the *BA/TAT* case, in which it does not have a direct interest; see Chapter 3 above, and the article headlined 'Air France attaque la Commission européenne' in *Le Figaro*, economic section, p. 1, 20 February 1993).

5. More precisely, in the two-period model (or in the model with an

exogeneously finite horizon) there is a unique equilibrium whose outcome tends to the efficient outcome as the discount rate tends to zero. The intuition is straightforward: the assumption that the discount rate tends to zero implies that 'last-minute' negotiations are virtually costless; therefore any blocked merger can always be renegotiated to a compromise deal at the last minute. There is also an infinite horizon example in which the same is true (Fudenberg and Tirole (1991), pp. 405–7).

6. It is clear that this may be an oversimplification. There may be situations where no feasible compromise deal exists; in this case there exist equilibria of the one-sided bargaining model that do not satisfy the Coase conjecture.

7. This view of the de Havilland case as a 'mistake' may sound a little far-fetched. But a number of individuals, both within the Commission and among lawyers advising firms, have expressed to us the view that the firms involved in that case significantly miscalculated the risk of refusal and would not with hindsight have adopted the same approach; just what alternative approach would have been open to it is not altogether clear, so this might instead represent a case where no compromise was feasible (we should emphasize that this conjecture does not rest upon any opinion expressed either publicly or privately to us by the parties to the de Havilland transaction or their lawyers). It has also been suggested that the Commission itself (and especially DG-IV) underestimated the vehemence of the criticism to which it was subsequently subjected, and might not in the future be so willing to turn a similar transaction down. Needless to say this conjecture, like the first, remains speculative.

8. In particular, the Commission, by making decisions too much on a case-by-case basis, may have failed to realize the reputational effects that spill over from one decision to the strategy of firms and their lawyers in future cases. In other words, it may have failed to take advantage of the fact that the Coase bargaining model is itself repeated in the way we described in footnote 4.

9. The distinction between assuming that compromises are costly, and that they may sometimes be infeasible, is clearly only a matter of degree.

10. We discussed the implications of this for the formal model in footnote 4.

11. This is not to say that there could not be a more complex justification in terms of criteria that are designed to impress other parties than firms (foreign governments, the voting public) without affecting the behaviour of firms; but the most plausible candidate explanations of this kind are not very reassuring from the point of view of the broader public interest.

6

Regulatory capture and the design of European merger policy

6.1 The theory of regulatory capture

6.1.1 *Introduction*

Previous chapters have examined the operation of the Merger Regulation as one means of diminishing the costs to the economy of the exercise of market power. We have taken its job and the manner of its institutional implementation as given and asked about the effectiveness with which that job is done. But we have not so far examined how far this view of the aims of the Regulation is consistent with the various pressures and constraints upon those who have to implement it. Is it reasonable to suppose that the European Commission, in applying the Regulation, is simply seeking to diminish the costs of market power? Is it not rather responding to a whole array of political pressures from various interest groups, including those that would benefit from the curbing of market power but including also many with a different agenda? Can an analysis of these pressures both explain the manner of its present implementation and offer guidance for the future?

Until a few years ago such a question would have been regarded as beyond the scope of economics even to ask, let alone to answer. Fortunately, academic and political contributors to the discussion of the role of the state in economic management have more recently reached a rare degree of consensus on one point: regulating the operation of the state's own organs and agencies is as central to the task of good government, and as deserving of systematic analysis, as is governing the activities of the private sector of the economy. It is no longer possible to regard government agencies as staffed by selfless and omniscient upholders of the common weal, nor to contrast them with the simple and ruthless pursuit of profits by private firms. For one thing, it has become abundantly clear that government agencies themselves respond to political and economic pressures and incentives, and that limitations on the information available to them may severely constrain the policies they can pursue; for another, the fact that firms may themselves be run by agents with interests of their own other than maximizing shareholders' wealth has become much harder to ignore. One of the tasks, therefore, for both firms and government agencies is to ensure that the individuals running them have incentives to do so in the wider interests of the parties whose welfare they affect.

What has become known as the theory of regulatory 'capture' attempts to describe the various influences on regulatory agencies to represent special interests rather than some idealized conception of the common good. There are two main components to this theory. The *first*, which has its origins in Marx's view of the influence of business interests over the state, but which was given significant impetus by the work of Stigler (1971), emphasizes that interest groups have various means to influence public decision-makers, both elected politicians and unelected officials. These means include direct bribes, indirect monetary inducements through campaign contributions, the hope of public decision-makers for future employment after they leave office (the 'revolving door'), the influence of voting lobbies in marginal constituencies, and – not least – the subtle influence that is exercised by proximity, through public officials' wish for good relations with the interest group representatives with whom they daily have to deal.[1] Though the study of regulatory capture is relatively modern, the phenomenon itself is not: Foster (1993) reports that Gladstone's attempts to regulate private railway companies in Britain in the 1840s were obstructed by the immense lobbying power of railway companies, who at one time numbered 132 MPs as directors.

In Stigler's work capture was conceived as subordination of the regulatory process to the interests of firms in the regulated industry, but more recent contributions (surveyed in Noll (1989)) have considered capture by many kinds of interest group (including consumer safety and environmental lobbying groups, for instance). And one can also contrast capture of a regulatory agency by the industry it oversees with capture by government (an instance of time inconsistency where the government is unable to commit itself not to interfere in the regulatory process for short-term electoral considerations, such as to preserve employment in firms threatened with reorganization in marginal constituencies). Both industry and government capture have their origins in a more fundamental notion, which can be called bureaucratic capture: when the aims of a regulatory agency come to reflect the individual aims of its staff – for larger budgets, a higher media profile, an enhanced reputation for winning legal cases, or whatever else those aims may comprise.[2] It is by working to influence these aims that interest groups can appropriate the regulatory process to their own ends. All these contributions imply that regulation will create and distribute rents, usually by restricting entry to the markets concerned.

The *second* component of the theory (particularly emphasized by Laffont and Tirole (1993), ch. 11) focuses on the constraints inherent in the regulatory process. As Laffont and Tirole point out, approaches based solely on the idea that regulators can be influenced suffer from a significant shortcoming. Interest groups may wish to influence public decision-making, but there are limitations upon their ability to do so, limitations due to the design of the regulatory institutions themselves when these are established to fulfil some public purpose. But if appropriate institutional design can limit the extent of regulatory capture, what constrains it from preventing regulatory capture altogether? Two major factors stand out. The first consists of the asymmetries of information that prevent the public at large from checking the actions of regulators and thus make capture possible. In the absence of these asymmetries, interest groups would be unable to extract rents from the regulatory process (and would thus have no incentive to influence regulatory outcomes). The second consists in the fact that most design of regulatory institutions is undertaken not by the ultimate principals (the voting public at large) but by politicians and officials who are themselves agents with delegated powers and whose incentives in designing institutions may in turn differ from those of the principals. In other words, regulation (like all political activity) involves hierarchies of delegation, and raises the question 'who regulates the regulators?' A detailed examination of the structure of regulatory institutions is therefore needed in order to explain not only why regulatory capture is possible but by what means it may be constrained.

Beginning, therefore, with the idea that any public agency must be run by individuals with aims and purposes of their own, the different contributions to this literature explore the various ways in which those aims and purposes may be harnessed by different interest groups to their own ends. As a matter of positive economics, capture by special interests is to be contrasted with influence by broader or more general interests, not with some mythical state of nature in which agencies respond to no interests at all. From the point of view of welfare economics, the fact that regulatory agencies respond to interest group pressures need not be seen as harmful (though the early literature tended admittedly to emphasize capture as a discredit to the very idea of regulatory intervention in the economy). The task for public policy is not somehow to prevent interest group pressures from affecting regulation, but rather to ensure that the pressures to which regulatory agencies respond are reasonably representative of society at large.

6.1.2   *Three tasks for a theory of regulatory capture*

The analysis of regulatory capture must therefore involve a number of distinct tasks. *First*, if it is to inform the welfare economics of institution design, it must formulate an explicit account of the interests regulation ought to serve. The overwhelming tendency in the economic literature on regulation has been to view its purpose as the promotion of economic efficiency, in line with the broad neo-classical consensus that other goals of public policy (such as the promotion of equity) are the province of different areas of government (such as the tax and benefit system).[3] This consensus has not been unchallenged: regulation of particular areas of economic life (such as health care) has often been argued to be based on goals other than efficiency (see Culyer (1989)), and hostile observers have often remarked that particular instances of regulation appeared to privilege other considerations over those of efficiency (see Franks and Mayer (1989) for a discussion of the 1986 Financial Services Act in the UK).

Even within the sub-field of competition policy, there are different juridical traditions, some of which emphasize goals of fairness and equity significantly more than efficiency. Nevertheless, the discussion in this chapter will use the promotion of economic efficiency as the main standard by which institutions involved in merger policy are to be assessed,[4] leaving open the question of whether such a criterion is adequate for the broader field of economic regulation as a whole.

Secondly, an analysis of regulatory capture should examine the aims and goals of those involved in implementing regulation on a day-to-day basis, in order to see what kinds of pressure different interest groups may be able to bring to bear. For instance, agencies headed by open political appointees (such as the US Department of Justice) may be expected to behave differently from those headed by civil servants (such as the German Bundeskartellamt or the UK Monopolies and Mergers Commission). In the context of a supra-national body such as the European Commission, it will make a difference whether individuals involved are from the Commission's own staff or are national civil servants on secondment: the latter are likely to be more sensitive to national interests, both when this is desirable and when it is not; the former may be more sensitive to pressures from within the Commission's own hierarchy. Regulators with fixed terms of appointment are less likely to respond to political pressures than those who can be dismissed at any time. Those with a background in the industries regulated may have both more knowledge of and more sympathy for their former employers. Different kinds of training – the law, economics or accountancy – will tend to imply different preferences and priorities, as well as different ambitions for future employment (see Coate and McChesney (1992)). Well-paid regulators may be more immune to financial inducements than those who are not, though they may be correspondingly more concerned not to threaten their livelihoods by offending the politically powerful.[5] It will make a difference to what extent those involved in regulation face clear terms of reference which not only define their goals but also constitute criteria for the evaluation of their performance and determination of their prospects for remuneration, promotion and reappointment.[6] And, finally, it will matter very much to what extent regulators see themselves as needing to establish a reputation for effective action and credible undertakings: a newly established agency with a relatively high profile may provide its staff with substantially different incentives (tending less towards industry capture and more towards government capture, perhaps) from those of an established agency whose activities have become routine.

Thirdly, the nature of regulatory capture will depend on the character of a number of constraints, some intrinsic to the regulatory process and some resulting from particular features of the institutions concerned. One kind of intrinsic constraint is informational: agencies have limited information about the activities of regulated firms, and the voting public have limited information about the activities of agencies. As emphasized by Laffont (1993), the first kind of information asymmetry leads to a fundamental trade-off: firms able to make high levels of productivity improvement can extract rents, and attempting to mitigate the social cost of these rents leads to inducing inefficiently low levels of productivity change from less able firms.[7] For example, a competition agency faces difficulties in distinguishing mergers that promote synergies and scale economies from those that simply increase market power. A policy of complete *laissez-faire* would give maximal incentives for efficiency gains; allowing only mergers that pass strict standards of proof would blunt incentives for those efficiency gains that were not sufficiently great to meet the standards.

And just as there are information asymmetries between regulators and firms, so the information asymmetries between the general public and their agents, the regulators, impose an analogous trade-off: allowing agencies complete discretion in their activities leaves them free to share rents with various interest groups; imposing a more restrictive framework of rules may mitigate this kind of capture at the cost of making policies more rigid and less sensitive to circumstances of the particular case. Where exactly the trade-off between discretion and rules should be made will depend upon intrinsic features of the regulatory task involved (such as how easily performance criteria can be quantified). But that there is such a trade-off is inherent in the nature of regulation under asymmetric information. It is particularly striking in the case of the efficiency defence in merger cases, which will be considered below.

It is sometimes thought that informational asymmetries can be resolved simply by reporting requirements: for example, firms can be required to report their costs. All such purported remedies run up against a difficulty that can be formally entitled 'incentive compatibility' or more colloquially the Mandy Rice-Davies problem.[8] This is that parties with private information will report what it is in their interests to report, no more and no less.[9] Any attempt to remove informational asymmetries has to work upon ensuring that it is in the parties' interests to report information accurately; and this in turn may significantly constrain what regulation can achieve.

The many other kinds of constraint that affect the nature of regulatory capture include the following: rules determining the publication of evidence or of reports about the agency's activities; rules about the extent to which and the circumstances under which regulators may meet with representatives of the industries concerned (rules that are much more restrictive in the United States than in Europe); rules determining when agency staff may accept employment in the industries; the policing of bribes and the rules governing indirect financial inducements; rules of procedure (including those governing the burden of proof); and the extent to which the agency's recommendations may be subject to scrutiny or overruling by other branches of government, including the courts.

There are in addition a number of features of the culture within which a regulatory agency operates that are difficult to classify formally as constraints, but which may nevertheless exercise a profound influence on the nature of regulatory capture.[10] One is the extent to which, regardless of what the formal rules may allow, other branches of government may feel free to disregard the agency's advice. In Germany, for instance, the Bundeskartellamt has a significant public standing and authority; its president appears on television talk shows and is a public figure in a way that cannot be said to be true of the head of any other anti-trust agency. This has not prevented various Economics Ministers from using their overruling powers, but has ensured that such exercises of power receive wide publicity and considerable critical scrutiny – and are consequently rarely exercised. Another cultural factor is the extent to which agencies and firms feel obliged to seek negotiated solutions to disagreements rather than being willing to resort to adversarial procedures such as the courts; the latter is much more routine in the United States than in Europe.[11] An additional consideration in the European Community is that the EC Commission has undoubtedly felt itself obliged to work gradually via consensus-building[12] to establish the legitimacy of its procedures in such fields as merger regulation, being aware that in a community of member states the formal existence of a regulation is not enough to guarantee political acceptability of the procedure it initiates.

The most intrinsic constraints on the regulatory process are therefore informational: in the absence of asymmetries of information between firms and regulators there would be no rents for captured agencies to distribute, and in the absence of asymmetries between regulators and the public at large there would be much less difficulty in ensuring that regulatory agencies fulfilled their public mandate to the letter – though there might be costs to the public of organizing to enforce this mandate even in the absence of information problems. The other constraints discussed above are all features of the particular constitution of a system of regulation. Some (like rules about publication of proceedings or the burden of proof) may mitigate the severity of the original asymmetries of information, by ensuring that those parties that have easiest access to important information are required to divulge it for the benefit of others. Others (like rules about financial inducements) affect the extent to which regulators' private incentives may be distorted by those of particular interest groups. Some (like legally enforceable rules) are features of the regulatory constitution that can be changed at will - they are constraints for the regulators but not for the lawmakers, one might say. Others (like aspects of the national culture) represent constraints for regulators and lawmakers alike. These constraints vary from situation to situation and from agency to agency, and a normative theory of constitution design must ask which kinds of constraint that can feasibly be imposed on agency conduct are most conducive to the wider public good. It would be a mistake to assume that the particular constitution of actual regulatory agencies will always or even usually be justified by such considerations: the design of regulatory institutions is no more likely to be carried out by disinterested representatives of the wider public good than is day-to-day regulation itself.[13] It is a process that involves politicians with constituencies to defend, bureaucrats with empires to enlarge, even academic specialists with axes to grind and consultancy income to solicit. Nevertheless, there are some broad principles that can clarify the normative aspects of institution design even if the extent to which they have operated historically may be a matter of greater dispute.

6.1.3   *Different responses to regulatory capture: accountability, independence, transparency*

6.1.3.1   Accountability

Awareness of the phenomenon of regulatory capture has prompted a number of general responses, both of a scholarly and a political character. One is a general scepticism about the powers that should be entrusted to government, and a belief that in many cases the unregulated market failure is a lesser evil than that of intervention. Such scepticism has provided the impetus behind much of the liberalization and deregulation of the 1980s in many countries. Where continued regulation has nevertheless been thought to be justified, several general principles have been advanced as helping to diminish the risks of capture. One is the principle of accountability: the idea that regulatory agencies should be held to account through the political process to the general public. In theory this means that greater political scrutiny should help to counterbalance the natural inequality in the ability of different interest groups to influence regulatory practice, including the well-known tendency for consumer interests to be less well organized than those of producers.[14] In practice it has meant: a greater attention to the oversight of regulatory bodies by legislative committees (such as the House of Commons Select Committees in the UK); arguments for increasing the powers of the European Parliament relative to those of the Commission; the incorporation of procedures such as environmental impact assessments into the practice of some government agencies (especially in the United States); scrutiny of regulatory proposals via institutions such as the US Office of Management and Budget and via publication (for example, in the *Federal Register*) to invite public reaction (see Viscusi *et al.* (1992), ch. 2); increased public funding for a number of bodies concerned with safety, consumer affairs and the environment; increased resort to public inquiries on contentious regulatory matters; and improved procedures (such as the establishment of ombudsmen) for representing public grievances.

One can model formally this process of increasing accountability in one of two main ways. One is as a shortening of the chain of delegation in a multi-tiered principal–agent problem. For example, instead of a chain in which responsibility is delegated from voters to a legislature, from a legislature to an executive, from an executive to a civil service, and perhaps again from a civil service to a separate regulatory agency (with at each stage some loss of precision in the degree of oversight possible due to an additional asymmetry of information), increased accountability may involve the establishment of direct oversight of the agency by the legislature.

Alternatively, one might view greater accountability as an increase in the influence of hitherto underrepresented interests in the regulatory process. For example, consumers or environmental interest groups may find it easier to exercise influence on the regulatory process through mechanisms such as public inquiries, or through legislative hearings, than directly on the separate agency concerned. (This may, of course, also be true sometimes of other, more powerful interests such as those of firms, but the implication of the argument is that increased accountability implies an increase in the *relative* power of the weaker interests.) Now these two interpretations of accountability are not equivalent: it will often be true that shortening the chain of delegation is the simplest way in which such changes in the influence of interest groups may be brought about, but it is not necessarily the only way. And nor will a shorter chain necessarily be sufficient to redress a prior imbalance in influence: regulatory institutions are complex hierarchies, and apparent increases in accountability may simply represent stronger oversight of one captured institution by another.

Under either interpretation, increases in accountability should not be presumed always to improve the quality of regulation from an objective standpoint. This is partly because, as is discussed in section 6.1.5.2 below, the costs to a principal of delegating oversight of the agent to an intermediary[15] may in some circumstances be offset by the fact that the intermediary's capacity to carry out supervisory functions (including threats) may be more credible than that of the principal; shortening the chain of delegation may therefore diminish credibility even as it increases accountability. It is also because of potential problems of the second best: partial responses to regulatory capture may be worse than no responses at all. For instance, as Laffont and Tirole (1992a) warn, where a regulatory agency is captured by producer interests, increasing the influence of hitherto excluded environmental pressure groups may worsen the quality of regulation: environmentalists share with producers an interest in restricting output below the optimum, and only if consumers are also sufficiently enfranchised will the reform improve efficiency.

6.1.3.2   *Independence*

A second general principle, paradoxically the apparent opposite to the first, is that of political independence. It has become particularly popular in recent years as a prescription for central banks (see Persson and Tabellini (1993)), though it was also influential in the establishment of sectoral regulatory agencies for the newly privatized utilities in the UK. It is based on the sentiment that politicians may be the source of more regulatory capture than they remedy; and it refers not to a complete absence of political accountability but rather to the view that such accountability should be exercised at occasional intervals and through clearly pre-specified criteria rather than on a day-to-day basis. There are really two distinct theoretical foundations for such a view. The first (and the one with the closer analogy to the rationale for central bank independence) is the belief that regulation faces a problem of time inconsistency: regulators would like the industries they regulate to invest optimally, but politicians will be more tempted than independent regulators to seek to expropriate any rents accruing to such investments after they have been made. In particular, they will tend to tighten the conditions of regulation if it turns out that profits have been higher than expected, while not being equally willing to loosen them if profits are low. Note that such expropriation might well be an optimal policy *ex post* (once investments have been sunk): nevertheless, regulatory independence is a means by which the politicians and regulators together can commit themselves *ex ante* to a policy that will establish the credibility needed to motivate future investment.

The second rationale for regulatory independence is the claim that the ability to exercise day-to-day influence is much more unequally distributed between different interest groups than is the ability to exercise influence at predetermined and infrequent intervals. Independent regulators (subject to periodic review) can therefore be expected to reflect the interests of the voting public better than those who are buffeted by the gusts of influence as they blow from day to day.

While the first of these two rationales does not presuppose any capture of government by special interest groups (just a capture of government, as it were, by its own short-term concerns), the second appeals essentially to interest group capture. The former is undoubtedly the more important for utility regulation, where the perceived problem is usually one of discouraged investment through populist disapproval of utility profits. By contrast, the latter is probably more relevant for regulation of mergers and for competition policy in general (where political pressures are more likely to err in the direction of underrepresentation of consumer interests, and where there is no obvious analogue to the time-inconsistency problem).

6.1.3.3 *Transparency*

A third general principle is that of transparency, which implies that regulatory agencies should be obliged to make public as much as possible of the information and reasoning upon which their decisions and actions are based. The case for transparency rests on three conceptually distinct arguments. First, by making more information public that might otherwise be private, it may reduce the informational asymmetries that give rise to the possibility of capture in the first place. In effect it facilitates monitoring of the agency by the voting public and enables them to check both its diligence and its competence (subject, of course, to the Mandy Rice-Davies problem). For this to be effective, all that is needed is publication of information *after* decisions have been taken (what may be called *ex post* transparency).

Secondly, transparency can aid a regulatory agency to commit itself (and, by extension, can aid those establishing such an agency to commit *it*) to a given regulatory policy by increasing the visibility of any departures from such a policy. This argument featured prominently in our discussion of bargaining in Chapter 5, where we emphasized that even without any risk of capture, an agency would typically have an interest in transparency in order to increase the credibility of signals it sends to firms of its unwillingness to be manipulated. It is no less important a consideration when there is a risk of capture, because then transparency, by increasing commitment, can diminish the efforts of firms to manipulate (and thus to capture) the agency. For this, though, what is required is both some form of visible commitment to a procedure before it undertakes bargaining (what might be called *ex ante* transparency, of the kind that might be established by procedural guidelines), *and* sufficient *ex post* transparency to ensure that this commitment can be effectively monitored.

The third argument for transparency rests on the view that one of the greatest sources of inequality in the influence exercised by different interest groups is the cost of gathering information, both about the issues concerned and about the nature of the regulatory process itself (and therefore about where influence may most effectively be exercised). Some interest groups (such as large firms) may gather such information as a by-product of their other activities; they may also have more at stake and may therefore be able better to spread the fixed costs of doing so.[16] Not only does information have some of the properties of a public good, in that the cost to the regulatory agency of publishing it once it has been acquired may be very small, but in addition the benefit of its publication to any particular interest group is related to the cost which that group would have had to incur to acquire it otherwise; enforcing publication therefore tends to offset some of the original inequalities in influence that were due to the cost of private information acquisition. Typically, though, for this kind of publication to make a difference there needs to be transparency of procedures *as they occur* (for example, through publication of analyses before these become incorporated into decisions), in order that interested parties can make use of the information while it still has some value. We can call this *procedural* transparency.

There is little doubt that transparency or lack of it can make a dramatic difference in practice to the influence of particular interest groups. A striking example was the calculation by the British Treasury in 1990 that the average British family of four paid an extra £16 per week in higher prices and taxes as a result of protection (over half of this sum being due to the Common Agricultural Policy). This sum was roughly equal to such a family's poll tax bill in the same year, and yet although the introduction of the poll tax had led to widespread public outrage and was generally believed to be the single most important factor underlying the fall from power of Mrs Thatcher, consumers had strikingly failed to agitate against protection, let alone to bring down prime ministers because of it. One can be sure that the political economy of trade reform would be very different if the resources to finance the CAP, the Multi-Fibre Arrangement and Voluntary Export Restraints were collected twice yearly from households in lump sum demands backed up by the threat of bailiffs instead of invisibly in higher prices.

Independence and transparency are not entirely separate principles but are intimately linked. First, effective transparency of regulatory procedures depends upon agencies' possessing at least enough independence to be able to resist pressures to modify what they publish to suit the preferences of those to whom they are politically responsible. Secondly, if regulatory agencies are notionally independent but the government retains (as it almost always does in a democracy) the right to override what the agency does, it is only the adverse publicity that such overriding would receive that will prevent a government from overriding the agency whenever it wishes to. Some economists have, indeed, thought it inconceivable that separate branches of government could continue to have disparate goals, presuming that the subordination of all such branches to a single central authority would be irresistible (see Hayek (1944), p. 64 and the discussion of this claim in Stigler (1988), pp. 141–7). It is only the presence of sufficient transparency to ensure that attempts to subordinate the branches receive adverse publicity, therefore, that can add substance to any formal constitutional provision of independence (we discuss this issue in more detail in the section on functional separation of powers in 6.1.5 below).

While all three broad principles of accountability, independence and transparency have considerable merit as responses to the problem of capture, they are too general to be of much guidance in specific issues of regulatory institution design. The next sections therefore consider some more specific applications.

6.1.4   *The assignment of regulatory powers: how centralized should regulation be?*

The question whether regulatory powers should be exercised at the level of European Community institutions or those of member states (or indeed those with even more local jurisdiction, such as the German Laender or the French Départements or Communes) has become one of the most contentious political issues of recent years in the Community. The principle of subsidiarity which appears in the Maastricht Treaty has often been criticized for vagueness, but it represents in fact a criterion for determining the burden of proof which has a great deal of theoretical and practical weight behind it. It states simply that regulatory powers should be exercised at the most local level unless there are compelling reasons for further centralization. It does not in itself specify what those reasons might be, but there is by now a growing literature discussing exactly that. Its theoretical foundation is Tiebout's (1956) model of the provision of local public goods. A schematic outline of the relationship between the Tiebout model and the conclusions that follow from subsequent applications of the model to regulatory centralization is given in Table 6.1.

Table 6.1   Applications of the Tiebout model to regulatory centralization.

Basic model	Assumptions	Conclusions
Tiebout (1956)	No spillovers Complete information	Decentralization
Easterbrook (1983)	Few spillovers Complete information	Decentralization
Rose-Ackerman (1981)	Spillovers Complete information No repeated interaction	Centralization
Gatsios & Seabright (1989) Neven (1992)	Spillovers Complete information Low discount rate	Decentralization with policy coordination
	Spillovers Complete information High discount rate	Centralization
Klibanoff & Morduch (1993)	Spillovers Incomplete information Local regulators better informed	Decentralization unless spillovers 'large'
	Spillovers Incomplete information Local regulators not better informed	Centralization

The presumption in favour of decentralization arises for two main kinds of reason. One kind is informational: on many questions, local authorities will be better informed than central authorities about conditions in the industries regulated; they will also be better informed about the needs and preferences of those citizens who are affected by the market failure the regulatory intervention is designed to redress; and the citizens themselves may well be better informed about the activities of the regulatory agencies. In other words, the asymmetries of information that lead to regulatory capture will often be simply less severe. The second kind of reason is that accountability may be easier to establish at a local level. This may be a feature of the political system, which gives local citizens a voice in their own affairs: national regulators, by contrast, are accountable to many other citizens than the ones directly implicated in a particular decision, and the influence of the preferences of the affected citizens on them may well be swamped by national trends. Alternatively, accountability may be enforced by the ability of citizens to leave a local jurisdiction whose regulatory policy does not meet their needs, and move to an alternative local jurisdiction that does (to exercise their right of 'exit', in Hirschman's (1970) phrase). Here local regulation is preferable because it increases the number of alternative regulatory jurisdictions between which footloose citizens may choose; it enhances the scope for 'competition between regulators' to offer solutions to the failure of competition between firms.

Applying the insight that a system of regulation can be considered a special case of a local public good enables us to use Tiebout's theory of local public goods to examine precisely the conditions under which decentralized regulation would be adequate to ensure efficiency. The most important (and restrictive) conditions for efficiency in the production and allocation of local public goods were shown by Tiebout to be the following:

1. Costless mobility of citizens between jurisdictions.
2. A large number of jurisdictions.
3. No external effects between jurisdictions.

These were in addition to technical assumptions such as that each public good has an optimal number of consumers (to ensure a determinate number of communities), and complete information about alternative possibilities. The absence of external effects meant that the costs of each good would be borne by the residents of the jurisdiction supplying it, and the excludability problem would be solved by the dependence of consumption upon location. Effectively, local jurisdictions would act rather like firms, supplying differentiated products to consumers, with a larger number of products required, the greater the variety in consumers' tastes. Centralization of regulation could not improve on local regulation, and would suffer from the same disadvantages in providing regulatory services as those faced by the command economy in providing goods and ordinary services.

It is evident that in reality the Tiebout conditions are very far from being met. This is particularly true where the issue is whether regulation should be carried out at a national or an EC level; here there are very major costs (including linguistic and cultural costs) to the mobility of citizens between member states, and 12 is a small number of competing jurisdictions given the large number of regulatory questions on which each pronounces. In addition there are many aspects of regulation in which the external effects between member states are quite significant.

However, the failure of the Tiebout conditions to be met does not by itself suggest when centralization of regulatory power will be the appropriate remedy. For one thing, limited mobility between juris-dictions may increase the likelihood of regulatory capture at a local level (since mobility is one of the best guarantors of accountability), but in no way implies that central regulation will improve matters. Centralization may alleviate problems of excessive capture of the regulatory process by national interests, but not when the capture is by interests other than national ones. A number of disputes between the European Commission and member states in recent years (those concerning drinking water pollution, for instance) have been based on the Commission's judgment that national regulation inadequately reflected even *national* interests. In other words, they have turned into simple clashes of view between national and EC regulators over the appropriate regulatory regime; in such circumstances there is no intrinsic reason to prefer the EC view, even if the EC's judgment happens to be the right one in a particular case.

International spillover effects between jurisdictions provide a more solid case for regulatory centralization. Table 6.1 summarizes the main arguments. Rose-Ackerman (1981) discusses the incentives for centralization arising from the presence of spillovers, on the assump-tion that the alternatives are centralization and uncoordinated decentralization. Easterbrook (1983) provides a specific interpreta-tion of competition among jurisdictions in the field of anti-trust policy, but doubts that spillovers are significant enough to outweigh the virtues of decentralization. Gatsios and Seabright (1989) admit the possibility of significant spillovers, but emphasize that these are not enough on their own to justify centralization, since localities are likely to be facing these interactions repeatedly. If spillovers were the only problem there might be nothing to prevent local jurisdictions from coordinating their regulatory policies to take account of the externalities.[17] A coordinated outcome might be enforceable by the threat of any locality (a member state, say) to revert to the non-cooperative policy if other member states reneged on their promise to implement the agreed policy.

However, several circumstances may arise in which coordination will not work. One is if parties discount the future too heavily (or alternatively, interact too rarely) to make the threat of retaliation a sufficient inducement for cooperation.[18] This fact may of itself encourage them voluntarily to give up to the EC the power to determine such matters, if it is hard to know beforehand which member states would be most likely to gain from breaking a voluntary agreement. Centralization then represents a kind of insurance policy for each state against the possibility that other states would gain more than it did itself from breaking a cooperative agreement.

Another circumstance in which coordination will not work is if there is incomplete information about whether each party is keeping its side of the bargain. This is especially likely if the regulation is of a significantly discretionary character. Centralization may solve this problem if jurisdictions can trust a central authority more than they can trust each other. Among the reasons why this might be so are the possibly greater incentives for a central regulator (with greater visibility and more frequent activity) to establish a reputation for sticking to an agreed policy.

Conversely, centralization that does not alleviate the asymmetric information problem may not improve matters. This has been shown in the context of the Tiebout model by Klibanoff and Morduch (1993). They extend the Tiebout framework by allowing for spillover effects; each locality can choose to undertake a project whose benefits flow partly to other localities. They assume that the benefits of the project to the locality itself are private information. They then assume that a central authority has the ability to undertake taxes and transfers (subject to overall budget balance), which it can use to induce localities to undertake privately unprofitable but socially beneficial projects. This central authority does not, however, have access to the information about the private benefits of each project, though it does know the magnitude of the spillovers. Klibanoff and Morduch show that unless spillover effects are large the central authority may not be able to improve on autonomous provision. The reason is that, in order to induce a locality to undertake a project with negative private but positive social value, the authority must offer some positive transfer. But incentive compatibility then requires it to offer the same level of transfer to all localities whose projects have the same or greater private value, otherwise the localities will understate the private value of their projects in order to qualify for a transfer. So moving from autonomous provision, which requires no transfers, to centrally coordinated provision requires a big overhang of transfer payments to those localities that would have produced on their own for free. And only if the spillover effects are large will the benefits outweigh the distortionary costs of financing the transfers.

The Klibanoff–Morduch result has a natural interpretation in the context of European merger policy. A merger between two firms in one member state that leads to some efficiency gains may nevertheless impose costs of market power that are partly borne by consumers outside the member state concerned. In order to ensure that national merger policies are coordinated in such a way as to reflect these spillover effects, the European Commission could choose to act as a broker, log-rolling between different issues of concern to member states to induce them to approve only those mergers whose Community-wide rather than merely national benefits were positive. This might, if effective, lead to the approval of some mergers that member states would otherwise have banned, and to the prohibition of some that member states would otherwise have approved. But even if the Commission's powers to effect political transfers of this kind were greater than in fact they are, it would still face the problem that member states had the incentive to overstate the private costs to them of a merger they wished to prohibit, and the private benefits of a merger they wished to approve, in order to extract additional (and costly) political concessions from the EC.

In this context, centralization of the power to regulate mergers with significant spillover effects does two things which a central power broker cannot. First, it removes from member states the ability to use the threat of autonomous decision-making as a lever to extract political concessions; and secondly, by enabling the EC to undertake its own investigation of the costs and benefits of mergers, it removes the asymmetry of information that makes this threat of leverage credible.

There are, naturally, a number of intermediate possibilities between full decentralization and full centralization of regulatory powers in a certain field. For instance, in some fields (such as measurement of the damage done by environmental pollution) decentralized information gathering can help to remove much of the information asymmetry, since it is possible to check that a member state has collected and published accurate statistics without repeating the whole information-gathering exercise. But in competition policy, where the concepts (the degree of competitiveness of a market, for instance) are much more fluid, contestable and discretionary, and where much of the necessary information needs to remain commercially confidential, the only way for the Commission to be sure that a fair analysis has been conducted may be to do the analysis itself.

6.1.5 *The functional separation of powers*

6.1.5.1 *The balance between sectoral and generic regulation*

The last section considered the question of how powers should be allocated between different *levels* of government. Now we consider the extent to which, at any given level, there is a case for separating different kinds of power between regulatory agencies charged with different tasks. There are two aspects to this question. First, is there sometimes a case for granting to distinct agencies similar kinds of regulatory power, but exercised in different sectors? For example, the UK formed a new regulatory body for each of the privatized utilities (telecommunications, gas, water and electricity). It could instead have formed a single (generic) office of utility regulation, or even have required the Monopolies and Mergers Commission to oversee all the utility companies. On what basis other than administrative convenience could one choose between these various options?

The chief advantage of having several sector-specific agencies lies in the possibility for comparing the performance of the agencies with each other. The literature on principal–agent relationships with several agents makes it clear that when the randomness in the circumstances affecting the outcome of the tasks is correlated between agents, relative performance evaluation acts as a spur to efficiency (Mookherjee (1984), Shleifer (1985), Holmstrom and Milgrom (1990));

the higher the correlation, the lower the agency costs of delegation.

The disadvantage of having sector-specific agencies lies in the possibly greater risk that these will be captured by producer interests. The intuitive reason sometimes adduced for such a claim is that multiplication of regulatory agencies raises the costs of organization to consumers (who have to lobby a large number of agencies) much more than it does to producers, who by and large continue to be regulated by a single agency. A very stylized example may help to make this clear. Suppose that in an economy there are n identical firms and m identical consumers ($n < m$). Profits per firm are π and income per consumer is y. Firms each invest resources $R(x)$ and consumers $r(x)$ in lobbying regulators, where x is the amount of their profits earned (or income spent, respectively) in the sector over which the regulator has control, and $R(.)$ and $r(.)$ are both increasing functions. Now suppose the regulatory system is organized into j different sectors; the issue is whether the same n firms should be divided into a small or a large number of sectors. Ignoring integer problems and assuming that each firm produces in only one sector, while each consumer divides his or her income equally between the products of each firm, yields the result that total investment in lobbying in each sector is equal to $nR(\pi)/j$ by firms and $mr(y/j)$ by consumers.

Now while we do not have much empirical evidence about the way in which expenditure on lobbying increases with income, we do have reason to believe the functions $R(.)$ and $r(.)$ are best represented as significantly convex, and therefore that expenditure increases more than proportionately with income. There are two reasons for this. One is direct observation, which suggests that most consumers and firms spend very little indeed on lobbying until the sums at stake become large. The other is the fact that in all countries *total* expenditure by firms on lobbying dramatically exceeds total expenditure by consumer organizations, in spite of the fact that aggregate consumer expenditure significantly exceeds total corporate profits. This suggests either that for some unexplained reason the function $R(.)$ lies everywhere well above $r(.)$, or that both functions are highly convex, and the discrepancy in total expenditures is due to profits per firm being much higher than income per head. Now if the functions are convex (as seems a more reasonable inference)[19], then as j (the number of sectors regulated separately) increases – holding n constant – total firms' expenditure on lobbying falls in a manner

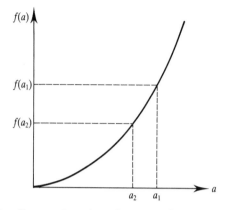

Figure 6.1 The effect on the value of a convex function of a reduction in its argument. f is a convex function of a: $\dfrac{f(a_1)}{a_1} < \dfrac{f(a_1) - f(a_2)}{a_1 - a_2}$.

inversely proportional to j, whereas consumers' lobbying expenditure falls by much more. Figure 6.1 illustrates that, for a convex function passing through the origin, a reduction in the argument of the function reduces the value of the function by more than proportionately. So increasing the number of sectors separately regulated is likely to tilt the balance of lobbying power in favour of producers.

To be sure, both the arguments for and against sectoral regulation presented here are somewhat stylized, but both receive a degree of corroboration from recent European regulatory experience. First, the advantages. It seems reasonable to suggest that the ability to make comparisons between the various newly established regulatory agencies in the UK has been to the benefit of the overall regulatory process, and has perhaps reinforced with a degree of rivalry the determination of the agencies to perform their task well and conscientiously. This has depended, however, on the agencies' having quite high profiles and fairly clear objectives by the standards of most regulatory agencies; in other cases where the goals are more diffuse, it could be that inter-agency rivalry would lead to concentration on more easily measurable aspects of performance to the possible detriment of overall policy. For example, in the United States anti-trust policy is divided more or less between the Federal Trade Commission and the Department of Justice on a loosely sectoral basis (with one or two exceptions, such as airline mergers which were dealt with by the Department of Transportation until the late 1980s); there is naturally a certain professional rivalry between these two agencies. Some observers such as Coate and McChesney (1992) have detected at certain periods a degree of political pressure on these two agencies to bring cases; the fact that it is possible to compare the cases each has brought may make this pressure harder to resist, whatever the merits of the cases themselves.[20]

There is also little doubt that, within Europe (both at the EC level and that of member states), those ministries or directorates with narrowly defined, sectoral responsibilities have been widely perceived as captured by the industries they were responsible for. In the EC, however, the nature of the relationship is not surprising given that the role of bureaucracies dealing with such industries as transport, energy and telecommunications has for most of the history of the Community been primarily promotional, attempting to develop Community policies or coordinate the actions of government departments and industries. Explicit regulatory responsibilities have been a relatively small part of their activities until recently. And these responsibilities have usually arisen as a consequence of the application of Community law, particularly in the area of competition policy, rather than as a natural consequence of policy formation by the directorates concerned (a responsibility that has been thrust upon them rather than one voluntarily acquired). Previously legitimate conduct (for example, a utility's exclusive right to market telecommunications equipment or to import electricity) has been challenged as contrary to the Treaty of Rome. However, although these sectoral directorates have responsibility for developing the policies, they often continue to identify with industry concerns. As a result the role of the horizontal regulatory authorities (particularly those responsible for competition and environmental protection) has become more important.

The growth in power of such generic or horizontal agencies at a period of overall deregulatory philosophy illustrates some of the dangers of seeing regulation or deregulation simplistically in terms of the degree of comprehensiveness of aggregate state intervention in the economy. And it also helps to explain the paradox that pressure for deregulation has come strongly in the 1980s from a bureaucratic body (namely, the Commission) rather than primarily from populist politics as in the United States. For deregulation can be expected to diminish the power of sectoral agencies far more than those of generic ones, and may even increase the latter. So there is no need to assume that generic regulatory authorities are intrinsically less susceptible to lobbying and rent-seeking than their more narrowly based national and sectoral counterparts. But the interests they represent are nevertheless different ones, and may favour outcomes that involve less rent-seeking in aggregate. The pressure for increasing competition in energy markets, for instance, has come primarily from large energy-intensive industries. And it seems evident that pro-competitive initiatives by the Competition Directorate have significantly increased the power and status of that Directorate at the expense of others, particularly since the application of general rules of competitive conduct (and the granting of derogations from those rules) remains very much a discretionary matter. Even if these developments have resulted in lower levels of rent appropriation overall (an outcome which is far from certain), the interests of the Competition Directorate will influence future regulation in ways that cannot always be assumed to be unambiguously in the public interest. Nonetheless, to the extent that its interventions have so far involved representing more effectively the interests of consumers, they are to be welcomed.

Overall, then, the use of sectoral agencies may yield some advantages, especially if the goals of the agencies concerned are clearly specified and are not confused with promotional activity on behalf of the sectors concerned. But many of the benefits of comparison can be achieved with rather little sectoral division of responsibilities, and these benefits in any case depend on a significant degree of correlation in the nature of the regulatory tasks. But the overall balance of advantage between primarily sectoral and primarily generic regulation will depend very much on historical and evolutionary features of the regulatory regimes concerned. And it is certainly not evident that a sectoral division of merger control responsibilities has much to recommend it.

6.1.5.2 *The separation of regulatory objectives*

A second issue in the regulatory division of powers at a given level of government concerns whether different kinds of task should be performed by the same or by different agencies. For example, it has already been argued in the preceding section that sectoral promotion tasks should be performed (if at all) by different agencies from those that perform regulatory tasks; the reason was that confusion between these two objectives makes it harder for political authorities to monitor whether the agencies are doing their job. Other issues concern whether the regulation of competition (which is an important part of overall public policy but is not its only desideratum) should be the concern of an agency that is to some degree at least functionally separate either from the rest of government in general or from any other agencies charged with industrial policy in particular.

Considerations of both independence and transparency are of relevance here. Consider the independence issue first. Tirole (1993)[21] discusses the benefits to the credibility of government action that may arise from the presence of multiple agencies, including some that have incentives to be much more 'tough' in fiscal matters than others. The knowledge, for example, that a public project facing cost overruns will see control transferred to an agency with incentives to terminate the project even if it has positive social value, may act to discourage cost overruns in the first place (a benefit which must be set against the cost of terminating some beneficial projects). Might this apply to competition agencies, or should instead such agencies have goals that are identical to the overall social goals of government? Some agencies do (like the UK Monopolies and Mergers Commission which is required to uphold 'the public interest'); others, like the EEC's Merger Task Force or Germany's Bundeskartellamt, are required to pursue more precise competition goals. Tirole's argument suggests that the latter has its costs (such as the prevention of mergers with adverse effects on competition but countervailing social benefits) which may be outweighed by the benefit of discouraging other forms of socially undesirable behaviour (analogous to the cost overruns on public projects). So what might such socially undesirable behaviour consist in?

One candidate for such a description is predatory action that has as its goal the weakening of rival firms to the point where being taken over by the predator is the only realistic alternative to quitting the market. The ideal solution to such a problem is more effective policing of predation, but given the well-known difficulties of doing so (see Kühn *et al.* (1992), section 8), it may be that a commitment to competition goals alone (and consequently a refusal to consider the failing firm defence) could in some circumstances be the right second-best policy. Nevertheless, the magnitude of the benefit from such a restriction of goals is not obviously very large. The failing firm defence is neither an overwhelmingly persuasive nor a very common one in practical merger policy, and competition agencies have some power to distinguish mergers that are the consequence of predatory behaviour from those that are not. Furthermore, a merger that is the only means to ensure that a firm stays in the market may not for that reason be desirable even on overall social grounds (the failing firm's assets may be more effectively deployable elsewhere), so a rigorous application of overall public policy criteria may help to discourage some such cases in any event. And the cost of excluding all other criteria from decision-making could in some circumstances be quite large.

A second, perhaps more serious, kind of activity that independence might aim to discourage is efforts by firms to subvert the authority's established policy (by lobbying and the mobilization of political support of various kinds). If it were successful in discouraging such activity, a formally independent agency might paradoxically need to try less hard to stick to its policy than another whose independence was more in doubt (we have suggested in Chapter 5 that something of this kind may be relevant to the position of the Commission in policing mergers).

In practice advocates of independent competition agencies almost never have in mind complete independence of the agency's decisions,[22] but rather a combination of transparency with a separation of powers that imposes some political cost to the government in overruling the agency. Such a policy limits the damage that might otherwise be caused by a single-minded pursuit of competition goals (because for really significant countervailing benefits the government will consider the political cost of overruling the agency worth paying) while keeping some of the benefits of greater credibility.

Transparency in such a context really consists of two kinds of requirement. One is that the recommendations, and as much of the reasoning as possible, of a competition agency should be published. In principle transparency in all three forms may be desirable: *ex ante* transparency through publication of guidelines, *ex post* transparency through publication of decisions, and procedural transparency by allowing the analysis of cases to become public in sufficient time to inform the public debate on a decision. As discussed above, these measures help to redress some of the inequalities in access to information faced by different lobbying groups, enable the voting public to monitor more easily how well the agency is doing its job, and send a more credible signal to firms. But there is a second, more subtle aspect of transparency, which consists in the possibility that the state may wish to restrict the kind of information that the agency may legitimately take into account in reaching its decisions.[23] Most judicial systems have rules of admissibility of evidence to diminish the incentives for investigators to use duress in its acquisition. Crémer (1992) provides an additional rationale for rules of inadmissibility of certain kinds of potentially relevant information within decision-making organizations: agents whose qualities or whose projects make them indispensable may thereby become prone to moral hazard, so it may help to deny them the opportunity to demonstrate their indispensability in the first place. In the context of competition policy, limiting the agency to consider only information directly relating to the degree of competition on the market (for example, during a merger) will discourage firms from presenting other information (for example, about efficiency gains) that will make them feel able to insert anti-competitive components into their merger proposals with impunity. If so, the ideal policy will be for the agency to discourage directly the anti-competitive aspects of proposed mergers; however, informational limitations will typically (and rightly) restrict the agency to approving or disapproving the proposals of firms, so that a procedural information restriction may after all have some benefit.

Once again, the gains from such a restriction of information may not seem very large: agencies charged with regulating mergers can and frequently do object to aspects of a proposed merger without threatening to veto the entire proposal. However, the credibility of their objections may then be in some doubt, and some of the measures adopted by the firms to meet those objections may be more cosmetic than real, so the benefits of a restrictive information policy are not negligible. The desirability of restricting the information available to the agency will then depend very much on the perceived costs of such a restriction, and here it must be said that the costs too are not as great as one might think.

The chief reason for this consists in the likely source of the information concerning countervailing benefits (such as efficiencies in a merger case). In most instances information about the degree of competition in a market will be available from a number of sources and can be verified by cross-checking. For instance, in merger cases a firm's estimates of its market share can be cross-checked against information from competitors, consumer organizations and official sources.[24] The same cannot be said of information about efficiency gains that are internal to the firm. Here it may be very difficult for a competition agency to verify the quality of the information it receives from the interested parties. Acceptance of submissions about efficiency gains therefore creates incentives for all firms to claim that these are very large, and the information content of such claims will consequently be very low.

What this implies is not that public policy should necessarily ignore all considerations of efficiency gains, but that for an agency evaluating the public policy implications of certain developments (such as mergers) there will be few costs to a policy of treating most information concerning such gains, if it comes from interested parties, as of little or no value. Not all information does come from interested parties: in some industries with common technology it may be possible to estimate efficiency gains rather more credibly. But it makes sense to treat claims to that effect with some circumspection.

To summarize, then, a degree of independence of competition agencies (in the sense of establishing goals for such agencies that differ from those of overall public policy, plus the power to make decisions in pursuit of those goals) has some value in discouraging anti-competitive behaviour that is difficult to prevent by other means, and perhaps a greater value in discouraging lobbying behaviour designed to subvert the agency's pursuit of its stated goals. But there is no real case for making that degree of independence very great (or to put it another way, for allowing countervailing considerations to enter public decision-making only at great political cost). Establishing a separate and transparent *function* for a competition agency is quite a different matter, and may be very important. This means that there are major benefits to the publication of such an agency's deliberations and decisions, and (somewhat less obviously but still persuasively) to ensuring that the agency is not distracted in its evaluation of competition concerns by being invited to consider a large amount of information about non-competition issues. It also means that the relationship between the agency and the political authorities will be more complex than that of simple monitoring of the agency's decisions: the political authorities will need from time to time to modify those decisions to ensure that the goals of public policy are given adequate weight.

There is, finally, a more fundamental theoretical issue about the relationship between independence and transparency, which was touched upon in section 6.1.3 above. This is that transparency may be the only means by which it is even possible for government agencies to be given goals which differ from those of the government itself. Most existing theoretical models of independent agencies simply assume that such agencies can be given the appropriate goals, and that the ability of government to override them can be bought only at significant political cost. However, political cost is not financial cost: if the constitution specifies that the government may override the decisions of an independent agency under certain circumstances, then provided those circumstances hold there is presumably no political cost to overriding the agency (since everyone knows that is what the constitution permits). Then what is to prevent the government continually broadening by small degrees its interpretation of what the constitution permits? Each small degree would presumably incur small political cost, and there would eventually be no way of halting the government's ability to override the agency whenever it saw fit.

Most economists would respond to this paradoxical claim by arguing that the incentive for governments to desist from overriding independent 'tough' agencies whenever they see fit is maintained by the value of a reputation for non-interference. If so (and this seems plausible), why can the government not acquire a reputation for toughness directly rather than do so via a reputation for non-interference with the decisions of an agency that is itself tough? The answer may lie in the fact that the real role for a 'tough' agency is to give maximum adverse publicity to any non-tough actions by the government, actions that might otherwise have been insufficiently noticed to harm the government's reputation. Such publicity of course requires transparency, and the extent to which transparency therefore underlies the very possibility of independence is a topic that the literature on regulatory capture has not yet sufficiently addressed.[25]

One evident problem is that if a government retains the power to override decisions of the agency, it presumably also retains the power to prevent the agency from publicizing the fact that it has done so.[26] The most plausible answer is that the very creation of an agency has a kind of 'announcement' effect which may add to the incentives for establishing a reputation. For example, by announcing that an agency will publish detailed reports justifying its decisions, the government invites the public to interpret the non-publication of any report as a sign of the agency's being overruled. If publication had not been made automatic, no such inference would be justified. Once again, transparency seems to be at the root of the constitutional conditions that can make independence even possible.

This chapter has so far reviewed the developing theory of regulatory capture and its remedies, illustrating it where possible with reference to competition policy in general and to merger policy in particular. It has not specifically considered the light this theory sheds on the case for merger control by the European Community, nor what form its procedures should take. These are the tasks of the next section.

6.2   Regulatory capture and European merger policy

6.2.1   *The costs of capture in merger policy*

In Chapter 2 we broached the question of how the design of a merger control procedure should attempt to take into account the costs imposed on society by a system of merger control. The costs on which our analysis focused consisted principally of the costs of delay imposed on firms and the costs of mistaken judgments about the approval or prevention of mergers. We argued that, compared to these, the resources directly commanded by a competition agency constituted in most circumstances a negligible fraction of the potential costs of overall competition policy.

To the costs of delay and mistaken decisions should be added costs of a third kind, namely those due to changes in corporate behaviour as a consequence of the merger procedure: the tendency to structure deals so as to increase the probability of a favourable interpretation under the regulation, any anti-competitive behaviour induced by the desire to exploit such procedures as the failing firm defence, the discouragement of otherwise beneficial merger activity through fear of the costs or the results of the merger control process, and the blunting of any incentives for managerial efficiency induced by the *threat* of takeover.[27] These costs would be present to some degree even with a merger policy that was optimally designed and as immune as possible to capture. But to what extent does regulatory capture contribute to these costs?

The answer depends to a considerable extent on the source and nature of the capture concerned. Bureaucratic capture of the simplest kind – namely, where the scale and intrusiveness of anti-trust activity reflect a desire for empire-building by bureaucrats – can impose costs that are potentially very large, chiefly by increasing the uncertainty and the delay to which firms are exposed. However, merger regulation is considerably less prone to this form of capture than are other areas of competition policy, since a merger is an event initiated by firms to which the authorities need to give a rapid response if the merger is not to be discouraged completely.[28] Furthermore, pressure from industry has been quite successful in ensuring that the time limit for merger approvals is kept low. This contrasts strikingly with other aspects of anti-trust activity, such as the investigation of monopoly and restrictive practices. It is particularly true in the United States, where major anti-trust cases usually take five to ten years and cost both plaintiffs and defendants many millions of dollars.[29] Not only are individual cases costly but many take place solely because of the incentive effects of triple damages in encouraging speculative complaints (Boner and Krueger (1991) report that 96% of US civil anti-trust suits are brought by private parties). Even in Europe the comparatively slower pace of Article 85 and 86 investigations by the Competition Directorate contrasts markedly with the streamlined nature of the merger procedure, and has led to a number of companies' seeking to have their transactions counted as mergers (instead of as cooperative joint ventures, for example) in order to avoid treatment under the slower procedures.[30] The outgoing Competition Commissioner, Sir Leon Brittan, has announced changes to the procedures under Articles 85 and 86, but at the time of writing it remains unclear exactly what the impact of these changes will be.

Concern about the effects of capture on merger procedures do not, then, typically focus on bureaucratic capture as such. There are four common worries: first, that the procedure may be excessively captured by industry interests, so that too many damaging mergers are approved; secondly, that the procedure may be excessively prone to government capture, so that mergers which will lead to desirable rationalizations of industry assets will be dissuaded by the pressure of politicians with electoral interests in the status quo; thirdly, that in an international context too many mergers are assessed by purely nationalistic criteria; and fourthly, that regardless of whether the procedure shows any particular bias, lobbying by various interest groups increases the randomness in the approval process, and this randomness increases the cost of the whole procedure.

The history and political context of the EC's Merger Regulation suggest that concern about the excessive capture of member states' procedures by national interests was one of the chief motivations for establishing the Regulation originally. This concern was expressed in a number of ways. First, many protagonists thought that national capture would simply lead to industry capture, namely to the emergence of pan-European monopolies that national authorities lacked the power or the incentive to control (especially if they could represent themselves as national or even European 'champions'). This was a danger particularly to be feared in the context of the Single Market Programme, which by liberalizing capital markets eased the way to trans-European corporate expansion through acquisition, and by liberalizing trading barriers gave firms the incentive to seek alternative ways to buttress their market power (see Emerson *et al.* (1988)). Since in response to this danger the European Commission had begun to intervene in merger cases in any event, a second concern was that of 'double jeopardy', namely the risk that firms would find themselves facing scrutiny from competing authorities vying with each other for jurisdiction. So the attraction of the Merger Regulation as establishing a 'one-stop shop' for companies was a very important part of the impetus behind its passage in 1989. And thirdly, the risk of double (or multiple) jeopardy was not just that it would increase uncertainty but that the effective decision about a merger would be taken by the most restrictively inclined authority. Some parties were therefore concerned that, in the absence of the Regulation, national authorities would intervene in the passage of many, quite harmless mergers on the basis of alleged threats to national interests (see Rosenthal (1992)).

So the passage of the Regulation was important not just for imposing a new European constraint on the operations of companies, but also for *removing* a number of (real or imagined) national constraints. Which of these two effects was the more significant is not a straightforward judgment to make. Some parties in the Commission (and outside – see Rosenthal (1992)) saw the Regulation as *facilitating* merger activity that might otherwise have been prevented on narrowly nationalistic grounds,[31] or simply discouraged by red tape and the risk of double jeopardy. Others have seen the Regulation as much more restrictive overall, and in particular as giving rein to a penchant within the Commission for supporting small and medium-sized firms (and by extension, for opposing the creation of large firms) as a matter of principle and regardless of the implications for efficiency (Glais (1992)).

Under either interpretation, the philosophy of the Merger Regulation contrasts markedly with that of the original anti-trust legislation in the United States, and much of anti-trust practice since. In the United States, anti-trust activity was seen as protecting citizens from the overweening power of corporations. And economic research has tended to express concern about government rather than industry capture in the process: it has been suggested (for example, by Coate and McChesney (1992)) that political pressures tend to distort anti-trust practice in the direction of greater intervention than would otherwise occur, though to a much less marked degree in the 1980s.[32] In Europe, by contrast, the Merger Regulation has been viewed at least as much as offering corporations a degree of protection against various threats. Those who see the Regulation as on balance a facilitator view the main threat against which it protects firms to be the excessive and inefficient interventionism of national governments (though, to be sure, some corporations benefit from such interventionism – especially those that receive state aids or protected markets). Those who see the Regulation as more restrictive believe its main beneficiaries to be small and medium-sized firms who are thereby protected from the power of large, efficient competitors.[33] Either way, the politicians and bureaucrats responsible for the passage of the Regulation appear clearly to have believed that most corporations would benefit from the protection it offered, and could therefore expect to favour the new regime.

On balance, too, it was hoped that industry would gain more than it lost from one of the other anticipated features of the new regime, namely its greater credibility compared to the fragmented patchwork of different national competition systems then in existence. The Commission, as a supranational body, would have greater weight in dealing with the many large multinational corporations than would the authorities of any single member state, and could therefore develop a more credible (and consequently coherent) competition policy (see Gatsios and Seabright (1989)). While this might lead to some firms being less able to escape the long arm of competition policy than they might otherwise have done, the overall increase in predictability should be favourable to industry overall.

Our discussions in Chapters 3 to 5 have led us to conclude that the actual practice of the Commission corroborates a view of the Regulation more as a facilitator of merger activity than as a restrictive influence. They have also suggested some reasons to doubt whether the gain in credibility of the procedure has been as great as was originally hoped. Whatever the verdict, it is worth noting the difference between the purpose and philosophy of the Merger Regulation and that of some other competition policy regimes (notably the United States), because it may help to explain the comparative absence of checks and incentives against industry capture embodied in the European system, as we discuss in Chapter 7. First, however, we need to review what may be concluded from the theory so far discussed about the case for European Merger control.

6.2.2   *The case for European merger control*

The discussion in section 6.1.4 has already indicated that a concern about an excessively national focus in the control of mergers is indeed one of the considerations on which a sound normative case could be based for allocating regulatory powers to a supranational agency such as the EC Commission in spite of the presumption of subsidiarity. Whether or not mergers are allowed to take place may have significant cross-border effects for companies whose activities take place in several countries. These effects will not be adequately internalized by national agencies, and typically the costs of market power to foreign customers will be given less weight than the rents of market power to domestic interests. At one time it was commonly argued that this was principally because shareholders were less dispersed internationally than consumers. But progressive removal of controls on international capital movements has changed the extent to which this is true[34] without substantially altering the importance of the asymmetry between the costs and the rents: in effect, lobbying responds more to the location of employment and of senior management than to the nationality of shareholders. The fact remains, though, that evaluation of international mergers according to purely national criteria not only would make merger control less accurate, but would be likely to bias it towards an excessive toleration of market power.

Just as importantly, these international spillovers are ones that do not lend themselves readily to resolution via cooperation between national agencies, because of the difficulty of monitoring the extent to which any cooperative agreement is being kept. Merger assessment involves collecting a great deal of information, some of it necessarily commercially confidential, and then evaluating it according to criteria whose application cannot be routine or automatic. It is hard for other national agencies to be sure that any one of their number is observing the spirit of a cooperative agreement in any particular case without duplicating most of the work involved in the investigation. In the circumstances the temptation to cheat on any voluntary coordination of national policies is extremely strong.[35]

Fortunately, however, the asymmetries of information are not intrinsic to the international character of the problem, but are themselves dependent upon the allocation of regulatory powers. In other words, under national merger control, national authorities have private information not because they are of the same nationality as the firms under investigation, but largely because they are the ones empowered to investigate. Allocating power to a supranational agency significantly alleviates this problem, a fact which the Klibanoff–Morduch model discussed above in section 6.1.4 implies will remove what might otherwise be significant impediments to the ability of international merger control to improve on the uncoordinated national outcome.

Though the case for some EC-level regulation of mergers is a strong one,[36] difficult questions naturally arise about where the boundaries should lie between the competencies of the EC and the various national-level agencies – questions made more difficult by the different scale and differing philosophies of existing national-level competition policies. At present the boundaries are determined by the interaction of three kinds of consideration:

1. The *scale* of the parties to the transaction, namely that their combined worldwide annual turnover must exceed ECU 5 billion, and that at least two of them must have EC-wide turnover exceeding ECU 250 million, if the transaction is to fall within the EC's sphere of competence. At the passage of the Regulation in 1989, the Commission expressed its wish to see the total turnover threshold reduced to ECU 2 billion when the Regulation was revised at the end of 1993. We discuss the pros and

cons of such a reduction in Chapter 8.

2. The extent of *international spillovers* from the transaction, as
    determined by the stipulation that mergers between firms
    conducting two-thirds or more of their business in one and the
    same member state fall outside the scope of the Regulation. This
    makes the importance of the spillovers in triggering EC inter-
    vention depend upon their size relative to the transaction rather
    than upon their absolute magnitude. If, as might seem more
    natural, it is the absolute size of the spillovers that determines
    whether national regulation will be distortionary, then any
    reduction in the aggregate turnover threshold may increase the
    potential for inconsistent treatment. For instance, under an ECU
    2 billion turnover threshold, suppose two firms with a turnover
    of ECU 1.1 billion each in a market involving a product with
    high transport costs were initially in a duopoly in the Benelux
    region and in North-East France. A merger between them would
    fall under the Regulation and might very well be prevented,
    provided they were independent firms. Suppose, however, each
    were the subsidiary of a German firm with a turnover exceeding
    ECU 3.3 billion; the transaction would then fall outside the
    Regulation, even if the damage done to competition in the larger
    German market were judged by the Bundeskartellamt to be
    small enough to justify approving the merger. To avoid this kind
    of distortion (and the associated regulatory advantage it would
    create for multinational companies based in the larger EC
    member states) it would be desirable for the EC to investigate
    transactions that give rise to international spillovers exceeding
    a certain absolute sum. For example, it could be stipulated that
    of the ECU 2 billion worldwide annual turnover (of which at
    least ECU 500 million takes place within the EC), at least ECU
    250 million of the latter must take place outside the member
    state with the largest share of the combined turnover.[37]

3. A series of *exceptions* to the two principles above. These are
    embodied in Article 9 (the 'German clause'), Article 22(3) (the
    'Dutch clause') and Article 21(3) (the 'legitimate interests' clause).
    This last raises issues beyond the scope of this chapter, but the
    first two involve important aspects of the subsidiarity question.
    Article 9 provides for a member state to apply to investigate
    itself a merger falling under the Regulation if it fears the creation
    or strengthening of a dominant position in a distinct market

within that state. However, Article 9 as it stands gives rise to significant ambiguities. Its chief rationale lies in the (justified) concern that the 'two-thirds rule' for turnover thresholds does not really capture what it purports to capture, namely the extent of economic spillover effects between member states. In particular, concentrations where the new economic entity operates independently of one or more of its parents may have an economic impact in only one member state even though (due to the turnover of the parent being counted for calculating the thresholds) the transaction is not exempted from the Regulation by the two-thirds rule. Since it is hard to think of any simple rule that captures economic spillovers better than the turnover rule, the only solution appears to be to give the Commission discretion to judge that, notwithstanding the turnover criterion, the case involves no real economic spillovers (either costs or benefits) and may therefore be judged by the appropriate national authority if the latter so wishes.

However, the history of Article 9 applications to date (and in particular the fact that the Commission has declined more applications than it has granted) suggests that some member states (particularly Germany) have viewed its purpose in a somewhat different light. Under this second interpretation, Article 9 embodies a principle to the effect that one member state should not be forced to suffer significantly damaging effects from a merger even if these are judged by the Commission to be outweighed by benefits elsewhere in the Community.[38] Since the whole point of centralizing merger control is to ensure that mergers are judged by their aggregate EC-wide effects rather than those in any one country, it is hard to see any long-term rationale for this interpretation of Article 9 based on subsidiarity considerations. Rather, its political origins appear to have lain in unallayed doubts by the German negotiators of the original text of the Regulation about the immunity of the merger control procedure to industry capture, and specifically to fears that the Task Force would approve mergers with more adverse consequences for market power than the German authorities themselves would be willing to tolerate.[39] If there is justification in such fears, the best long-term response to them lies in strengthening the MTF's procedures against industry capture – and perhaps in measures that increase the extent to which they are seen to be strengthened against capture – rather than in the use of a measure like Article 9. And the purpose of Article 9 itself could usefully be clarified by an explanation that it is intended to apply to circumstances where the Commission judges the turnover rule to have given the misleading impression that there were significant economic spillover effects between member states.

Related points can be made about Article 22(3), which is in any case due to be reviewed with the turnover thresholds at the end of 1993. It allows states without merger control legislation of their own to ask the Commission to apply the Merger Regulation to deals that would otherwise fall below the thresholds. While in principle a desirable transitional step, it is somewhat at odds with the spirit of the subsidiarity principle, which implies that whether or not member states choose to have merger authorities should be a matter for the member states themselves. A state choosing to have weak or non-existent competition regulation should be free to do so for those aspects of competition without substantial cross-border effects. Firms choosing to establish themselves there should also be able to do so in the clear ability to anticipate the regulatory regime they have to face, without fearing that the rules will be changed by a government appealing to Brussels against a merger that would not normally fall under the Regulation but which the government happens not to like. Of course, subsidiarity implies that the member state may choose to change the rules if it wishes, but there is no reason for the European Commission to connive in this, which is in effect what Article 22(3) does.

Nevertheless, both Article 9 and Article 22(3) raise somewhat difficult political issues, and it would be best not to be dogmatic about the boundaries between national and European competition policy. A useful compromise, very much within the spirit of subsidiarity, would be to allow some possibility for national authorities to be represented in MTF investigations for certain borderline Article 9 cases (for example, those in which it is unclear how much impact a concentration will have outside the main member state concerned). Likewise, what are now Article 22(3) cases could be resolved by enabling member states who presently lack competition legislation to establish small-scale competition agencies with the right to request technical assistance from either the MTF or from other member states.

Finally, though, chief among the risks inherent in the uncoordinated national outcome is the tolerance of excessive market power. This could as easily imply use of merger control to stop efficient mergers threatening firms who have enjoyed their rents in the form of high costs or 'the quiet life', as the waving through of mergers that diminish competition. But either way, it implies that the procedures embodied in European merger control need to be adequately resistant to industry capture, to ensure that any gains from the internationalization of merger control are not dissipated in increased tolerance of regulatory capture by those who benefit from market power. It is to an assessment of these procedures that we shall turn in Chapter 7. But first we should consider the most significant aspects of the criteria for assessment under which a European agency should operate.

6.2.3 *Criteria for merger assessment*

6.2.3.1 *Competition and the efficiency defence*

It is not, and could not be, the function of any merger control authority to decide whether a given merger is on balance 'a good thing'. This is partly because the information required to reach such a judgment would be far more substantial than the authority could obtain for every case; more fundamentally because in a market economy there is a presumption that private agents should be free to pursue their own interests as they see fit unless this pursuit has adverse consequences for the interests of third parties. It is therefore to the external effects of a merger that the investigation process necessarily directs itself in the first instance, and if there are no adverse external effects a merger will and ought to be approved. This need not imply any naive optimism on the part of the authorities that mergers will always be beneficial to the parties undertaking them. There is by now a substantial literature (see Ravenscraft and Scherer (1987) for the US, and Hughes (1992) for a survey of the UK evidence) casting serious doubt on the average long-term efficiency of mergers, and suggesting that either systematic over-optimism or (more probably) managerial motives of empire-building and the like are often responsible for promoting growth by acquisition rather than through growth by market expansion.[40] While this certainly should restrain the authorities from any positive promotion of the merger process as such, it does not suggest that merger policy can or should in any way concern itself with insisting that firms do what is good for them.

This simple prescription becomes more difficult to apply, however, once the authorities judge that there are negative external effects (such as an increase in market power). For clearly these effects can be more or less serious, and if they are only mildly serious in a given case it may be questionable whether they should automatically override any positive private benefits that the merger may generate. It becomes inescapable to form some, if only tentative, judgment about the significance of the private benefits in order to know whether and when they should be able to offset an adverse impact on market power.

The discussion in section 6.1.5.2 above has therefore a relatively straightforward application to the questions of European merger control. It would be hard to make any kind of serious case that the question of whether a proposed merger was harmful to competition was the only issue of importance from the point of view of social welfare; it would be hard likewise to deny that mergers which do harm competition may nevertheless have redeeming features. In order to decide whether a European merger control procedure should take explicit account of what is sometimes called 'the efficiency defence', what we must ask is not 'can countervailing efficiency sometimes make an otherwise anti-competitive merger worth while?' – to which the answer is obviously 'yes'. Instead the relevant question is whether the evident benefits of a procedure that acknowledges the efficiency defence outweigh its (perhaps less evident) costs. The benefits of an efficiency defence are obvious: they consist in the value of genuinely efficiency-enhancing mergers which could not otherwise be approved under the existing procedure since they harm competition too much. The costs of an efficiency defence consist principally in the harm done by genuinely undesirable mergers which are approved as a result of spurious claims about the magnitude of the efficiency gains to which they give rise.[41]

The important question is therefore how reliably a merger control agency might be able to assess the validity of claims about efficiency gains. There is one, somewhat purist view, which says 'never'. It points to the adverse findings about the average efficiency of mergers and draws the inference that a merger control agency would never be able to tell *ex ante* which mergers would do better than the average. Therefore, according to this view, it should not even try, but should prevent all mergers which harm competition regardless of any arguments about countervailing benefits. On its own, however, this view has little merit. Even the negative findings of studies such as that of Ravenscraft and Scherer (1987) do not imply that all types of merger have the same *ex ante* prospects: some (principally conglomerate mergers between parties of very unequal size) do much worse than average while others (horizontal mergers between nearly equal parties) do substantially better. Furthermore, even a relatively cursory merger investigation will reveal more about the firms in question (such as whether there are prospects for the rationalization of overhead costs) than is available in the large-scale data sets used for scholarly evaluation of mergers *ex post*. Even if an academic study based on a large data set could not predict *ex ante* which mergers would 'beat the average', it would not imply that the merger authorities with their different and more specific information could not do so.

However, it was pointed out in section 6.1.5.2 that the evidence available to merger authorities about efficiency gains is subject in a serious way to the Mandy Rice-Davies problem. The information required for the assessment is supplied by parties with a shared interest in exaggerating the benefits, and there is little scope for third-party corroboration. Furthermore, the fact that information about efficiency benefits might be of very little value does not imply that its inclusion will make little difference to the outcome, for an agency prone to industry capture might well be able to use such information more effectively to escape scrutiny of the degree to which it was captured.[42]

This implies that two questions need to be answered satisfactorily before there are reasonable grounds for thinking that an explicit[43] efficiency defence will improve merger control. The first is whether the Commission can put in place procedures to compensate for the distorted nature of the information supplied to it by the parties to the merger. At the very least this must imply a very explicit burden of proof: for example, a statement that the efficiency defence will be considered only when, in the absence of convincing evidence to the contrary, the merger will be prohibited (see our discussion of burdens of proof below). Secondly, there should be some specialized investigation by an independent body of the empirical basis for any

efficiency defence. One possible means for this might be the establishment of an efficiency audit unit within the Merger Task Force,
with powers to conduct detailed internal enquiries within firms
claiming efficiency gains – any firm not wishing to open its premises
to such a unit would be presumed to have no efficiency gains worth
claiming. It would be desirable for such a unit to operate independently of the MTF team investigating the merger, in order to ensure
that its findings were not distorted by the desire to fit in with the
conclusions of the team (though it would need to have access to
MTF files). And in order to give the unit the right incentive to gain
a reputation for accuracy in its evaluations, it would be desirable
for it to be enabled to offer its services on a consultancy basis to
national authorities (and even, where appropriate, to private sector
firms provided conflicts of interest could be avoided).

The second relevant question is whether there are grounds for
thinking the existing merger control procedure sufficiently robust to
the danger of industry capture to be able to resist the temptation to
use an efficiency defence as an excuse to rubber-stamp otherwise
doubtful deals. We shall consider how robust is the current EC
procedure in Chapter 7; first we examine what conclusions emerge
from the analysis of regulatory capture about other criteria for merger
assessment.

6.2.3.2 *Criteria for assessing competition*

The question of what criteria a merger control agency should use
for assessing the external effects of a merger on competition raises
mainly technical issues that are unrelated to problems of regulatory
capture as such, and which we discussed in Chapters 2 and 3.
Nevertheless our discussion of questions of bargaining and reputation in Chapter 4 does have one very clear implication for these
procedures: other things being equal, it is important to have clear
and transparent procedures that can be not only implemented but
seen to be implemented. This is because preventing mergers is
potentially politically costly for the agency; firms (who enjoy a
first-mover advantage in the bargaining process, since it is they who
make the proposals that the agency must accept, modify or reject)
may be tempted to exploit the agency's understandable preference
for avoiding confrontation in order to induce it to accept anti-
competitive proposals. The agency's sole defence against such

manipulation is reliance on a *reputation* for performing its competition analysis objectively, and it can only acquire such a reputation if it commits itself to procedures sufficiently transparent to enable third parties to see whether it has in fact employed those procedures. If distortions of the analysis are invisible to third parties they are costless for the reputation of the agency; if they are costless for the agency they increase the temptation of the firms to manipulate the bargaining process. Paradoxically, therefore, an agency with a commitment to objective analysis has an interest in increasing its own potential for embarrassment by making its procedures as transparent as possible, in order to signal to firms its unwillingness to be manipulated.

Two themes in particular emerge. First, that procedures that can be (at least approximately) replicated are preferable to those that cannot. So, for example, tests of product or geographic market definition that are backed by some quantitative survey evidence of the intentions of buyers are preferable to those that rely on the (albeit well-informed) hunches of case rapporteurs. Rough breakdowns of production costs into fixed, variable and sunk components are preferable to general statements about entry barriers being high or low. And secondly, it is desirable for the agency to publish as much of its reasoning in individual cases as possible (this has the additional advantage of enabling firms involved in future cases to anticipate the agency's procedure of analysis). How this kind of transparency might be achieved in the context of European merger control is a question we shall consider in more detail in Chapter 8.

6.2.3.3 *Burdens of proof*

One kind of rule of procedure deserves more explicit consideration, and this concerns standards of proof. Of particular significance is the question of whether firms should be required to establish that merger proposals are not anti-competitive (subject to some pre-screening to ensure that obviously harmless mergers were not troubled), or whether the burden should lie instead on the agency. It is important to note that the significance of the burden of proof lies not so much in the proportion of cases which are approved or prevented as a result – it is always possible to have more or less stringent rules for any given allocation of burden of proof. Much more important are the incentives given to firms under investigation to reveal information in their possession to the agency. When the burden of proof is on the firm, the knowledge that information it conceals may count against it in the investigation provides a powerful incentive in favour of revelation. When the burden of proof is on the agency, the likelihood that any private information of the firm that is adverse to the firm's chances of approval will be concealed makes the agency's task much harder. Since that private information has a social value that is not fully captured by the firm (revelation of information in favour of the firm's case has positive value for the firm, but revelation of information counting against it has negative private and positive social value), rules that help to internalize that social value to the firm's own decision-making have much to commend them.

There is therefore a significant case for placing the burden of proof at least on those firms whose merger proposals have failed an initial screening – that is, those which apparently give rise to substantial competition concerns. Similar reasoning applies to procedural rules designed to increase the incentive for firms to supply information in good enough time for it to be adequately analyzed (such as 'stopping the clock' for merger investigations during the time it takes the parties to respond to information requests). Certainly, it is preferable to design incentives for firms to reveal information of their own accord rather than relying on the uncertain and intrusive nature of powers of search and subpoena. However, it should also be said that the gains from revealing such information will themselves depend upon the extent to which the competition agency is restricted in its ability to make use of information that cannot adequately be corroborated other than by the parties to the transaction. If, for reasons of minimizing the risk of capture, the agency is limited to analyzing purely competition concerns on the basis of publicly corroborated information, placing the burden of proof on firms may have little effect. Conversely, a shift in the burden of proof may have some effect in alleviating the asymmetry of information that prompted the original intention to restrict the discretion of the agency.

6.3   Concluding remarks

This concludes our discussion of the theory of regulatory capture and its implications for the design of European merger policy. We have argued that there is a strong case for centralization of at least some merger control powers within the European Community, and that a well-implemented European merger policy should be able to overcome some of the distortions that would arise from competition between national jurisdictions. We have also indicated some of the principles that could help to ensure the effective implementation of such a policy. The time has come to look in more detail at how merger control in the Community actually operates, and to assess it in the light of the principles we have outlined. This will be the task of Chapter 7.

Notes

1. It should be evident that capture is by no means to be equated with corruption, and many of the mechanisms of capture are not ones that could reasonably be prevented by the criminal law – especially since the risk of error makes very large penalties undesirable.
2. For an account of utility regulation that incorporates the individual aims of regulators, see Evans and Garber (1988); for empirical evidence that lawyers in the US Federal Trade Commission have been systematically more keen than other officials to initiate legal proceedings, see Coate and McChesney (1992).
3. For the purposes of this discussion, economic regulation will be understood to mean the formulation and policing by the state of rules governing the conduct of economic activity by other non-state parties; it is thus distinct from other areas of state activity, such as taxation, the enforcement of contracts or the direct public provision of goods and services, for all of which a more persuasive case can be made that other goals besides efficiency are concerned.
4. This need not imply that the social welfare function to be maximized is the simple sum of producers' and consumers' surplus and government revenue. For instance, giving greater weight to public than private income may reflect a judgment about the distortionary costs of raising such revenue through taxation (see Little and Mirrlees (1974)). None of the arguments of this chapter will turn on questions of the precise weights to be given to components of the surplus in the social welfare function.
5. In any case, when regulators have ambitions subsequently to run for office in systems where politics requires a great deal of money, it is doubtful whether any realistic salaries could significantly diminish the power of indirect financial inducements.
6. Tirole (1993) discusses why employees of government might be given lower-powered monetary incentives than those of the private sector (that is, they are paid a smaller fraction of their marginal product).

One factor, he argues, is that quality of service considerations are at least as important for government activity, and high-powered incentives tend to lead to under-investment in quality, especially in the absence of performance indices incorporating quality considerations (such as a firm's share price). Another way of putting this is that measuring output is more difficult in the government sector; an additional reason for low-powered incentives may also be the greater difficulty of measuring an individual employee's *marginal* contribution to output.

7. This may sound counter-intuitive in the light of the complaint often made against competition policy that it unnecessarily shackles the *most* efficient firms. But the point of such a complaint is precisely that shackling the most efficient firms is unnecessary and a policy that does so is a bad policy. It is the less efficient firms for whom some blunting of incentives is unavoidable if the extent of market power is to be contained.

8. After a prostitute in the famous Profumo case in Britain in the 1960s who, on being told in court that the minister denied ever having met her, replied 'Well he would say that, wouldn't he?'

9. This does not necessarily mean that regulated firms required to report their costs will always lie. They might find it easier to report correctly their accounting costs, especially if these are subject to auditing, but simply to take less effort than they would otherwise have done to keep those costs low.

10. One way to view them is as different ways in which particular societies reward the acquisition of reputation.

11. A study by Vogel (1986) compares the relatively voluntarist approach to environmental regulation in the UK with that of the United States, and concludes that in spite of their different styles these approaches have produced remarkably similar compliance records. 'The more adversarial mode of regulation adopted by the United States makes voluntary compliance problematic; to the extent that regulations are regarded by the private sector as unreasonable, firms are likely to comply with them only if they are forced to do so.' In effect, more adversarial systems may impose larger monitoring costs. Vogel draws similar conclusions in the fields of occupational health and safety, chemical and drug regulation, consumer protection and financial services, though his comparison of the effects of the different national systems is more sketchy.

12. Exceptions to this (such as the Commission's use of directives under Article 90 to push through reform of the telecommunications sector in opposition to member states) have only underlined the validity of the generalization by the intense controversy they have provoked (see McGowan and Seabright (1992)).

13. McGowan and Seabright (1992) consider the history of the allocation of powers between EC institutions and those of member states in the fields of competition and environmental regulation, and conclude that 'the actual assignment of responsibilities [has been] determined much more by fashion, historical accident, the discovery of dormant legal

powers and the outcome of bureaucratic power struggles than by an objective consideration of the normative criteria'.

14. Ironically, some of the earliest 'economic theories of the state' (Downs (1957)) assumed that political influence was wielded by voting, and that the interests of the (actual or potential) median voter therefore had a disproportionate influence on policy-making. Such theories had some difficulty in explaining why producer interest groups usually appear to wield more power than consumers, since corporations as such have no votes (though employees of certain corporations in marginal constituencies may have very vital votes). Later theories of 'rent-seeking' activity (Krueger (1974)) emphasized the financial resources of producer groups; the effectiveness of lobbying is likely to increase more than proportionately with the resources (including time) spent upon it, thereby disadvantaging those interest groups whose members have less at stake per capita.

15. One such cost, modelled in Anderlini (1987), consists in the fact that intermediaries who design reward schemes for agents will tend to distort them in ways designed to emphasize the intermediaries' indispensability: for instance, by reducing the scope for responsibility on the part of the agent in order to increase the need for direct monitoring. This is one plausible explanation of the notorious reluctance of politicians and civil servants to allow public sector enterprise to operate with significant autonomy – how could the politicians and civil servants justify their jobs?

16. This may seem strange given the well-known view of Olson (1965) that large interest groups (such as consumers) face greater free-rider problems. But there is no contradiction: for a given economic stake, the larger the number of individuals sharing it the greater the free-rider problem among them; but if the stake increases proportionately with the number of members the fixed costs of information acquisition may be more easily borne. The former explains why firms are more powerful lobbyists than consumers; the latter explains why large firms are more powerful lobbyists than small firms.

17. It is true that on any one regulatory issue there may be no satisfactory compromise (the core of the game may be empty). But then it may be possible to undertake intertemporal compromises or trade-offs between different issues, which will be subject to the same kinds of advantage and disadvantage as the compromises discussed here.

18. There is little doubt that, had merger control remained in member states' hands, the purchase of the de Havilland aircraft company by Aerospatiale and Alenia would have been approved. Likewise, a foreign bid for some significant national firm such as Dassault, MBB or GEC would have been at risk of nationalistic prohibition even if it were not intrinsically anti-competitive.

19. If resources are spent on lobbying in proportion to their expected effectiveness, then the convexity in the expenditure functions would reflect a more basic convexity in the outcome of lobbying as a function of resources expended.

20. The fact that the cases all have to be won is a counterweight to this pressure, however, which may not be present in more administrative systems such as those in Europe, where judicial review is only an occasional event. It is also possible that the markedly higher success rate of the FTC than the DOJ in winning cases owes something to the greater complexity of the cases the DOJ handles (such as those involving financial institutions).

21. Based on work with Mathias Dewatripont.

22. Independence of the agency's *decisions* is still possible even without complete independence of the agency, if the only way for the government to overturn the agency's decisions is to fire the director of the agency and force the new director to consider the decision again.

23. Of course, practical considerations will limit the information the agency can process; the question here is whether the agency itself should be free to decide what to count as the most relevant.

24. These are not identically credible. For instance, some mergers are very much in competitors' interests, so competitors may be the last parties to wish to challenge them.

25. It is true that the government could give itself financial costs of overruling the agency by requiring the head of the agency to be paid a very large indemnity if forced to resign. One reason we do not see such contracts is that they would make accountability of such an agency very difficult. The paradox remains: pure accountability or pure independence seem to be relatively stable states; partial accountability and partial independence seem to require transparency to make them possible.

26. This is related to a problem studied by Caillaud *et al.* (1993), which concerns the circumstances under which a principal can commit to 'tough' actions against a competitor by writing an appropriate publicly observable contract with an agent, if such a contract can be secretly renegotiable at any time. It turns out that even the presence of secret renegotiation may not deprive contracts of all commitment power. The intuition is that, because the agent has private information about his or her type, he or she will in some circumstances be able to extract a rent from the original (public) contract. Renegotiating this in secret will not, therefore, leave things just as they were before, because to induce the agent to agree to the renegotiation he or she will have to be offered a payoff higher than he or she would have received in the absence of any contract. Unfortunately, this model is not obviously applicable to our present problem, because it is hard to see what is the informational asymmetry that prevents the government from simply overruling its 'tough' agency and then requiring it to keep quiet about the fact.

27. For example, Schumann (1988) found that the 1985 New York takeover statutes requiring greater time and information to be available to shareholders to consider tender offers *both* improved the benefit to shareholders of actual consummated takeovers *and* diminished the credibility of the takeover threat, thereby diminishing shareholder wealth overall. This is a particularly significant finding, because it is

the threat of takeover rather than actual takeover that is supposed to improve managerial efficiency. However, the takeover threat may have undesirable as well as desirable effects, and neither the theoretical nor the empirical literature has reached a consensus on which kind of effect outweighs the other.

28. One way of thinking of this is as like a monopolist's pricing decision. The number of mergers is fairly elastic with respect to the cost imposed on them by regulation, a fact that limits the costs imposed more than in other, less cost-elastic areas of anti-trust activity.

29. Stigler (1988), p. 165. He reports that 'in the IBM case, [it was said that] the budget by the company for the defence was not limited, but nevertheless exceeded that limit'. It must be said, however, that the high costs of US anti-trust action are much more to be blamed upon the legal system than on excessive zeal of the anti-trust agencies. Coate and McChesney (1992) remark on the high proportion of cases won by the FTC, which certainly suggests no inclination to initiate weak or frivolous cases.

30. However, one critic of the Commission's judgment in the de Havilland case has suggested that it shows the Commission to be much more reluctant to grant approval to cooperation between firms on a once-and-for-all basis (as under the Merger Regulation) than in the temporary and reversible way possible under Article 85 exemptions. Consequently he suggests that the promoters of a cooperative project 'might sometimes receive a more favourable hearing if they chose to opt for a "non-concentrative" formula' (Glais (1992), p. 114).

31. And perhaps also on ideological grounds. There were some marked national differences in this: the French, in particular, were inclined to see the Germans and (in different ways) the British as dogmatically opposed either to mergers in general or to mergers of certain kinds (such as those where the acquiring company was publicly owned).

32. This needs some qualification. By political pressure, we are here referring to pressure from political sources external to the FTC and the DOJ (from Congress, in particular). However, the DOJ is headed by the Attorney General who is a member of the Cabinet, and the Assistant Attorney General and his or her deputies are all political appointees. This means that the tendency of the DOJ can be strongly politically influenced, but from its head rather than from outside. This influence during the 1980s can certainly be argued to have been determined strongly by a pro-business ideology.

33. There is said to have been vigorous lobbying of the Commission against the de Havilland merger by a number of de Havilland's competitors. The Commission has also given some ammunition to those who hold this interpretation in its decision on the *AT&T/NCR* case, in which possible cost savings from the transaction were considered a negative factor since 'potential advantages flowing from synergies may create or strengthen a dominant position' (see Chapter 3).

34. It is likely that remaining barriers to mobility within Europe in terms of language and culture will soon be more significant for goods than

they are for capital – and for labour they will be the most significant of all.

35. Stronger, certainly, than for almost any other form of international policy coordination (certainly including monetary and fiscal policy).

36. It is nevertheless interesting to compare the justification for European merger control with the procedure for cooperation between the EC and EFTA competition authorities initiated by the Agreement establishing the European Economic Area (see Stragier (1993)). The latter is a prime example of internalizing spillovers by voluntary coordination (albeit between only two parties, so of a somewhat simpler character than would be entailed by coordination between the 12 members states of the EC). Seeing how this coordination works in the future will provide an interesting test of the subsidiarity argument.

37. At the time of writing (March 1993) there have been press reports of growing opposition by some member states to the lowering of the turnover thresholds, allegedly on grounds of respect for subsidiarity. The arguments discussed above make it clear that scale of the transaction as such is not really a relevant consideration for subsidiarity; small transactions with substantial spillovers will still risk leading to distorted judgments if handled purely by national agencies. It may be, of course, that this opposition is based more on a distrust of any increase in the powers of the Commission than on a proper concern for subsidiarity as such; such distrust may furthermore reflect a concern (for different reasons in different member states) at the implementation of the Regulation so far.

38. There is yet another, somewhat different rationale for Article 9, which is that on certain questions national authorities may have a major intrinsic informational advantage over those of the EC. If so there is certainly a case for their undertaking their own investigations, and perhaps in their interests' being represented in some more formal way in the MTF's procedures than merely by membership of the Advisory Committee. But the case for their having a veto on such mergers depends on those cases' not being characterized by large spillovers, which will not always be the case.

39. For example, discussions with officials of the Bundeskartellamt suggested to us that the BKA would have been very unlikely to approve the Varta–Bosch merger. However, the extent to which this represents a difference of opinion about what the Commission should have decided, as opposed to the different interests the BKA and the Commission are supposed to reflect, is harder to say.

40. Such evidence may of course raise the possibility of a legitimate role for public regulation to protect the interests of shareholders that may be damaged by the managers who nominally act on their behalf. However, such regulation if justified is not obviously the province of merger policy, but should rather be pursued with respect to the standing mechanisms of corporate governance to ensure that decisions regarding all corporate investments (not just mergers) adequately reflect the interests concerned.

41. There are other potential costs: first, any unpreventable predatory behaviour before the merger designed to increase the attractiveness of the merger outcome; and secondly, any increase in lobbying and rent-seeking to which the apparently more easily influenced procedure might give rise. Reference has already been made to such costs in section 6.1.5.2.

42. A notorious example is the evaluation by the UK Monopolies and Mergers Commission of the merger in 1987 between British Airways and British Caledonian. This case was admitted to raise significant competition concerns. Not only was the sole evidence of countervailing efficiency gains that supplied by British Airways, but publication of this evidence (the magnitude of the gains as well as their source) was prevented by the Secretary of State, making its evaluation by outside observers impossible. The efficiency defence was accepted in spite of the fact that even the regulatory body concerned (the Civil Aviation Authority), which *had* examined the evidence, remained unconvinced by it.

43. There are already two respects in which efficiency considerations could be argued to have some implicit weight in the EC's existing procedures: one is a reference in the Regulation to technical and economic progress (albeit with the rider that it benefits consumers and is not an obstacle to competition); the other is the fact that arguments within the Commission about the merits or otherwise of particular controversial mergers frequently refer to efficiency benefits whether these are formally recognized or not. This last was especially true of the de Havilland decision.

7

The procedures of merger control

7.1 The EC and elsewhere: an international comparison

In this section we shall consider the steps by which mergers are assessed in the European Community, in the process comparing it with the equivalent steps in a number of other jurisdictions. Beginning with notification, continuing with investigation, and going on to decision and judicial review, we shall ask at each step: who is responsible? what are the factors determining the objectives of the regulators concerned? what are the constraints upon their decisions? and what are the risks of capture to which these factors particularly give rise?

7.1.1 *Notification*

Firms contemplating a merger in the European Community that may fall within the scope of the Regulation will typically discuss it confidentially with officials of the Merger Task Force (MTF), the body established within the Competition Directorate to undertake the day-to-day implementation of the Regulation. The purpose of pre-notification discussions is to speed up the evaluation of non-controversial cases, and also to minimize the costs of proceeding with a merger that is subsequently judged unacceptable. The latter rationale also underlies the requirement that mergers falling within the scope of the Regulation be notified to the MTF within a week of the triggering event (signing of contract, announcement of bid, etc.), and may not be put into effect for an extendable three-week period after Notification.[1]

Table 7.1 compares, in a very simplified and schematic way, a number of aspects of the merger control procedure in the EC with those in Germany, the UK, France and the United States. One feature that will be noticed is that a single body is responsible for notification and investigation in the EC, as in Germany and France, but contrary to the situation in the United States, where two parallel bodies operate (albeit with coordination of their role in merger control). And in the UK, the body responsible for investigation (the MMC) is neither the party deciding whether an investigation is warranted (who is the Secretary of State for Trade and Industry) nor even the party advising the Secretary of State on that decision (who is the Director General of Fair Trading). This unification of roles in the EC undoubtedly helps to enhance the efficiency of the procedure and its clarity to the parties concerned, since it allows those officials who undertake the preliminary discussions with the merging parties to speak with some authority about the way in which the investigating agency will approach the case. However, it also carries certain risks, namely that officials will commit themselves implicitly in pre-notification discussions (and therefore without adequate investigation) to approving certain kinds of transaction.[2] It is notable that a number of recent EC mergers that either involved high market shares or raised sufficiently serious competition issues to warrant the negotiation of remedies were nevertheless approved within the one-month preliminary investigation period (see Chapter 3). The current procedure places greater emphasis on efficiency and predictability from the point of view of the parties than on transparency from the point of view of the general public.

7.1.2   *Investigation*

So what are the incentives and constraints at work in the investigation procedure? As Table 7.1 makes clear, the investigating agency in the EC is more directly under political control than in the other jurisdictions, except the US Department of Justice which is under the direct control of a cabinet minister, the Attorney General.

Table 7.1 Merger control procedures in various jurisdictions.

Merger jurisdiction	Notification	Notification requirement	Investigation	Decision	Decision criteria
European Community	Competition Directorate (Merger Task Forced)	Pre-merger	Competition Directorate (Merger Task Force)	European Commission	Dominance
Germany	Bundeskartellamt	Pre-merger for largest Post-merger for others	Bundeskartellamt	Bundeskartellamt subject to overrule by Minister of Economics	Market power
United Kingdom	Director General of Fair Trading	Pre-merger voluntary Post-merger for others	Monopolies and Mergers Commission	Secretary of State for Trade and Industry	Public interest, with emphasis on market power
France	Ministry of Economic Affairs	Pre-merger voluntary	Conseil de la Concurrence	Minister of Economic Affairs	Market power
United States	Federal Trade Commission, Department of Justice	Pre-merger for largest	Federal Trade Commission Department of Justice	Federal District Courts	Market power

Table 7.1 (*cont.*) Merger control procedures in various jurisdictions.

Merger jurisdiction	Efficiency defence	Advice	Head of investigating agency	Publication of guidelines, recommendations	Review or appeal
European Community	Not explicit	Advisory Committee on Concentrations	Politician	Brief decisions Annual report	European Court of Justice, Court of First Instance
Germany	No for BKA, yes for Minister of Economics	Monopolkommission	Civil servant	Biennial report	Berlin Court of Appeals/ Supreme Court
United Kingdom	Yes		Civil servant	Detailed case reports Policy document in 1991	None
France	Yes	Conseil de la Concurrence	Administrative law judge	Brief recommenda-tions Annual report	Administrative Supreme Court (Conseil d'Etat)
United States	Yes, though not very influential in practice		Politician (DOJ) Politically balanced group of Commissioners (FTC)	Merger Guidelines	Appeal Courts/ Supreme Court

Notes

1. The column headed 'Decision criteria' has sought to distinguish between jurisdictions that base decisions primarily on competition criteria according to whether these are mainly single-firm based ('dominance') or take multi-firm interaction into account ('market power').
2. The head of the EC's investigating agency is the Competition Commissioner (a politician). The head of the Merger Task Force, which is a body within the Competition Directorate, is a civil servant.

European Commissioners are not, however, like national politicians – they are, in particular, required to forswear national allegiances on joining the Commission. While it would be naive to think that this removes all risk of national capture it does nevertheless point to the fact that Commissioners have a significant stake in establishing a reputation for transcending their political origins. However, this does not turn Commissioners into civil servants, and there is little doubt that political influence (in particular, a general preference for relatively restrictive or relatively permissive approaches to merger control) can be more easily exercised through the control structure of the European Commission than in the other agencies (again with the significant exception of the US Department of Justice). This conclusion is strengthened by noting that the Advisory Committee on Concentrations, which consists of representatives of the member states, meets with the Commission's staff during the investigation and *before* any publication of the results of the investigation. There are in addition numerous informal contacts with national administrations; there are the 'inter-service' meetings at which the MTF consult with staff from other parts of the Commission, many of whom have already been vigorously lobbied by different interested parties (our surveys in Chapter 4 showed that substantial numbers of firms mobilize heavy lobbying support, particularly from officials in member states). MTF staff therefore feel the impact of political pressures surrounding the cases under investigation at a relatively early stage in the procedure. They are also aware that political pressure is exerted liberally at points above them in the Commission's hierarchy: one MTF rapporteur told us that 'I sometimes get only ten minutes to present the outlines of the case analysis to the Commissioner; and I know that after I've done so the firms will get half an hour to talk to him'.

It is only fair to recognize that these political pressures are, nevertheless, somewhat muted compared to what they might be if decisions on merger control were taken by the European Council. Competition policy is - unlike many other areas – specifically delegated to the Commission, and Regulation 17 of 1962 further delegates to the Commission substantial powers (of investigation, prosecution and the definition of liability) to enable it to implement such policy.

The distinction between political and administrative mechanisms is in any case a matter of degree. No merger control procedure lacks mechanisms for the exertion of political influence, and the presence of such mechanisms in the EC is neither surprising nor in itself a cause for concern. But there are two features of the way in which such influence may be exerted that are neither necessary nor desirable, and both arise from the procedure's comparative lack of transparency. One is that the political influence can easily be exerted before an investigation into the facts of the case has proceeded very far,[3] and certainly before any publication of findings. A preliminary report is prepared by the MTF before the meeting of the Advisory Committee, but this report is not published. The decision that is eventually published (besides being much shorter than the reports of, for example, the UK's Monopolies and Mergers Commission) is supported by reasoning that may well have been substantially redrafted since the basic facts of the case were established, and will be constrained by the need to justify a decision of the Commission as a whole. It will typically have been redrafted in the light not only of technical commentaries but of an awareness of the political pressures on the decision (see our discussion of drafting inconsistencies in section 3.7). Not only will this tend to distort the actual analysis of the competition aspects of the case; it may also tend to obscure which kinds of political pressures were actually most influential in determining the outcome.[4] The aim of greater transparency, by contrast, is not to banish the influence of political pressures, but enable those pressures to be visible without disguise.

The second consequence of the nature of the political accountability of the MTF is that it facilitates the exertion of pressure on a case-by-case basis. It is common – and desirable – for merger control agencies to be responsive to swings in general policy towards mergers. For instance, the 1984 Tebbit Guidelines indicated that references to the UK Monopolies and Mergers Commission would be made more consistently on competition grounds than previously; while these guidelines had no power to bind the MMC itself, they were a clear and transparent indication of political preferences for giving emphasis to certain of the MMC's criteria over others. Such pressure is very different from pressure to approve or block particular mergers. Pressure of the latter kind can be and is exerted in all jurisdictions (for instance, the decision by the German Economics Minister to overturn the decision of the BKA blocking the Daimler-Benz/MBB merger in 1989), but it takes place more visibly in some than in others.

Transparency is assisted by the publication of details of the analysis and recommendations of an investigating agency without the constraint of its having to support the decisions of the political authorities. Whether the agency is headed by a politician or a civil servant is not nearly so significant on its own. For instance, the Conseil de la Concurrence, though notionally independent of the French Economics Ministry since its foundation in 1986, is subject to much more activist political review than the MMC or (especially) the BKA (see Boner and Krueger (1991)). Likewise the fact that the MMC is headed by a civil servant and makes only recommendations, not decisions, has not prevented it from coming under some political pressure - but the fact that it publishes very detailed reports makes such pressure more visible, as a glance at the report on the British Airways–British Caledonian merger will confirm[5] (see footnote 42 to Chapter 6). Furthermore, what makes the MMC most vulnerable to pressure is not its *procedures*, which are comparatively transparent, but the vagueness of its *criteria* (in particular the broad range of factors it is entitled to consider under the public interest heading). Another way to express this is that what the MMC most needs is *ex ante* transparency. The Commission has neither *ex ante* nor procedural transparency, and its *ex post* transparency is much less than that of the MMC.

The problem of vagueness of criteria is not resolved, however, simply by restricting criteria to competition rather than more broadly public interest concerns. We have already presented evidence in Chapter 4 that firms and especially their lawyers view the criteria that are used to apply the Regulation as sufficiently flexible to give them significant bargaining power. It is not only from the side of the merging parties that there is this perception: one member of the MTF told us that 'the case rapporteurs themselves do not know what policy they should be following. If you ask a rapporteur what the policy is, the best thing he could say would be "Look at Article 2 and think about it".' By contrast, the explicit rationale of the US Merger Guidelines is that the notion whether a merger harms competition is too vague by itself either to be reasonably predictable by firms or to ensure that the agency follows a consistent (and credible) procedure. The same reasoning surely applies to European circumstances: guidelines, detailing a check-list of procedures to be followed, do not prevent an agency from departing from them, but may at least provide some pressure to ensure that such departures are made for defensible reasons rather than capriciously. *Ex ante* transparency, in criteria as well as procedures, would have much to recommend it in the European context.

7.1.3 *Decision*

Although the analysis of a merger case is undertaken by the EC's Competition Directorate (and specifically by its Merger Task Force), the *decision* regarding a particular case is taken by the Commission as a whole. Consequently, in any controversial case the Competition Commissioner must make a careful assessment of the extent to which he can carry support within the Commission for his preferred decision. On competition matters the views of the Competition Commissioner naturally have great weight, but it is not absolute. The nature of the political process by which a judgment by the Merger Task Force on the intrinsic merits of a case is transmuted into a political compromise is unfortunately very opaque. Good press discussion of particular cases can help, but by its nature it tends to be limited to reporting the more obvious instances of disagreements, such as when a Commissioner is overruled by the rest of the Commission. However, such cases will always be rare, and give little insight as to whether the eventual decision is one that the Competition Commissioner (let alone the MTF) would have preferred. Commissioners wish (like all politicians) to gain a reputation for success in persuading their colleagues. They will therefore minimize instances of overt disagreement, usually by adapting their case to be congenial to the perceived views of the majority on the Commission instead of forcing an unmodified recommendation to a vote there is a serious risk of losing. This is neither surprising nor undesirable, nor is it undesirable that the investigation of a merger should be subject to subsequent political review. What *is* unfortunate is that, given the fogginess of the boundary between the investigation and the subsequent review, the nature of the political negotiation risks distorting the character of the investigation.[6] And the distortion becomes all the more important the earlier in the procedure the parties begin explicit or implicit negotiations, a fact that has implications for the extent to which the Commission should be empowered to accept legally binding undertakings in first-stage investigations, a matter we discuss in Chapter 8.

7.1.4 *Judicial review*

Judicial review constitutes a much more transparent procedure, but unfortunately this is due partly to its very slow and cumbersome nature. An appeal brought by a member state to the European Court of Justice (ECJ) is likely to take up to two years, and although private parties can bring cases more rapidly to the Court of First Instance, these face the possibility of further appeal to the ECJ. The consequence has been that both the Commission and the parties concerned have been extremely anxious to avoid judicial review, which would jeopardize the very speed and efficiency which has been one of the hallmarks of the Merger Regulation's first two years. In the Commission's case there has been the additional important need to establish legitimacy for its procedures, which would have been difficult to do if significant numbers of its early decisions had been subject to challenge by the courts. However, the wish to avoid judicial review is not neutral in its effects on the investigation and decision procedure, but will tend to distort decision-making in favour of those interest groups that are most likely to resort to the courts if the decision is not to their liking. In an uncontested merger the parties who gain from the deal (in particular, the merging firms) are likely to be better organized and informed, and consequently more likely to seek judicial review, than those who might lose (such as consumers). Consequently the pressures to avoid judicial review will tend to bias the procedure in favour of approval in such cases; this applies less to contested mergers, where the management of the acquired firm face fewer organizational obstacles, and where the threat of judicial review can even be thought of as a kind of 'poison pill'.

To an extent, the Commission can reduce the risk of review by negotiating remedies with the parties concerned; it is hard for a party to a merger convincingly to bring a legal appeal if it has already indicated willingness to agree to proposed remedies. Once again, though, this is not neutral in its effects: it encourages resort to cosmetic remedies, or to ones that rely on excessive optimism about the future development of competition, or to ones that involve the Commission in inappropriately detailed positive intervention in the structure of firms and of markets (see our discussion in section 3.6). It may particularly encourage such remedies in cases that involve the Commission breaking new ground, or otherwise making general policy in a merger case. Such criticisms were levied at the Commission in the 1992 *Nestlé/Perrier* case, which involved the first explicit use of the concept of collective dominance. It has been suggested that the Commission was particularly keen to avoid judicial challenge by the firms to this innovative decision; if there is any truth in this, it is ironic that the decision has indeed been challenged, only by a party (namely the Perrier workforce) opposed to rather than supportive of the deal.

Furthermore, it is in the nature of many remedies that they are negotiated very much at the last minute and at the level of the Commission rather than at the level where the analysis is performed (as one MTF rapporteur put it to us, 'we often learn about the remedies after the handshaking has taken place'). They do not receive, therefore, the kind of economic analysis that they need: the analysis that appears in published decisions has often been written in the awareness of a *fait accompli*. And in the absence of objective analysis it is hard to see how remedies can help being as *ad hoc* as we have noted them to be in Chapter 3.[7]

Paradoxically, therefore, the most transparent component of the EC's merger control procedure (namely judicial review) imposes sufficient costs on the parties concerned that, in a quite reasonable wish to avoid it, they may in practice resort to procedures that carry a risk of increasing the opacity and the distortions in the process as a whole. This suggests a need to seek less costly ways of ensuring transparency.

7.2 Strengths and weaknesses of the EC's procedure

The discussion so far has suggested the following important strengths in the EC's merger control procedure by comparison with that of other jurisdictions:

1. It is fast, with the great majority of cases decided within a month, and the remainder within four months.
2. It is flexible, with the pre-notification discussions in particular enabling the Merger Task Force to waive unnecessary information requirements.
3. The fact that a single body is responsible for notification and investigation makes it possible for firms to be better informed

before they commit themselves about the kind of investigation they will face.

4. It has removed some pre-existing ambiguities about the boundaries between EC and national jurisdiction with its 'one-stop shop', though ambiguities about the treatment of joint ventures have been very significant.

The main weakness of the procedure, however, is its lack of transparency, particularly for an agency that is under more direct political control than most. This is evident both in the fact that there is no report of the analysis of individual cases that is written independently of the need to justify the eventual decision, and in the somewhat less systematic character of the criteria for analysis than those of (for example) the US Department of Justice (see Chapter 3). It applies especially to negotiated remedies, which often receive no systematic analysis at all prior to being agreed.

The comparative precision of the Commission's decision criteria, as embodied in the emphasis on competition criteria in the Regulation, is not enough of an advantage to compensate. This is particularly so because, in the absence of transparency, it is not clear how free the decision-making process can continue to be of covert appeal to non-competition criteria; what is certain is that such criteria are not given systematic examination.

This lack of transparency may well lead to a greater degree of capture in the future than it has done up to now, as the work of the MTF becomes more routine and its presence on the European scene less of a novelty (and as the various interest groups become more skilful at applying effective pressure). But is it possible to say anything about the *kind* of capture which might result?

A number of considerations suggest that, because of regulatory capture, future distortions of the merger control procedure are likely to be in the direction of excessive tolerance of market power, especially by firms with a strong base of national or regional political influence (a combination of national and industry capture, in other words). To some extent this is because of the pressures that were noted in section 6.2.2 and which an EC-based procedure may be only partly successful at offsetting. It is partly also because political influence in the Community will continue to coalesce around national interest groups to a significant extent for the foreseeable future.[8] To some extent the Commission as a transnational body can help to overcome these tendencies. But even so the Commission is not organized exactly as a transnational civil service: certain posts are by convention reserved for nationals of certain member states, for instance. Some of those who work in the Commission (and a greater number in the MTF than elsewhere, given the necessary speed with which it was established) are appointed for temporary periods, either as 'agents temporaires' or as national civil servants on secondment to the EC, often on terms more favourable than their appointments in their home countries. It may be difficult in such circumstances for the officials concerned to build up the continuity and sense of collective professional identification that may be needed to resist the national and sectional pressures that surround an institution like the Commission.

A degree of capture by national interests need not imply industry capture (indeed it is compatible with excessive controls upon industry by governments prone to blocking mergers on nationalistic grounds). But in the present circumstances national pressures are more likely to lead to industry capture than the reverse. This is partly because in most contexts firms are more effective at lobbying national governments than are other interest groups. It is also because the speed and lack of transparency of European procedures, plus the reluctance of the Commission to provoke resort to judicial review, encourages the strategic manipulation of the procedure by well-informed firms, as was noted above.[9] Firms know that expressing a willingness to compromise on some aspects of a doubtful merger invites a degree of compromise from the Commission in turn (this is especially so when the arguments take place to a considerable extent informally prior to Notification). But the first move in this bargaining game is not made by the Commission – it is made by the firms. The knowledge that concessions from the Commission can be 'bought' by concessions from firms therefore invites firms to make initial proposals even more anti-competitive than they need be in order to leave scope for concessions. The bargaining process is one that encourages a certain extremism in opening proposals, in other words.[10] At the very least it diminishes the pressure on firms to diminish any anti-competitive impact of a transaction before they come to the Commission. Market conditions may not always permit this kind of strategic manipulation, since they may constrain feasible deals quite tightly. But where they do leave room for flexibility, well-advised firms are likely in future to exploit the bargaining procedure to the full,[11] in a way considerably facilitated by the lack of transparency of that procedure.

Most of all, the procedure leaves very little scope for the exercise of any countervailing power to that of the Commission itself, subject as it is to pressure from the parties to the transaction. Third parties have very little time in which to make representations (and no time at all where negotiated remedies are concerned). Competitors often have little interest in doing so since they may be beneficiaries of market power (and where their interests are potentially more directly affected – namely, in the imposition of remedies - they have no opportunity to complain). Buyers may take an interest, but only in cases where they are well organized and prompt. In fact, in some respects the most significant countervailing power to the Commission comes from member states (a fact which may explain the reluctance of some to cede more power by downward revision of the turnover thresholds); yet it was the very fact that member states' interests may lead to distortion of the merger control procedure that provided the most coherent rationale for the European Merger Regulation in the first place. What this highlights therefore is that, given the opacity of current procedures, some more credible countervailing power is needed. Member states at present provide what little of this there is, but it is not enough, and it comes from the wrong source.

Some of the risks we have discussed are hard to avoid in any procedure that places a premium – as the EC's rightly does – on speed and responsiveness to firms' concerns.[12] However, there are a number of kinds of general reform that might help to reduce these risks. These are the subject of Chapter 8.

Notes

1. Pre-notification usually therefore minimizes the cost of merger control to firms, but it may also raise the credibility of the procedure by ensuring that the costs are ones firms could reasonably be expected to bear. By way of contrast, the purchase of DFK Gas AB by AGA AB, a Swedish carbonic gas manufacturer, in 1987, was not notified to the Swedish authorities since Sweden has no pre-merger notification requirement. By the time the Competition Ombudsman sought to prevent the merger, which gave the new firm a 97% share of the Swedish carbonic acid market, the Market Court judged that integration of the firms' operations had proceeded so far that separating the

operations would have been extremely costly, so the merger was allowed to proceed (see Boner and Krueger (1991), p. 70).

2. Officials from the MTF have no explicit power of commitment, of course. Nevertheless, since the purpose of pre-notification discussions is partly to signal to firms whether or not their transactions are likely to prove problematic, the risk is that officials who have (in good faith) encouraged the notification of a transaction that subsequently turns out to be potentially problematic, may be tempted to pursue the investigation less vigorously than they should, in order to avoid making their earlier encouragement appear incompetent. There is an analogy here with well-known incentive problems in banking regulation, where regulators who have failed to spot solvency problems at a particular bank may be tempted subsequently to cover up the fact in order to avoid drawing attention to their earlier failure to discover the difficulties (we are grateful to Jean Tirole for this point).

3. To some extent, direct political accountability of the agency may substitute for more subterranean channels of influence. For instance, one official of the US Department of Justice interviewed by us was asked whether he had faced attempts to pressurize him directly in the investigation of a case. He could recall only one such intervention (by a Senator from the same party as the President then in office seeking lenient treatment of the firm concerned) which he had been able without too much difficulty to ignore. But he added that most Senators would have found it unnecessary to seek to exert pressure on officials of the Justice Department when they could do so directly via their political representative, the Attorney General, especially when the kind of pressure they might exert was in a direction congenial to that individual's political views. Consequently, an agency not headed by a politician might find itself open to more frequent attempts to pressurize its officials in order to influence investigations before their results become public. The seriousness of this risk would depend on the incentives for individual officials to resist covert pressure of this kind (including the strength of the professional ethic in the bureaucracy).

4. A number of participants at inter-service meetings have told us that it is not uncommon for efficiency gains to be urged in favour of particular transactions even though their consideration is not a formal part of the Regulation. Whether such arguments are influential is hard to evaluate; what is certain is that, if they are, this fact will not be evident from the Commission's published decision. And claims about the magnitude of such gains will not have been subjected to the kind of rigorous empirical examination that an explicit efficiency defence might require. Similar points apply to the comments made to us by a number of lawyers (see Chapter 4) that they find it important to 'get the Commission to like the deal as a whole'.

5. For instance, while the responsible politician was able to prevent publication of details of the alleged efficiency gains (on grounds of commercial confidentiality) he would have found it much harder, in a full and detailed report of this kind, to justify preventing publication

of the CAA's opinion that BA's resort to the efficiency defence was unconvincing.

6. In particular, Commissioners who have previously been ministers in their member states may think of an investigating agency as essentially in the business of providing advice to political decision-makers, and may therefore view the avoidance of political embarrassment as at least as important as the provision of objective analysis.

7. There are some reasons also to be concerned about whether the nature of the Commission's decision-making process allows even that economic analysis that has been carefully performed to be as influential as it should be. One (unconfirmed) story reported to us of the Commission's hour-long discussion of the *ICI/Dupont* case claimed that after 45 minutes the Competition Commissioner had to remind his colleagues that the relevant market was not the market for carpets. *Se non è vero, è ben trovato.* Perhaps that explains why so few firms bother to hire economic consultants (see Chapter 4).

8. This will not necessarily be much diminished by any future shift in the balance of political power away from the Commission and Council of Ministers and towards the European Parliament, since voting blocs in the Parliament are likely to be at least as much influenced by national and regional divisions as is the distribution of power within the Commission itself (which matters more than the Council as far as competition policy is concerned). Only the formation of genuinely pan-European political parties is likely to change this, and linguistic and cultural factors make this a distant prospect.

9. Firms are becoming increasingly well informed. The first head of the Merger Task Force left the Commission in early 1993 to work for the Brussels office of a British law firm (the Commission does not restrict this kind of 'revolving door' appointment).

10. There is an analogy here with arbitration procedures in industrial relations, where it is well known that some apparently unreasonable procedures (such as final-offer arbitration) encourage moderation in the parties' demands. More apparently reasonable procedures (such as 'splitting the difference') encourage unreasonable claims.

11. Our discussions with law firms, in particular, have revealed many of them to be fully aware that the Commission is keen (in the words of one) 'to let the deal get done if at all possible', and to realize the significant bargaining power this gives them.

12. Nevertheless, our calculations in the appendix to Chapter 2 indicate that a gain of an extra month or two in a merger investigation is not worth having at the price of increasing the risk of a wrong decision by more than a few percentage points. It is quite likely that in discussions with the Commission, firms exaggerate the costs to themselves of delaying a merger (for example, by proceeding to a second-stage investigation). It would be in their interests to do so, particularly if they believe that an over-hasty investigation is likely to increase the overall probability of approval.

8

Some options for change

The objective of this last chapter is to evaluate possible changes to the Merger Regulation and its implementation in light of our discussion so far. We distinguish between: (i) changes to the procedure that can be entertained in the current legislative and institutional framework; (ii) changes in the design of the institutions and the allocation of their powers; (iii) changes in the terms of the Regulation; and (iv) changes in the methods of merger analysis.

8.1　Modifications to the current procedure

Our discussion of institutions in Chapter 7 has highlighted the considerable lack of transparency of the process of EC merger control. We emphasized that this lack of transparency stems in part from the fact that different stages in the procedure are blurred into each other. To separate out these stages would require significant institutional changes, and several options are discussed in the next section. Nevertheless, transparency might still be enhanced by a number of changes which, although significant, are compatible with the existing institutional arrangements.

First, draft decisions could be published by the Merger Task Force before the case is put forward to the Commission. These draft decisions could also be more detailed than the decisions currently published. Similarly, the opinion of the Advisory Committee on Concentrations could be published immediately after the Committee has met, and before the case is brought in front of the Commission. Non-publication of any information supplied to the MTF would be solely on the basis of necessary commercial confidentiality, as judged by the MTF and interpreted by the courts. The Commission would have the power to enforce publication of any information withheld by the MTF, but not to prevent publication of information which the MTF wished to publish.

At present, the opinion of the MTF in difficult cases is often leaked to third parties or to the press. But in terms of transparency, leaks are a very poor substitute for proper reporting. Transparency requires that information should be verifiable and widely available.

It is essential that proposed remedies should be given a proper evaluation by the MTF. If the proposals appear early enough in the process, an evaluation can be included in the draft decision; otherwise there is a strong case for requiring a minimum breathing-space after the proposal of remedies, in order to invite third-party comments, to give the MTF time to undertake a proper evaluation, and to ensure that the Commission itself has time to reflect without being bounced into a decision. The present negotiation of remedies is one of the most opaque parts of the whole procedure, opaque in some cases even for the case rapporteurs. At the same time, remedies may sometimes affect significantly the competitors of the merging firms. It would seem important to let these competitors have the opportunity to voice their opinion and to give them sufficient time to do so.

The benefits of proper reporting should not, however, be exaggerated; without institutional separation between the agency publishing its decision and the Commission, the independence of the MTF will still be limited. There will still be a tendency for the MTF's report to be written to justify decisions, the outline of which can already be foreseen. Publication of draft decisions can reduce this tendency, but not as much as would be desirable.

Secondly, there is a case for placing the burden of proof on firms whose proposals fail the initial screening (phase I). As we have discussed, this provides the firms with a strong incentive to reveal necessary information. This incentive could be further enhanced by 'stopping the clock' for investigations during the time it takes the parties to respond to information requests. Currently such suspension occurs only exceptionally, when the Commission has to request information by decision or to order an investigation by decision.

Thirdly, *ex ante* transparency of the procedure could be improved by publishing guidelines for the analysis of mergers, as is done in the United States. As we discussed in Chapter 3, the analysis of mergers published in Commission decisions is currently less consistent than it could be, and the reasoning behind decisions is often vague and insufficiently motivated. This increases uncertainty for firms but also provides the Commission with much discretion which can be abused. Publication of guidelines and a check-list of procedures diminishes this discretion to some extent. But as we emphasized in Chapter 7, *ex ante* transparency is likely to be properly effective only if it is accompanied by some transparency *ex post*; the detail of published decisions should be such as to enable the consistency or lack of it between the guidelines and the actual analysis undertaken in decisions to be assessed. In is only in those circumstances that the Commission will have an adequate incentive to establish a reputation for adhering to these guidelines. Deviations will then presumably be exceptional and well motivated.

Fourthly, cases which involve negotiated remedies (that is, anything which depends upon an undertaking by the firm as to its future behaviour) should automatically proceed to the second stage of investigation. This need not prevent the MTF from reporting well within its deadline (or even within the deadline for the first stage if the case is sufficiently urgent), but it would ensure that the MTF had adequate powers to require information sufficiently detailed to enable it to assess the case properly.

8.2   Institutional changes

As we have discussed, the lack of transparency in EC merger control results partly from the fact that the different stages of the procedure are blurred into each other in a way that is difficult to distinguish from the outside. Yet clearly speed and flexibility may partly be compromised by separating out all the stages of the procedure, and separating these in turn from the normal processes of political compromise within the Commission itself. At what stages in the process, therefore, is separation most important, and how can it best be achieved?

Figure 8.1 shows a very schematic outline of six stages of the merger control procedure: notification, investigation, negotiation, decision, political review and judicial review. This is not a chrono-

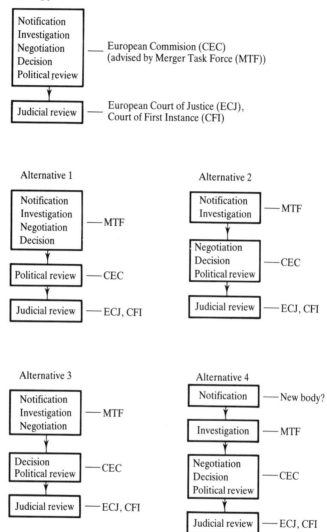

Figure 8.1 Division of responsibility for stages of procedure.

logical but a logical division since in practice a number of the stages (investigation and negotiation, for example) overlap with each other.

At present the EC's procedures effectively assign all the first five stages to one body (the European Commission). It is true that at least the first two are carried out by a notionally separate body (namely, the Merger Task Force), but for the reasons already discussed this acts more as a support unit to the Commission than as a genuinely and visibly separate agency. The fourth and fifth stages (namely, decision and political review) are not distinct in the EC's procedures since the Council has no power to overturn the Commission's decisions.

What, then, are alternative ways of dividing responsibility for this procedure, and what in each case would division effectively mean? Let us distinguish four possible proposals, and examine the pros and cons of each:

1. A division could be established between the decision stage and the stage of political review (between stages 4 and 5). Stages 1 to 4 would be the responsibility of a separate agency, probably working according to quite tightly defined competition criteria. The division of functions would allow for the possibility of political modification of the agency's decisions by the Commission only after such decisions had been taken and a report published. This arrangement appears to be roughly what advocates of an 'independent' European competition agency have in mind. It is not tantamount to complete independence since the Commission would still be able to overturn particular decisions, but it represents – at least formally – as much independence as that enjoyed by the BKA.[1]

   An important point to be made about this and indeed all the four proposals is that, for a division of responsibilities for the different stages to be more than cosmetic, it is necessary not only that there be publicly available information about the procedure at its different stages (for instance, that the agency publish its report separately from any overriding of its decision by the Commission), but that the goals set for the responsible agency at each stage be distinct from each other. A competition agency that published notionally independent reports but which was still a sub-department of the European Commission and whose head reported to the Competition Commissioner or Director General would be independent only in name. There would still be the same tendency for the agency's reports to be written to justify decisions already taken; and those decisions themselves would be taken under the political pressures of the Commission. So an 'independent' agency would need its head to be appointed for a fixed term, probably by the Commission as a whole; its officials would likewise have to have secure appointments and to be enabled to carry out their work on a daily basis without interference.

How realistic this option is within the structure and political culture of the European Commission is not straightforward to assess. It is not clear whether a structure similar to that of the Bundeskartellamt could be easily implemented within the Commission; the BKA is actually organized around a number of independent units whose decisions cannot be overturned even by the President of the BKA. Such an organization would be a major departure from the traditions and habits of the Commission, in which consensus is emphasized and in which a politician is nominated, with much power, as the head of each directorate. Whether in the medium term the Commission could be persuaded to accept such a reform is hard for us to say; it seems improbable in the short term, if only because it is hard to imagine agreement between the member states about how such an agency should be set up and what its criteria of assessment should be. We believe such a reform would have some merits; however, and more practically, we believe that a less apparently radical division of functions could go a very long way towards achieving the same benefits, and at somewhat less political cost.

2.   A division could be made between the stages of notification/investigation and negotiation/decision (between stages 2 and 3). In other words, there might be an independent agency responsible for investigation, while decision-making power remained with the Commission. In order to ensure the independence of the investigation process, the head of the agency would need to be appointed on a fixed-term basis by the Commission as a whole.

Given that the MTF under this system would have no decision-making power, the value of the reform would consist principally in its publishing detailed reports, unamended by any deliberations by the Advisory Committee on Concentrations (which could be published separately), and consequently relatively undistorted by the need to justify decisions already taken.

Whether the MTF's reports should make precise recommendations or lay out for the Commission a series of options, with the pros and cons of each, is a more difficult matter to decide. Very precise recommendations, coupled with a presumption that the Commission would not normally act against them, would make the MTF *de facto* more like an independent agency; a menu of options would place the decision capacity more clearly in the Commission's hands.

How effective such a reform would be would depend very much on how strongly the Commission felt bound by the agency's analyses in taking its decisions. That in turn would be influenced by the agency's own ability to establish a reputation for persuasive and objective analysis, as well as on the kind of publicity received when this analysis was ignored. Nor is it inconceivable that some of those interests in the Community at present opposed to an explicit efficiency defence in the procedure might be reassured that the presence of an independent source of competition analysis would at least ensure that any claims about efficiency gains received a full and objective evaluation, instead of operating on the basis of hunch and suggestion.

3. A third possibility is that investigation could still be kept separate from decision, but negotiation could be made the responsibility of the investigating agency rather than the decision-making agency. The main purpose of such a proposal would take account of concerns that separating the negotiation from the investigation stages would slow down the process of agreeing and evaluating remedies.

However, it is not clear that such a proposal would be very practical, as the agency would be seriously limited in the conviction with which it could enter into negotiations if it were truly independent of the decision-making body. And one of the persistent themes in our discussions so far has been the potential distortion to the objectivity of competition analysis induced by the nature of the negotiation process.

Nor is it very clear how much delay the separation of investigation from negotiation and decision-making would in fact impose upon the process of negotiating remedies. Firms would negotiate with the Commission; all that would be required would be for the MTF to have prepared a report on the proposed remedies before the Commission reached its decision. There might be a small delay, but a delay well worth accepting for the benefit of significantly improved transactions. One thing it would make more difficult would be for the Commission to succumb to the temptation of accepting a remedy first and performing the analysis later – but that is hardly the most damning objection imaginable.

4. Notification could be separated from investigation (stage 1 from stage 2). We have discussed the possible risks that might arise from implicit undertakings being made during the pre-notification process. However, it has also become clear that the benefits of pre-notification discussion with the same agency that will perform the analysis are very substantial (both in increasing speed and in avoiding the costs of firms' misunderstanding their chances of approval). The risks in pre-notification discussion would seem to arise chiefly through an insufficiently clear separation of the investigation from the decision-making bodies; if that can be achieved, the benefits of a unified notification and investigation procedure seem comfortably to outweigh the costs.

Overall, therefore, of the four different ways we have discussed of increasing the degree of separation between different components of the European merger control procedure to assist transparency, the most persuasive seems to be to separate the notification/investigation procedures from the remaining ones, though there are some arguments in favour of the other changes.

8.3   The terms of the Regulation

The turnover thresholds which determine the applicability of the Merger Regulation are due to be reviewed, and possibly lowered to ECU 2 billion, by the end of 1993. Doubts have been expressed, however, that the Commission will pursue the matter further, given that France, Germany and the UK are apparently not favourably inclined towards such a revision.[2]

The immediate implication of a reduction in the worldwide turnover thresholds would be to shift some work from member states' agencies to the MTF. According to a simulation undertaken[3] by the BKA, some 60–70 additional mergers would have been reviewed by the MTF rather than the BKA in the period until the end of 1992 if the threshold had been set at ECU 2 billion from the outset. This would have represented roughly a doubling of the number of German transactions reviewed by the MTF. A doubling in the number of cases provides therefore a reasonable approximation to the increased workload that the MTF would face with a 2 billion threshold.[4] The administrative implications for the MTF of such an increased caseload are a relatively minor issue; what matters is whether the further centralization implied by the reduction in the threshold is appropriate.

As we discussed in Chapter 6, the appropriate degree of decentralization rests on the balance between the costs of national decisions which do not internalize the effects of mergers across borders, and the benefits of competition between jurisdictions in terms of reduced capture and decisions which more closely reflect national preferences. The size of the externality across countries can be approximated by the volume of sales which occurs outside the member states where the merger occurs or where the highest combined turnover of the merging parties is found (though subject to some qualifications we note in our discussion of Article 9 in section 6.2.2). In turn, national authorities will take inadequate decisions to the extent that the balance between costs and benefits arising from the merger varies across countries; if the net effects of a merger outside a country are similar to those within its borders, decisions by national authorities applying identical criteria will be adequate and independent of the distribution of sales across countries. Accordingly, in ideal circumstances a rule allocating jurisdiction should take into account the correlation between the internal and the cross-border effects of a merger proposal. In practice, this correlation can hardly be assessed before jurisdiction is assigned, so that a rule based on the absolute size of the turnover externality seems a more practical response.

The benefit from reducing the threshold would arise from the internalization of cross-border effects; this has to be weighted against the cost of imposing decisions on member states in which the assessment of competitive effects within their territory diverges from their own assessment. Accordingly, the precision of the procedure used to sort mergers with a European dimension from the others matters a great deal; a very imprecise procedure is likely to enhance the net cost of centralization.

As we argued in section 6.2.2, the combination of a turnover threshold with a two-thirds rule for capturing spillover effects (rather than the more appropriate use of an absolute spillover rule) has a number of distortionary effects that are likely to become more serious if the thresholds are lowered. We would strongly recommend the adoption of an absolute spillover rule.

It is hard to assess whether the benefits from internalizing spillover effects for transactions that would fall under the Merger Regulation in the range of 2 to 5 billion would outweigh the costs of further centralization. The somewhat negative attitude of the national governments towards a change in the thresholds, as reported in the press, indicates that the cost of centralization is perceived to be significant; national governments are clearly not entirely happy with the way in which mergers have been dealt with by the Commission, albeit for very different reasons.[5] These governments presumably consider that some decisions would have been different if they had been taken at the national level, and vice versa. Evaluating such a counter-factual is a highly speculative exercise; some German cases like *Varta/Bosch* would very probably have been blocked at the national level. The French government might have cleared *Aero-spatiale/Alenia/de Havilland*. Whether decisions taken by national authorities would have been different at the EC level is equally difficult to evaluate. Since October 1990, four German mergers have been blocked by the BKA. This is accordingly an upper bound to the number of mergers that have been blocked in Germany but could have been cleared at the EC level. Interestingly, none of the eight cases blocked by the MMC would have gone to the EC if the threshold had been set at 2 billion.[6]

The cost of centralization is therefore perceived by member states to be significant. If externalities across countries are taken seriously, though, it is not clear that the appropriate response to such dissatisfaction is to resist further centralization. An alternative response, and a more positive one, would be to undertake changes in the current procedure to make sure that it better performs the task that it is assigned to do. A number of the suggestions we discuss should be understood in this spirit.

On the whole, it does not seem that the reduction of the thresholds should be a priority; improving the procedure to enhance transparency and changing the rule for allocating jurisdictions to reflect better the absolute size of externalities should, in our opinion, come first.

The review of thresholds is the only change which is formally contemplated by the end of 1993 and a decision would require only a qualified majority in the Council. There is no reason, however, why additional modifications could not be entertained, or at least debated. Two issues warrant particular attention: namely, the legal standing of undertakings by firms and the explicit consideration of efficiency.

As we discussed in Chapter 3, positive decisions taken after one month of investigation (under Article 6.1b) sometimes include remedies. For instance, decisions on *Air France/Sabena*, *BA/TAT* and *TNT/Post offices* have been taken under article 6.1b and include important remedies. It is, however, clear from Article 8 of the Regulation that the Commission is legally entitled to negotiate and impose remedies only in the context of a full inquiry (and a decision under Article 8). The question then arises whether undertakings by firms which have been negotiated during a short (one-month) procedure can be enforced in court. Remedies negotiated during the short procedure were initially meant to involve only structural elements which would be difficult to overturn, precisely to avoid possible litigation regarding the actual *ex post* realization of firms' undertakings. However, remedies negotiated under recent airline cases (*Air France/Sabena* and *BA/TAT*) cannot be said to be structural, and require explicit actions by the undertakings concerned after the decision has been cleared.

Two alternative modifications can be entertained. On the one hand, the regulation could be changed in such a way that the Commission would become legally entitled to negotiate remedies during the first month of investigation. On the other hand, a full proceeding (phase II) could be automatically initiated for all cases which involve remedies. This second solution would, in our opinion, be preferable. It would ensure that the MTF had adequate power to require information sufficiently detailed to enable it to assess the case properly. In addition, as mentioned above, the negotiation of remedies may greatly affect competitors and it would seem appropriate to give them enough time to make their opinion known. It is also worth noticing that the initiation of a proceeding does not necessarily prevent the MTF from reporting well within its deadline, or even within the deadline for the first stage if the case is sufficiently urgent.

As we indicated above, it is clear as a matter of principle that efficiency considerations can make an otherwise anti-competitive

merger worth while. It is also naive to think that efficiency considerations are not currently taken into account during the process of
merger review. Commission services other than the MTF will often
insist on efficiency during inter-service meetings; it is also reported
by members of the MTF that in private hearings with the Commissioner, firms will insist on efficiency gains in particular when remedies
are being negotiated. According to some rapporteurs, apparently lax
remedies or a favourable assessment of dominance will often hide
some concern for efficiency. The main weakness of the current
procedure is therefore that efficiency is considered even though it is
not really supposed to be mentioned; as a result, potentially distorted
efficiency claims by firms are not given a serious hearing.

The scope for introducing efficiency claims through the back door
will be reduced if some of the proposals for increased transparency
discussed above are implemented. Whether an explicit consideration
of efficiency would then improve matters depends on whether
the Commission could implement a procedure through which the
information provided by the firms could be reasonably verified. The
organization of an efficiency audit unit, independent from the MTF,
might help in this regard.[7] The report of the efficiency audit might
also be a separate document, though the MTF could provide
comments on whether, in its opinion, the magnitude of the gains
identified offsets any damage to competition. In any event, it seems
that giving efficiency claims a serious hearing could only improve
matters over the current situation, even for those who are currently
sceptical about the merits of efficiency considerations. In a sense,
efficiency considerations are inevitable at the EC level, and treating
them seriously is probably more effective than pretending to ignore
them.

8.4   Changes in the analysis of mergers

Our discussion of actual decisions in Chapter 3 has pointed to a
number of areas where the analysis undertaken by the MTF could
be improved. There are two areas which, in our opinion, warrant
special attention.

First, the definition of markets is not consistent across cases and
in many instances is likely to be excessively narrow; this arises
because product and geographic markets are considered sequentially

and also because supply substitutability is often ignored. The assessment of dominance in excessively narrow markets can hardly appeal to systematic measures like market shares; a large number of additional factors are then considered which involve a great deal of judgment and accordingly leave the procedure more open to manipulation than it need be. It would therefore help if the MTF could first decide on the methodology which it deems appropriate to define markets; we would recommend taking both demand and supply substitutability into account and considering product and geographic markets simultaneously. It might then be appropriate for the MTF to publish this methodology in widely available guidelines.

The MTF rarely makes use of quantitative information to define markets, and prefers instead to emphasize product characteristics. Our analysis in Chapter 3 has highlighted the shortcomings of this approach. There is no reason why more quantitative assessments could not be undertaken at reasonable cost, within the time frame for decisions imposed by the Regulation. To provide a rough estimate of demand elasticities takes no more than a few days' work for a competent econometrician if the data is available.

Problems of data gathering should not be exaggerated. First, the MTF could maintain and constantly update a data bank of the most important markets. The MTF could also purchase data when necessary from marketing firms; market records covering a few years back are usually available directly and at reasonable cost. The quality of data can also only improve over time as bar codes are used more extensively for billing purposes. Finally, it is likely that in most cases firms have access to at least some of the information which is necessary for estimating demand elasticities. Such information is obtained as part of the routine activities of market monitoring. The MTF could very well ask for the data to be made available.

The cost of permanently employing an econometrician and of maintaining a data bank is also rather small compared to the cost associated with incorrect decisions. So, even if econometric evidence would improve decisions only marginally, it is worth taking it seriously (as indeed it is taken seriously by the US anti-trust authorities).

In conclusion, all of these proposals for procedural reform have some rationale in the considerations that have emerged from our discussion of general principles and our examinations of existing procedures. To some extent the components come as a package, in the sense that – as our discussion in Chapter 6 reminded us – piecemeal implementation of reforms in organizational design can sometimes worsen the very phenomena of regulatory capture they are designed to alleviate. But it should be stressed that the precise weight that should be accorded to each component is a matter of judgment. And for such judgment no general principles can be an adequate substitute.

Notes

1. It is arguable that the different political culture of the Community from that of Germany would lead the Commission to use its right to overrule much more than is done in Germany. 'The only way to make a Eurokartellamt work would be to put it in Berlin', was how one Commission official expressed it to us.
2. See *Financial Times*, 1 March 1993.
3. This was an internal study, but the BKA has kindly made its findings available to us.
4. The UK authorities have not performed a similar analysis, partly because of the significant workload in obtaining the relevant EC turnover figures. The Office of Fair Trading suggested to us that its impression was that a lowering of thresholds to 2 billion would have rather less than doubled the load of British cases reviewed by the MTF.
5. It seems fair to assume that Germany would prefer an institutional set-up closer to that of the BKA, while France would like to see an efficiency defence.
6. Three cases would have been reviewed by the EC with a threshold at 1 billion.
7. The MTF could also commission consultants' reports from the private sector.

Appendix I

Chronological list of decisions taken between 21 September 1990 and 25 March 1993

Case	Title	Main market	Date of decision	OJ publication*
(1) IV/H.0004	RENAULT/VOLVO (SWE;FRA)	Manuf. of motor vehicles, trailers semi-trailers	01/11/90 7.4 decision 07/11/90 6.1a decision 07/11/90 6.1b decision	281 90/11/90 281 90/11/90
(2) IV/M.0018	AG/AHEV (BEL;NET)	Insurance and pension funding, except compulsory social security	21/11/90 6.1b decision	304 04/12/90
(3) IV/H.0023	ICI/TIOXIDE (UKI;UKI)	Manuf. of chemicals and chemical products	28/11/90 6.1b decision	304 04/12/90
(4) IV/H.0025	ARJOMARI/WIGGINS TEAPE (FRA;UKI)	Manuf. of pulp, paper and paperboard	10/12/90 6.1a decision	321 21/12/90
(5) IV/M.0027	PROMODES/DIRSA (SPA;FRA)	Retail sale in non-specialized stores	17/12/90 6.1b decision	321 21/12/90
(6) IV/M.0026	CARGILL/UNILEVER (USA;UKI)	Wholesale of agricultural raw materials and livestock	20/12/90 6.1b decision	327 29/12/90
(7) IV/H.0024	MITSUBISHI/UCAR CARBON (JAP;USA)	Graphite and carbon electrodes	04/01/91 6.1b decision	005 90/01/91
(8) IV/H.0037	MATSUSHITA/MCA (JAP;USA)	Motion picture and video activities	10/01/91 6.1b decision	012 18/01/91
(9) IV/M.0050	AT&T/NCR (USA;USA)	Manuf. of office machinery and computers	18/01/91 6.1b decision	016 24/01/91
(10) IV/M.0021	BNP/DRESDNER BANK (OKHB) (FRA;GER)	Monetary intermediation	04/02/91 6.1b decision	034 09/02/91
(11) IV/H.0058	BAXTER-NESTLE/SALVIA (USA;SWI;GER)	Clinical nutrition products	06/02/91 6.1a decision	037 13/02/91
(12) IV/H.0009	FIAT GEOTECH/FORD NEW HOLLAND (ITA;NET)	Manuf. of agricultural and forestry machinery	08/02/91 6.1b decision	118 03/05/91
(13) IV/N.0065	ASKO/OMNI (GER;SWI)	Labour recruitment and provision of personnel	21/02/91 6.1b decision	051 27/02/91
(14) IV/M.0057	DIGITAL/KIENZLE (USA;GER)	Manuf. of office machinery and computers	22/02/91 6.1b decision	056 05/03/91
(15) IV/M.0017	MBB/AEROSPATIALE (FRA;GER)	Helicopters	25/02/91 6.1b decision	059 08/03/91
(16) IV/M.0069	KYONA/SAITANA (JAP;JAP)	Monetary intermediation	07/03/91 6.1b decision	066 14/03/91
(17) IV/H.0070	OTTO/GRATTAN (GER;UKI)	Retail sale not in stores	21/03/91 6.1b decision	093 11/04/91
(18) IV/H.0042	ALCATEL/TELETTRA (FRA;ITA)	Manuf. of radio, television and communication equipment	21/01/91 6.1c decision	122 17/05/91
(19) IV/M.0080	REDOUTE/EMPIRE STORES (FRA;UKI)	Retail sale not in stores	12/04/91 8.2 dec, with cond. 25/04/91 6.1b decision	156 14/06/91
(20) IV/M.0063	ELF/ERTOIL (FRA;SPA)	Manuf. of refined petroleum products	29/04/91 6.1b decision	124 14/05/91

Chronological list of decisions taken between 21 September 1990 and 25 March 1993

Case	Title	Date of decision	Main market	OJ publication*
(21) IV/M.0073	USINOR/ASD (FRA;FRA)	29/04/91 6.1b decision	Manuf. of basic iron and steel and of ferro-alloys (ECSC)	193 24/07/91
(22) IV/M.0082	ASKO/JAKOBS/ADIA (GER;SWI;SWI)	16/05/91 6.1b decision	Labour recruitment and provision of personnel	132 23/05/91
(23) IV/H.0043	CEAC/MAGNETI HARELLI (FRA;ITA)	21/01/91 6.1c decision 29/05/91 8.2 dec., with cond.	Manuf. of accumulators, cells and primary batteries	222 10/08/91
(24) IV/M.0010	CONAGRA/IDEA (USA;FRA)	30/05/91 6.1b decision	Manuf. of food products and beverages	175 06/07/91
(25) IV/M.0092	RVI/VBC/HEULIEZ (FRA;FRA;SWE)	03/06/91 6.1b decision	Manuf. of motor vehicles, trailers and semi-trailers	149 08/06/91
(26) IV/M.0081	VIAG/CCE (GER;UKI)	06/06/91 6.1b decision	Packaging products in aluminium	156 14/06/91
(27) IV/M.0072	SAMOFI/STERLING DRUGS (FRA;USA)	10/06/91 6.1b decision	Manuf. of pharmaceuticals, medicinal and botanical products	156 14/06/91
(28) IV/H.0085	ELF/OCCIDENTAL (FRA;UKI)	13/06/91 6.1b decision	Extraction of crude petroleum and natural gas	160 20/06/91
(29) IV/M.0098	ELF/BC/CEPSA (FRA;SPA;SPA)	18/06/91 6.1b decision	Manuf. of refined petroleum products	172 03/07/91
(30) IV/M.0093	APOLLINARIS/CADBURY SCHWEPPES (GER;UKI)	24/06/91 6.1a decision	Manuf. of beverages	203 02/08/91
(31) IV/M.0097	PECHINEY/USINOR (FRA;FRA)	24/06/91 6.1b decision	Manuf. of basic iron and steel and of ferro-alloys (ECSC)	175 06/07/91
(32) IV/H.0099	NISSAN/RICHARD NISSAN (JAP;FRA)	28/06/91 6.1b decision	Manuf. of motor vehicles, trailers and semi-trailers	181 12/07/91
(33) IV/H.0101	DRAEGER/IBH/HMP (GER;USA;FRA)	28/06/91 6.1b decision	Software consultancy and supply	236 11/09/91
(34) IV/H.0076	LYONNAISE DES EAUX/BROCHIER (FRA;GER)	11/07/91 6.1b decision	Pipeline construction	188 19/07/91
(35) IV/H.0105	ICL/NOKIA DATA (UKI;FIN)	17/07/91 6.1b decision	Manuf. of office machinery and computers	236 11/09/91
(36) IV/H.0112	BDS/SD-SCICON (USA;UKI)	17/07/91 6.1b decision	Software consultancy and supply	237 12/09/91
(37) IV/N.0068	TETRA PAK/ALFA-LAVAL (SWI;SWE)	05/03/91 7.2 decision 19/03/91 6.1c decision 22/07/91 8.2 dec., without cond.	Packaging machines and foodstuffs	290 22/10/91

No. / Case	Parties	Decision	Activity	Ref. / Date
(38) IV/M.0088	ELF/ENTERPRISE (FRA;UKI)	24/07/91 6.1a decision	Extraction of crude petroleum and natural gas	203 02/08/91
(39) IV/H.0111	BP/PETRONED (UKI;SPA)	29/07/91 6.1b decision	Hydrocarbons	208 09/08/91
(40) IV/H.0062	ERIDANIA/ISI (ITA;ITA)	30/07/91 6.1b decision	Sugar	204 03/08/91
(41) IV/M.0012	VARTA/BOSCH (GER;GER)	12/04/91 6.1c decision / 12/04/91 Art. 9 dec., non-referral / 31/07/91 8.2 dec., with cond.	Manuf. of accumulators, cells and primary batteries	320 22/11/91
(42) IV/M.0116	KELT/AMERICAN EXPRESS (UKI;USA;UKI)	12/08/91 7.4 decision	Extraction of crude petroleum and natural gas	223 28/08/91
(43) IV/N.0124	BNP/DRESDNER BANK (CS) (FRA;GER)	20/08/91 6.1b decision	Monetary intermediation	266 31/08/91
(44) IV/M.0129	DIGITAL/PHILIPS (USA;NET)	26/08/91 6.1b decision	Computer and related activities	235 10/09/91
(45) IV/M.0110	ABC/GENERALE DES EAUX/CANAL+/WH SMITH (USA;FRA;FRA;UKI)	02/09/91 6.1b decision / 10/09/91 6.1b decision	Radio and television activities	244 19/09/91
(46) IV/H.0130	DELTA AIRLINES/PAN AM (USA;USA)	13/09/91 6.1b decision	Air transport	289 07/11/91
(47) IV/H.0134	MANNESMANN/BOGE (GER;GER)	23/09/91 6.1b decision	Shock absorbers	265 11/10/91
(48) IV/H.0053	AEROSPATIALE/ALENIA/DE HAVILLAND (FRA;CAN;ITA)	03/06/91 7.2 decision / 12/06/91 6.1c decision / 02/10/91 8.3 decision	Manuf. of aircraft and spacecraft	334 05/12/91
(49) IV/M.0119	METALLGESELLSCHAFT/DYNAMIT NOBEL (GER;GER)	14/10/91 6.1b decision	Mining of metal ores	276 23/10/91
(50) IV/M.0122	PARIBAS/MTH (FRA;GER)	17/10/91 6.1b decision	Wholesale of machinery, equipment and supplies	277 24/10/91
(51) IV/H.0086	THOMSON/PILKINGTON (FRA;UKI)	23/10/91 6.1b decision	Electro-optical equipment for missiles	279 26/10/91
(52) IV/N.0137	BANK AMERICA/SECURITY PACIFIC (USA;USA)	24/10/91 6.1b decision	Monetary intermediation	289 07/11/91
(53) IV/M.0146	METALLGESELLSCHAFT/SAFIC ALCAN (GER;FRA)	08/11/91 6.1b decision	Trading of rubber	300 21/11/91
(54) IV/M.0141	UAP/TRANSATLANTIC/SUN LIFE (SAF;FRA;UKI)	11/11/91 6.1b decision	Insurance and pension funding, except compulsory social security	296 15/11/91
(55) IV/M.0156	CEREOL/CONTINENTALE ITALIANA (ITA;ITA)	27/11/91 6.1a decision	Manuf. of vegetable and animal oils and fats	? 11/01/92
(56) IV/H.0102	TNT/GD NET (AUL;FRA;GER;NET;SWE;CAN)	02/12/91 6.1b decision	Post and courier activities	322 13/12/91
(57) IV/H.0149	LUCAS/EATON (UKI;USA)	09/12/91 6.1b decision	Manuf. of parts and accessories for motor vehicles	328 17/12/91
(58) IV/H.0164	MANNESHANN/VDO (GER;GER)	13/12/91 6.1b decision	Electrical and electronic parts for vehicles	88 09/04/92

Chronological list of decisions taken between 21 September 1990 and 25 March 1993

Case	Title	Date of decision	Main market	OJ publication*
(59) IV/M.0121	INGERSOLL RAND/DRESSER (USA;USA)	18/12/91 6.1b decision	Pumps	86 07/04/92
(60) IV/M.0147	EUROCOM/RSGC (FRA;FRA)	18/12/91 6.1b decision	Advertising	332 21/12/91
(61) IV/M.0165	ALCATEL/AEG KABEL (FRA;GER)	26/11/91 7.2 decision	Manuf. of insulated wire and cable	
		18/12/91 6.1b decision		6 10/01/92
		18/12/91 Art. 9 dec., non-referral		
(62) IV/M.0113	COURTAULDS/SHIA (FRA;ITA;USA)	19/12/91 6.1b decision	Manuf. of man-made fibers	333 24/12/91
(63) IV/M.0138	CAMPSA (UKI;FRA,SPA,SPA,SPA,SPA)	19/12/91 6.1b decision	Retail sale of automotive fuel	334 28/12/91
(64) IV/M.0139	VIAG/BRUHL (GER;GER)	19/12/91 6.1b decision	Motor blocks and cylinder heads	333 24/12/91
(65) IV/M.0159	MEDIOBANCA/GENERALE (ITA;ITA)	19/12/91 6.1a decision	Insurance and pension funding, except compulsory social security	334 28/12/91
(66) IV/M.0167	GAMBOGI/COGEI (ITA;ITA)	19/12/91 6.1b decision	Building of complete constructions or parts	334 28/12/91
(67) IV/N.0176	SUNRISE (UKI;UKI;UKI;UKI;UKI)	13/01/92 6.1a decision	JV – Breakfast television franchise	18 24/01/92
(68) IV/M.0178	SAAB ERICSSON SPACE (SWE;SWE)	13/01/92 6.1b decision	Electronics for space applications	17 23/01/92
(69) IV/M.0152	VOLVO/ATLAS (SWE;SWE)	14/01/92 6.1b decision	Hydraulic mechanisms	17 23/01/92
(70) IV/M.0183	SCHWEIZER RUCK/ELVIA (SWI;SWI)	14/01/92 6.1b decision	Insurance and pension funding, except compulsory social security	27 04/02/92
(71) IV/H.0182	INCHCAPE/IEP (UKI;UKI)	21/01/92 6.1b decision	Car dealing	21 28/01/92
(72) IV/H.0133	ERICSSON/KOLBE (GER;USA)	22/01/92 6.1b decision	Telecommunications	27 04/02/92
(73) IV/M.0179	SPAR/DANSK SUPERMARKET (GER;DEN)	03/02/92 6.1b decision	Discount shops	29 06/02/92
(74) IV/M.0184	GRAND METROPOLITAN/CINZANO (UKI;ITA)	07/02/92 6.1b decision	Manuf. of beverages	47 21/02/92
(75) IV/M.0180	TARMAC/STEETLEY (UKI;UKI)	12/02/92 6.1b decision	Manuf. of bricks, tiles and construction products	50 25/02/92
		12/02/92 Art. 9 dec., referral		
		12/02/92 Art. 9 dec., non-referral		
(76) IV/N.0162	JAMES RIVER/RAYNE (USA;ITA;VIR)	13/02/92 6.1b decision	Manuf. of articles of paper and paperboard	43 18/02/92
(77) IV/M.0090	BSH/NESTLÉ/COKOLADOVNI (FRA;SWI)	17/02/92 6.1a decision	Chocolates and biscuits	47 21/02/92

No.	Case	Parties	Decision	Activity	Ref./Date
(78)	IV/M.0166	TORRAS/SARRIO (KUW;SPA;SPA)	24/02/92 6.1b decision	Manuf. of pulp, paper and paper products	58 05/03/92
(79)	IV/M.0187	IFINT/EXOR (LUX;FRA)	21/02/92 7.2 decision	Farm produce	
(80)	IV/H.0186	HENKEL/NOBEL (GER;SWE)	02/03/92 6.1b decision / 23/03/92 6.1b decision	Manuf. of detergents, cleaning and toilet preparations	88 09/04/92 / 96 15/04/92
(81)	IV/N.0189	GENERALI/BCKA (ITA;SPA)	06/04/92 6.1b decision	Insurance and pension funding, except compulsory social security	107 28/04/92
(82)	IV/M.0168	FLACHGLAS/VEGLA/JVC (UKI;FRA)	13/04/92 6.1a decision	Recycling	120 12/05/92
(83)	IV/M.0192	BANESTO/TOTTA (SPA;POR)	14/04/92 6.1b decision	Banking	107 28/04/92
(84)	IV/M.0202	THORN EMI/VIRGIN (UKI;UKI)	27/04/92 6.1b decision	Recorded music, music publishing	120 12/05/92
(85)	IV/H.0207	EUREKO (NET;DEN;SWE;UKI)	27/04/92 6.1a decision	Insurance (life and non-life)	113 01/05/92
(86)	IV/M.0126	ACCOR/WAGONS-LITS (FRA;BEL)	05/12/91 7.2 decision / 13/12/91 6.1c decision / 28/04/92 8.2 dec., with cond.	Hotels and restaurants	
(87)	IV/M.0188	HERBA/IRR (ITA;SPA;KUW)	28/04/92 6.1a decision	Rice dealers	204 21/07/92
(88)	IV/M.0197	SOLVAY/LAPORTE (BEL;UKI;UKI)	30/04/92 6.1a decision / 30/04/92 6.1b decision	Manuf. of chemicals and chemical products	120 12/05/92 / 165 02/07/92 / 165 02/07/92
(89)	IV/N.0210	HONDI/FRANTSCHACH (SAF;AUS)	12/05/92 6.1b decision	Manuf. of pulp, paper and paper products	124 16/05/92
(90)	IV/M.0218	EUCOM/DIGITAL (NET;GER)	18/05/92 6.1b decision	Freight management information system	140 03/06/92
(91)	IV/H.0213	HONG KONG+SHANGHAI BANK/MIDLAND BANK (HOK;UKI)	21/05/92 6.1b decision	Financial intermediation, except insurance and pension funding	157 24/06/92
(92)	IV/H.0224	VOLVO/LEX (SWE;UKI)	21/05/92 6.1b decision	Manuf. of cars and trucks; sale, maint., repair of motor vehicles	142 04/06/92
(93)	IV/M.0221	ABB/BREL (SWI;UKI)	26/05/92 6.1b decision	Railway rolling stock and equipment	142 04/06/92
(94)	IV/M.0220	BIBBY/FINANZAUTO (UKI;SPA)	29/06/92 6.1b decision	Sale and leasing of earth-moving equipment	275 23/10/92
(95)	IV/H.0236	ERICSSON/ASCOM (SWE;SWI)	08/07/92 6.1b decision	Manuf. of insulated wire and cable	201 08/08/92
(96)	IV/M.0241	EUROCARD/EUROCHEQUE-EUROPAY (BEL;BEL;BEL)	13/07/92 6.1a decision	Other financial intermediation	182 18/07/92
(97)	IV/M.0242	PROHODES/BRMC (FRA;FRA)	13/07/92 6.1b decision	Other wholesale; retail sale in non-specialized stores	232 10/09/02
(98)	IV/H.0229	THOMAS COOK/LTU/WEST LB (UKI;GER;GER;UKI)	14/07/92 6.1b decision	Travel agent	199 06/08/92
(99)	IV/M.0234	GECC/AVIS (USA;UKI)	15/07/92 6.1b decision	Vehicle fleet leasing for corporate customers	201 08/08/92

Chronological list of decisions taken between 21 September 1990 and 25 March 1993

Case	Title	Date of decision	Main market	OJ publication*
(100) IV/M.0190	NESTLÉ/PERRIER (SWI;FRA)	17/03/92 7.2 decision	Mineral water	
		17/06/92 7.4 decision		
		25/03/92 6.1c decision		
		22/07/92 8.2 dec., with cond.		356 05/12/92
(101) IV/M.0117	KOIPE-TABACALERA/ELOSUA (ITA;ITA;ITA;SPA)	28/07/92 6.1a decision	Manuf. of crude oil and fats	227 03/09/92
(102) IV/M.0160	ELF ATOCHEM/ROBM & HAAS (FRA;USA)	28/07/92 6.1b decision	Polymethyl methacrylate (PMMA)	201 08/08/92
(103) IV/M.0232	PEPSI CO/GENERAL MILLS (USA;USA)	05/08/92 6.1b decision	Snack foods	228 04/09/92
(104) IV/H.0198	PECHINEY/VIAG (FRA;GER)	10/08/92 6.1b decision	Manuf. of basic precious and non-ferrous metals	307 25/11/92
(105) IV/M.0206	RHONE-POULENC/SNIA (FRA;ITA)	10/08/92 6.1b decision	Polyamide fiber (used in the manufacture of carpets)	212 18/08/92
(106) IV/M.0249	NORTHERN TELECOM/MATRA COMMUNICATION (CAN;FRA)	10/08/92 6.1b decision	Telecommunications	240 19/09/92
(107) IV/M.0253	BTR/PIRELLI (UKI;ITA)	17/08/92 6.1b decision	Antivibration systems and automotive weatherscaling	265 14/10/92
(108) IV/M.0261	VOLVO/LEX (2) (SWE;UKI)	03/09/92 6.1b decision	Manuf. of cars and trucks, sales, maintenance	239 18/09/92
(109) IV/H.0235	ELF AQUITAINE THYSSEN/MINOL AG (FRA;GER;GER)	10/08/92 7.4 decision	Refinery and distribution of petrochemical products	232 10/09/92
(110) IV/M.0239	AVESTA/BRITISH STEEL/NCC (SWE;UKI;SWE)	04/09/92 6.1b decision	Manuf. of basic iron and steel and of ferro-alloys	258 07/10/92
(111) IV/M.0251	ALLIANZ/DKV (GER;GER)	10/09/92 6.1b decision	Insurance	258 07/10/92
(112) IV/H.0258	CCIE/GTE (UKI;USA;GER)	25/09/92 6.1b decision	Lamps and lighting products	258 07/10/92
(113) IV/H.0256	LINDE AG/FIAT ON CARRELLI ELEVATORI (GER;ITA)	28/09/92 6.1.b decision	Materials handling equipment	258 07/10/92
(114) IV/N.0263	ANOLD/JERONINO MARTINS (NET;POR)	29/09/92 6.1b decision	Main marketing	261 10/10/92
(115) IV/M.0214	DU PONT/ICI (USA;UKI)	20/05/92 7.2 decision	Manuf. of nylon fibers	
		02/06/92 6.1c decision		
		30/09/92 8.2 dec., with cond.		007 13/01/93

No.	Case	Parties	Decision	Sector	Ref
(116)	IV/H.0517	AIR FRANCE/SABENA (BEL;FRA)	05/10/92 6.1b decision	Air transport	272 21/10/92
(117)	IV/M.0265	VTG/BPTL (GER;GER)	12/10/92 6.1a decision	Transport	279 28/10/92
(118)	IV/M.0254	FORTIS/LA CAIXA (BEL;SPA)	05/11/92 6.1b decision	Insurance	297 13/11/92
(119)	IV/M.0222	MANNESMANN/HOESCH (GER;GER)	13/07/92 6.1c decision 13/07/92 Art. 9 dec., non-referral 12/11/92 8.2 dec., without cond.	Steel tubes	
(120)	IV/M.0266	RHONE POULENC CHIMIE/LYONNAISE DES EAUX (FRA;FRA)	26/11/92 6.1b decision	Industrial waste processing	319 05/12/92
(121)	IV/M.0259	BRITISH AIRWAYS/TAT (UKI;FRA)	27/11/92 6.1b decision	Air transport	326 11/12/92
(122)	IV/M.0277	DEL MONTE/ROYALE FOODS/ANGLO-AMERICAN (USA;SAF;SAF)	09/12/92 6.1b decision	Canned food	331 16/12/92
(123)	IV/M.0283	WASTE MANAGEMENT/SAE (FRA;UKI)	21/12/92 6.1b decision	Waste processing	010 15/01/93
(124)	IV/M.0289	PEPSI CO/KAS (USA;SPA)	21/12/92 6.1b decision	Non-alcoholic drinks	008 13/01/93
(125)	IV/M.0290	SEXTANT/BGT-VDO (FRA;GER;GER)	21/12/92 6.1b decision	Avionics – instruments for aircraft	009 14/01/93
(126)	IV/M.0238	SIEMENS/PHILIPS (GER;NET)	23/12/92 6.1c decision	Telecommunications and power cables	
(127)	IV/M.0296	CREDIT LYONNAIS/BFG BANK (FRA;GER)	11/01/93 6.1b decision	Banking and finance	045 17/02/93
(128)	IV/M.0291	KNP/BUHRMANN TETTERODE/VRG (NET;NET;NET)	18/01/93 6.1c decision	Paper	
(129)	IV/H.0293	PHILIPS/THOMSON/SAGEM (NET;FRA;FRA)	18/01/93 6.1a decision	Liquid crystals (for watches, computers, etc.)	022 26/01/93
(130)	IV/M.0301	TESCO/CATTEAU (UKI;FRA)	04/02/93 6.1b decision	Food and grocery retailing	045 17/02/93
(131)	IV/M.0304	VWAG (VOLKSWAGEN)/VAG UK (GER;UKI)	04/02/93 6.1b decision	Automotive products	038 12/02/93
(132)	IV/M.0299	SARA LEE/BP FOOD DIVISION (USA;UKI)	08/02/93 6.1b decision	Packaged heat	039 13/02/93
(133)	IV/M.0278	BRITISH AIRWAYS/DAN AIR (UKI;UKI)	17/02/93 6.1b decision	Air transport	068 11/03/93
(134)	IV/H.0216	CEA INDUSTRIE/FRANCE TELECOM/SGS-THOMSON (FRA;FRA;FRA;ITA)	22/02/93 6.1b decision	Semiconductors	068 11/03/93
(135)	IV/M.0286	ZUERICH/MNI (UKI;SWI)	08/03/93 7.4 decision	Insurance	
(136)	IV/M.0292	ERICSSON/HEWLETT PACKARD (SWE;USA)	12/03/93 6.1b decision	Telecommunication in informatics sector	
(137)	IV/M.0312	SANOFI/YVES ST-LAURENT (FRA;FRA)	15/03/93 6.1b decision	Perfumes and cosmetics	
(138)	IV/M.0272	NATRA/CAP 6EMINI 506ETI (FRA;FRA)	17/03/93 6.1b decision	Military information	
(139)	IV/M.0295	SITA-RPC/SCORI (FRA;FRA;FRA;FRA;FRA;FRA)	19/03/93 6.1b decision	Industrial waste	
(140)	IV/M.0300	KINGFISHER/DARTY (UKI)	22/03/93 6.1b decision	Retailing of brown goods + white goods	

Notes
17 Article 6.1a decisions have been taken between 21 September 1990 and 25 March
    1993
113 Article 6.1b decisions
 11 Article 6.1c decisions
  1 Article 9 decision, referral
  4 Article 9 decisions, non-referral
  6 Article 8.2 decisions, with conditions/obligations
  2 Article 8.2 decisions, without conditions/obligations
  1 Article 8.3 decision
  7 Article 7.2 decisions
  5 Article 7.4 decisions
Official Journal of the European Communities publication

Statistics

1 *Notifications*

Number of decisions

Decision	Number
6.1a dec., not in scope of reg	17
6.1b dec., no serious doubt	113
6.1c dec., serious doubt	11
8.2 dec., with cond./oblig.	6
8.2 dec., without cond./oblig.	2
8.3 dec., prohibition	1
9 dec., referral to MS	1
9 dec., non-referral to MS	4
7.2 dec., suspension of consent	7
7.4 dec., derogation to suspension	5
Total	167

Miscellaneous

Number of notifications terminated	141
actually in phase I	8
actually in phase II	1
Number of notifications received	150
Number of Article 9 letters received	5

2 *Prenotifications and backup cases*

Classification according to the conclusion

Code	Title	Number
214	Not notif., not a concent.	52
215	Not notif., aborted	29
212	Not notif., <250 million	22
211	Not notif., <5 billion	20
23	Pending for developments	14
213	Not notif., 2/3 rule	13
219	Not notif., miscellaneous	7
20	Before regulation	5
29	Closure of back-up case	1
Total		163

NACE codes

11: extraction of crude petroleum and natural gas; service activities incidental to oil and gas extraction excluding surveying

32: manufacture of radio, television and communication equipment and apparatus

33: manufacture of medical precision and optical instruments, watches and clocks

50: sale, maintenance and repair of motor vehicles and motorcycles, retail sale and automotive fuel

51: wholesale trade and commission trade except of motor vehicles and motorcycles

52: retail trade, except of motor vehicles and motorcycles; repair of personal and household goods

63: supporting and auxiliary transport activities of travel agencies

71: renting of machinery and equipment without operator and of personal and household goods

3 *Other classifications*

Classification according to the type of concentration

Code	Type of concentration	Notif.
JVEN	Joint venture/control	70
AMAJ	Acquisition of majority	61
MERG	Merger	6
AMIN	Acquisition of minority	2
CBID	Contested bid	3
ABID	Agreed bid	6
SPLT	Split up/demerger/divestment	1
HCAS	Hypothetical case	0
CSHR	Cross-shareholding	1
Total		150

Classification according to the categories of products

Code description	Notif.
10 Mining of coal and lignite; extraction of peat	0
11 Extraction of crude petroleum and natural gas	3
12 Mining of uranium and thorium ores	0
13 Mining of metal ores	1
15 Manuf. of food products and beverages	15
17 Manuf. of textiles	0
21 Manuf. of pulp, paper and paper products	6
22 Publishing, printing and reproduction of recorded media	1
23 Manuf. of coke, refined petroleum products and nuclear fuel	4
24 Manuf. of chemicals and chemical products	14
25 Manuf. of rubber and plastic products	1
26 Manuf. of other non-metallic mineral products	1
27 Manuf. of basic metals	5
28 Manuf. of fabricated metal products, except machinery and equipment	2
29 Manuf. of machinery and equipment nec	6

Classification according to the categories of products

Code description	Notif.
30 Manuf. of office machinery and computers	4
31 Manuf. of electrical machinery and apparatus nec	7
32 Manuf. of radio, television and communication equipment	6
33 Manuf. of medical instruments, watches and clocks	2
34 Manuf. of motor vehicles, trailers and semi-trailers	12
35 Manuf. of other transport equipment	6
36 Manuf. of furniture; manufacturing nec	0
37 Recycling	5
40 Electricity, gas, steam and hot water supply	0
41 Collection, purification and distribution of water	0
45 Construction	3
50 Sale, maintenance and repair of motor vehicles	5
51 Wholesale trade and commission trade	8
52 Retail trade, except of motor vehicles and motorcycles; repair of buildings and civil engineering constructions	9
55 Hotels and restaurants	3
60 Land transport; transport via pipelines	0
61 Water transport	1
62 Air transport	4
63 Supporting and auxiliary transport activities of travel agencies	1
64 Post and telecommunications	3
65 Financial intermediation, except insurance and pension funding	7
66 Insurance and pension funding, except compulsory social security	8
70 Real estate activities	1
71 Renting of machinery and equipment without operator	2
72 Computer and related activities	8
74 Other business activities	3
75 Public administration and defence; compulsory social security	2

92	Recreational, cultural and sporting activities	3
93	Other service activities	1
Total		172

Classification of the companies according to their origin

Code	Country	Notif.
FRA	France	77
UKI	United Kingdom	59
GER	Germany	51
USA	USA	35
ITA	Italy	24
SPA	Spain	20
NET	Netherlands	13
SWE	Sweden	17
BEL	Belgium	11
SWI	Switzerland	13
JAP	Japan	5
DEN	Denmark	2
POR	Portugal	4
CAN	Canada	5
SAF	South Africa	4
FIN	Finland	1
LUX	Luxemburg	1
IRL	Ireland	1
KUW	Kuwait	2
HOK	Hong Kong	2
GRE	Greece	0
AUS	Austria	1
AUL	Australia	1
VIR	Virgin Islands	1
NZL	New Zealand	0
NOR	Norway	0
IND	Indonesia	0
HUN	Hungary	0
ARG	Argentina	0
Total		351

Classification according to cross-border versus non-cross-border operations (each country)

	Notif.
Non-cross-border operations	39
Cross-border operations	111
Total	150

Classification according to cross-border versus non-cross-border operations (CE12 = one country)

	Notif.
Non-cross-border operations	95
Cross-border operations	55
Total	150

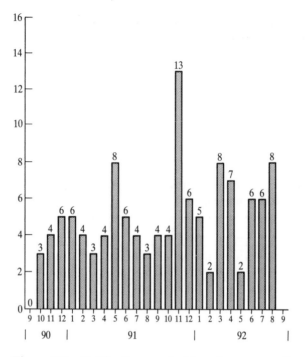

Figure AI.1 Notifications received (number per month).

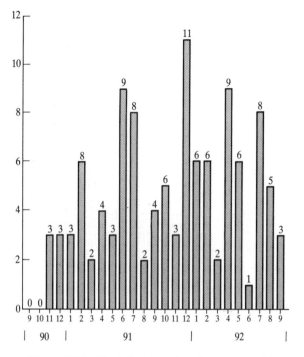

Figure AI.2 Final decisions (number per month).

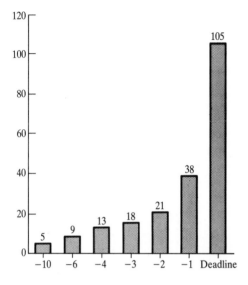

Figure AI.3 Timeliness of final decision (phase I cases, cumulative graph). Decisions taken X days before deadline.

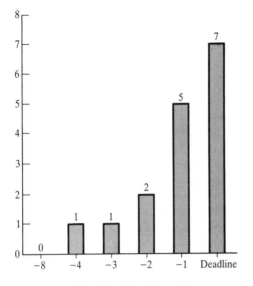

Figure AI.4 Timeliness of final decision (phase II cases, cumulative graph). Decisions taken X weeks before deadline.

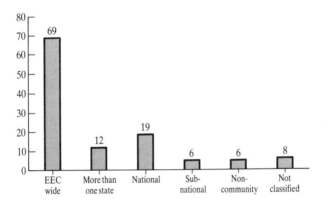

Figure AI.5 Geographic market definition (as set out in the decisions).

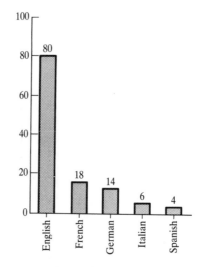

Figure AI.6 Language of procedure (number of cases treated in ...).

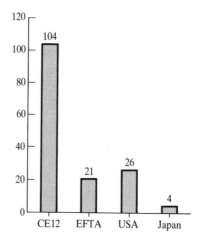

Figure AI.7 Nationality breakdown (number of cases involving ...).

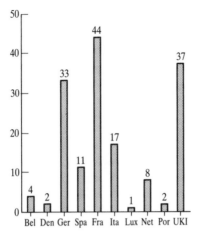

Figure AI.8 CE12 nationality breakdown (number of cases involving . . .).

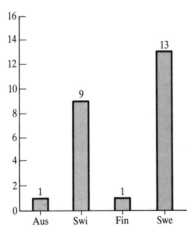

Figure AI.9 EFTA nationality breakdown (number of cases involving . . .).

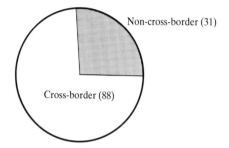

Figure AI.10   Cross-border cases (all countries).

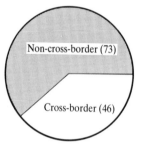

Figure AI.11   Cross-border cases (CE12 = one country).

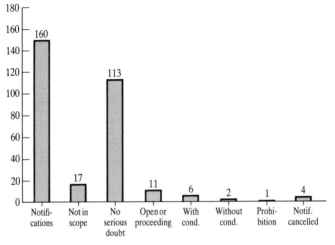

Figure AI.12 Notifications and decisions.

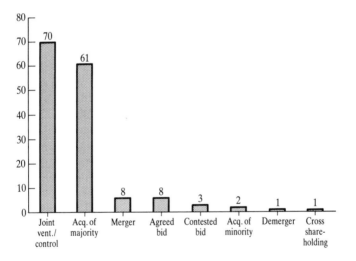

Figure AI.13 Type of concentration.

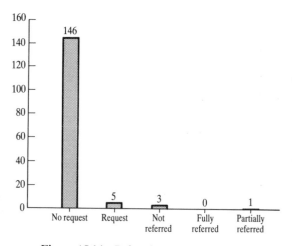

Figure AI.14 Referral to member states.

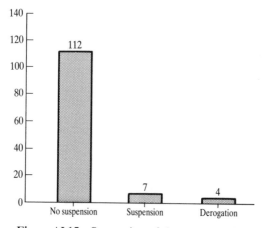

Figure AI.15 Suspension of the concentration.

Appendix II

COUNCIL REGULATION (EEC) No 4064/89
of 21 December 1989
on the control of concentrations between undertakings

THE COUNCIL OF THE EUROPEAN COMMUNITIES,

Having regard to the Treaty establishing the European Economic Community, and in particular Articles 87 and 235 thereof,

Having regard to the proposal from the Commission ('),

Having regard to the opinion of the European Parliament (²),

Having regard to the opinion of the Economic and Social Committee (³),

(1) Whereas, for the achievement of the aims of the Treaty establishing the European Economic Community, Article 3 (f) gives the Community the objective of instituting 'a system ensuring that competition in the common market is not distorted';

(2) Whereas this system is essential for the achievement of the internal market by 1992 and its further development;

(3) Whereas the dismantling of internal frontiers is resulting and will continue to result in major corporate reorganizations in the Community, particularly in the form of concentrations;

(4) Whereas such a development must be welcomed as being in line with the requirements of dynamic competition and capable of increasing the competitiveness of European industry, improving the conditions of growth and raising the standard of living in the Community;

(5) Whereas, however, it must be ensured that the process of reorganization does not result in lasting damage to competition; whereas Community law must therefore include provisions governing those concentrations which may significantly impede effective competition in the common market or in a substantial part of it;

(6) Whereas Articles 85 and 86, while applicable, according to the case-law of the Court of Justice, to certain concentrations, are not, however, sufficient to control all operations which may prove to be

incompatible with the system of undistorted competition envisaged in the Treaty;

(7) Whereas a new legal instrument should therefore be created in the form of a Regulation to permit effective control of all concentrations from the point of view of their effect on the structure of competition in the Community and to be the only instrument applicable to such concentrations;

(8) Whereas this Regulation should therefore be based not only on Article 87 but, principally, on Article 235 of the Treaty, under which the Community may give itself the additional powers of action necessary for the attainment of its objectives, including with regard to concentrations on the markets for agricultural products listed in Annex II to the Treaty;

(9) Whereas the provisions to be adopted in this Regulation should apply to significant structural changes the impact of which on the market goes beyond the national borders of any one Member State;

(10) Whereas the scope of application of this Regulation should therefore be defined according to the geographical area of activity of the undertakings concerned and be limited by quantitative thresholds in order to cover those concentrations which have a Community dimension; whereas, at the end of an initial phase of the application of this Regulation, these thresholds should be reviewed in the light of the experience gained;

(11) Whereas a concentration with a Community dimension exists where the combined aggregate turnover of the undertakings concerned exceeds given levels worldwide and within the Community and where at least two of the undertakings concerned have their sole or main fields of activities in different Member States or where, although the undertakings in question act mainly in one and the same Member State, at least one of them has substantial operations in at least one other Member State; whereas that is also the case where the concentrations are effected by undertakings which do not have their principal fields of activities in the Community but which have substantial operations there;

(12) Whereas the arrangements to be introduced for the control of concentrations should, without prejudice to Article 90 (2) of the Treaty, respect the principle of non-discrimination between the public and the

(') OJ No C 130, 19. 5. 1988, p. 4.
(²) OJ No C 309, 5. 12. 1988, p. 55.
(³) OJ No C 208, 8. 8. 1988, p. 11.

private sectors ; whereas, in the public sector, calculation of the turnover of an undertaking concerned in a concentration needs, therefore, to take account of undertakings making up an economic unit with an independent power of decision, irrespective of the way in which their capital is held or of the rules of administrative supervision applicable to them ;

(13) Whereas it is necessary to establish whether concentrations with a Community dimension are compatible or not with the common market from the point of view of the need to maintain and develop effective competition in the common market ; whereas, in so doing, the Commission must place its appraisal within the general framework of the achievement of the fundamental objectives referred to in Article 2 of the Treaty, including that of strengthening the Community's economic and social cohesion, referred to in Article 130a ;

(14) Whereas this Regulation should establish the principle that a concentration with a Community dimension which creates or strengthens a position as a result of which effective competition in the common market or in a substantial part of it is significantly impeded is to be declared incompatible with the common market ;

(15) Whereas concentrations which, by reason of the limited market share of the undertakings concerned, are not liable to impede effective competition may be presumed to be compatible with the common market ; whereas, without prejudice to Articles 85 and 86 of the Treaty, an indication to this effect exists, in particular, where the market share of the undertakings concerned does not exceed 25 % either in the common market or in a substantial part of it ;

(16) Whereas the Commission should have the task of taking all the decisions necessary to establish whether or not concentrations with a Community dimension are compatible with the common market, as well as decisions designed to restore effective competition ;

(17) Whereas to ensure effective control undertakings should be obliged to give prior notification of concentrations with a Community dimension and provision should be made for the suspension of concentrations for a limited period, and for the possibility of extending or waiving a suspension where necessary ; whereas in the interests of legal certainty the validity of transactions must nevertheless be protected as much as necessary ;

(18) Whereas a period within which the Commission must initiate proceedings in respect of a notified concentration and periods within which it must give a final decision on the compatibility or incompatibility with the common market of a notified concentration should be laid down ;

(19) Whereas the undertakings concerned must be afforded the right to be heard by the Commission when proceedings have been initiated ; whereas the members of the management and supervisory bodies and the recognized representatives of the employees of the undertakings concerned, and third parties showing a legitimate interest, must also be given the opportunity to be heard ;

(20) Whereas the Commission should act in close and constant liaison with the competent authorities of the Member States from which it obtains comments and information ;

(21) Whereas, for the purposes of this Regulation, and in accordance with the case-law of the Court of Justice, the Commission must be afforded the assistance of the Member States and must also be empowered to require information to be given and to carry out the necessary investigations in order to appraise concentrations ;

(22) Whereas compliance with this Regulation must be enforceable by means of fines and periodic penalty payments ; whereas the Court of Justice should be given unlimited jurisdiction in that regard pursuant to Article 172 of the Treaty ;

(23) Whereas it is appropriate to define the concept of concentration in such a manner as to cover only operations bringing about a lasting change in the structure of the undertakings concerned ; whereas it is therefore necessary to exclude from the scope of this Regulation those operations which have as their object or effect the coordination of the competitive behaviour of undertakings which remain independent, since such operations fall to be examined under the appropriate provisions of the Regulations implementing Articles 85 and 86 of the Treaty ; whereas it is appropriate to make this distinction specifically in the case of the creation of joint ventures ;

(24) Whereas there is no coordination of competitive behaviour within the meaning of this Regulation where two or more undertakings agree to acquire jointly control of one or more other undertakings with the object and effect of sharing amongst themselves such undertakings or their assets ;

(25) Whereas this Regulation should still apply where the undertakings concerned accept restrictions directly related and necessary to the implementation of the concentration ;

(26) Whereas the Commission should be given exclusive competence to apply this Regulation, subject to review by the Court of Justice ;

(27) Whereas the Member States may not apply their national legislation on competition to concentrations with a Community dimension, unless this Regulation makes provision therefor ; whereas the relevant powers of national authorities should be limited to cases where, failing intervention by the Commission, effective competition is likely to be significantly impeded within the territory of a Member State and where the competition interests of that Member State cannot be sufficiently protected otherwise by this Regulation ; whereas the Member States concerned must act promptly in such cases ; whereas this Regulation cannot, because of the diversity of national law, fix a single deadline for the adoption of remedies ;

(28) Whereas, furthermore, the exclusive application of this Regulation to concentrations with a Community dimension is without prejudice to Article 223 of the Treaty, and does not prevent the Member States from taking appropriate measures to protect legitimate interests other than those pursued by this Regulation, provided that such measures are compatible with the general principles and other provisions of Community law ;

(29) Whereas concentrations not covered by this Regulation come, in principle, within the jurisdiction of the Member States ; whereas, however, the Commission should have the power to act, at the request of a Member State concerned, in cases where effective competition could be significantly impeded within that Member State's territory ;

(30) Whereas the conditions in which concentrations involving Community undertakings are carried out in non-member countries should be observed, and provision should be made for the possibility of the Council giving the Commission an appropriate mandate for negotiation with a view to obtaining non-discriminatory treatment for Community undertakings ;

(31) Whereas this Regulation in no way detracts from the collective rights of employees as recognized in the undertakings concerned,

HAS ADOPTED THIS REGULATION :

Article 1

Scope

1.   Without prejudice to Article 22 this Regulation shall apply to all concentrations with a Community dimension as defined in paragraph 2.

2.   For the purposes of this Regulation, a concentration has a Community dimension where :

(a) the combined aggregate worldwide turnover of all the undertakings concerned is more than ECU 5 000 million ; and

(b) the aggregate Community-wide turnover of each of at least two of the undertakings concerned is more than ECU 250 million,

unless each of the undertakings concerned achieves more than two-thirds of its aggregate Community-wide turnover within one and the same Member State.

3.   The thresholds laid down in paragraph 2 will be reviewed before the end of the fourth year following that of the adoption of this Regulation by the Council acting by a qualified majority on a proposal from the Commission.

Article 2

Appraisal of concentrations

1.   Concentrations within the scope of this Regulation shall be appraised in accordance with the following provisions with a view to establishing whether or not they are compatible with the common market.

In making this appraisal, the Commission shall take into account :

(a) the need to maintain and develop effective competition within the common market in view of, among other things, the structure of all the markets concerned and the actual or potential competition from undertakings located either within or outwith the Community ;

(b) the market position of the undertakings concerned and their economic and financial power, the alternatives available to suppliers and users, their access to supplies or markets, any legal or other barriers to entry, supply and demand trends for the relevant goods and services, the interests of the intermediate and ultimate consumers, and the development of technical and economic progress provided that it is to consumers' advantage and does not form an obstacle to competition.

2.   A concentration which does not create or strengthen a dominant position as a result of which effective competition would be significantly impeded in the common market or in a substantial part of it shall be declared compatible with the common market.

3.   A concentration which creates or strengthens a dominant position as a result of which effective competition would be significantly impeded in the common market or in a substantial part of it shall be declared incompatible with the common market.

Article 3

Definition of concentration

1.   A concentration shall be deemed to arise where :

(a) two or more previously independent undertakings merge, or

(b) — one or more persons already controlling at least one undertaking, or

— one or more undertakings

acquire, whether by purchase of securities or assets, by contract or by any other means, direct or indirect control of the whole or parts of one or more other undertakings.

2.   An operation, including the creation of a joint venture, which has as its object or effect the coordination of the competitive behaviour of undertakings which remain independent shall not constitute a concentration within the meaning of paragraph 1 (b).

The creation of a joint venture performing on a lasting basis all the functions of an autonomous economic entity, which does not give rise to coordination of the competitive behaviour of the parties amongst themselves or between them and the joint venture, shall constitute a concentration within the meaning of paragraph 1 (b).

3.   For the purposes of this Regulation, control shall be constituted by rights, contracts or any other means which, either separately or in combination and having regard to the considerations of fact or law involved, confer the possibility of exercising decisive influence on an undertaking, in particular by :

(a) ownership or the right to use all or part of the assets of an undertaking ;

(b) rights or contracts which confer decisive influence on the composition, voting or decisions of the organs of an undertaking.

4.   Control is acquired by persons or undertakings which :

(a) are holders of the rights or entitled to rights under the contracts concerned ; or

(b) while not being holders of such rights or entitled to rights under such contracts, have the power to exercise the rights deriving therefrom.

5.   A concentration shall not be deemed to arise where :

(a) credit institutions or other financial institutions or insurance companies, the normal activities of which include transactions and dealing in securities for their own account or for the account of others, hold on a temporary basis securities which they have acquired in an undertaking with a view to reselling them, provided that they do not exercise voting rights in respect of those securities with a view to determining the competitive behaviour of that undertaking or provided that they exercise such voting rights only with a view to preparing the disposal of all or part of that undertaking or of its assets or the disposal of those securities and that any such disposal takes place within one year of the date of acquisition ; that period may be extended by the Commission on request where such institutions or companies can show that the disposal was not reasonably possible within the period set ;

(b) control is acquired by an office-holder according to the law of a Member State relating to liquidation, winding up, insolvency, cessation of payments, compositions or analogous proceedings ;

(c) the operations referred to in paragraph 1 (b) are carried out by the financial holding companies referred to in Article 5 (3) of the Fourth Council Directive 78/660/EEC of 25 July 1978 on the annual accounts of certain types of companies (¹), as last amended by Directive 84/569/EEC (²), provided however that the voting rights in respect of the holding are exercised, in particular in relation to the appointment of members of the management and supervisory bodies of the undertakings in which they have holdings, only to maintain the full value of those investments and not to determine directly or indirectly the competitive conduct of those undertakings.

Article 4

Prior notification of concentrations

1.   Concentrations with a Community dimension defined in this Regulation shall be notified to the Commission not more than one week after the conclusion of the agreement, or the announcement of the public bid, or the acquisition of a controlling interest. That week shall begin when the first of those events occurs.

2.   A concentration which consists of a merger within the meaning of Article 3 (1) (a) or in the acquisition of joint control within the meaning of Article 3 (1) (b) shall be notified jointly by the parties to the merger or by those acquiring joint control as the case may be. In all other cases, the notification shall be effected by the person or undertaking acquiring control of the whole or parts of one or more undertakings.

(¹) OJ No L 222, 14. 8. 1978, p. 11.
(²) OJ No L 314, 4. 12. 1984, p. 28.

3. Where the Commission finds that a notified concentration falls within the scope of this Regulation, it shall publish the fact of the notification, at the same time indicating the names of the parties, the nature of the concentration and the economic sectors involved. The Commission shall take account of the legitimate interest of undertakings in the protection of their business secrets.

Article 5

Calculation of turnover

1. Aggregate turnover within the meaning of Article 1 (2) shall comprise the amounts derived by the undertakings concerned in the preceding financial year from the sale of products and the provision of services falling within the undertakings' ordinary activities after deduction of sales rebates and of value added tax and other taxes directly related to turnover. The aggregate turnover of an undertaking concerned shall not include the sale of products or the provision of services between any of the undertakings referred to in paragraph 4.

Turnover, in the Community or in a Member State, shall comprise products sold and services provided to undertakings or consumers, in the Community or in that Member State as the case may be.

2. By way of derogation from paragraph 1, where the concentration consists in the acquisition of parts, whether or not constituted as legal entities, of one or more undertakings, only the turnover relating to the parts which are the subject of the transaction shall be taken into account with regard to the seller or sellers.

However, two or more transactions within the meaning of the first subparagraph which take place within a two-year period between the same persons or undertakings shall be treated as one and the same concentration arising on the date of the last transaction.

3. In place of turnover the following shall be used :

(a) for credit institutions and other financial institutions, as regards Article 1 (2) (a), one-tenth of their total assets.

As regards Article 1 (2) (b) and the final part of Article 1 (2), total Community-wide turnover shall be replaced by one-tenth of total assets multiplied by the ratio between loans and advances to credit institutions and customers in transactions with Community residents and the total sum of those loans and advances.

As regards the final part of Article 1 (2), total turnover within one Member State shall be replaced by one-tenth of total assets multiplied by the ratio between loans and advances to credit institutions and custo-

mers in transactions with residents of that Member State and the total sum of those loans and advances ;

(b) for insurance undertakings, the value of gross premiums written which shall comprise all amounts received and receivable in respect of insurance contracts issued by or on behalf of the insurance undertakings, including also outgoing reinsurance premiums, and after deduction of taxes and parafiscal contributions or levies charged by reference to the amounts of individual premiums or the total volume of premiums ; as regards Article 1 (2) (b) and the final part of Article 1 (2), gross premiums received from Community residents and from residents of one Member State respectively shall be taken into account.

4. Without prejudice to paragraph 2, the aggregate turnover of an undertaking concerned within the meaning of Article 1 (2) shall be calculated by adding together the respective turnovers of the following :

(a) the undertaking concerned ;

(b) those undertakings in which the undertaking concerned, directly or indirectly :

— owns more than half the capital or business assets, or

— has the power to exercise more than half the voting rights, or

— has the power to appoint more than half the members of the supervisory board, the administrative board or bodies legally representing the undertakings, or

— has the right to manage the undertakings' affairs ;

(c) those undertakings which have in the undertaking concerned the rights or powers listed in (b) ;

(d) those undertakings in which an undertaking as referred to in (c) has the rights or powers listed in (b) ;

(e) those undertakings in which two or more undertakings as referred to in (a) to (d) jointly have the rights or powers listed in (b).

5. Where undertakings concerned by the concentration jointly have the rights or powers listed in paragraph 4 (b), in calculating the aggregate turnover of the undertakings concerned for the purposes of Article 1 (2) :

(a) no account shall be taken of the turnover resulting from the sale of products or the provision of services between the joint undertaking and each of the undertakings concerned or any other undertaking connected with any one of them, as set out in paragraph 4 (b) to (e) ;

(b) account shall be taken of the turnover resulting from the sale of products and the provision of services between the joint undertaking and any third undertakings. This turnover shall be apportioned equally amongst the undertakings concerned.

Article 6

Examination of the notification and initiation of proceedings

1.   The Commission shall examine the notification as soon as it is received.

(a) Where it concludes that the concentration notified does not fall within the scope of this Regulation, it shall record that finding by means of a decision.

(b) Where it finds that the concentration notified, although falling within the scope of this Regulation, does not raise serious doubts as to its compatibility with the common market, it shall decide not to oppose it and shall declare that it is compatible with the common market.

(c) If, on the other hand, it finds that the concentration notified falls within the scope of this Regulation and raises serious doubts as to its compatibility with the common market, it shall decide to initiate proceedings.

2.   The Commission shall notify its decision to the undertakings concerned and the competent authorities of the Member States without delay.

Article 7

Suspension of concentrations

1.   For the purposes of paragraph 2 a concentration as defined in Article 1 shall not be put into effect either before its notification or within the first three weeks following its notification.

2.   Where the Commission, following a preliminary examination of the notification within the period provided for in paragraph 1, finds it necessary in order to ensure the full effectiveness of any decision taken later pursuant to Article 8 (3) and (4), it may decide on its own initiative to continue the suspension of a concentration in whole or in part until it takes a final decision, or to take other interim measures to that effect.

3.   Paragraphs 1 and 2 shall not prevent the implementation of a public bid which has been notified to the Commission in accordance with Article 4 (1), provided that the acquirer does not exercise the voting rights attached to the securities in question or does so only to maintain the full value of those investments and on the basis of a derogation granted by the Commission under paragraph 4.

4.   The Commission may, on request, grant a derogation from the obligations imposed in paragraphs 1, 2 or 3 in order to prevent serious damage to one or more undertakings concerned by a concentration or to a third party. That derogation may be made subject to conditions and obligations in order to ensure conditions of effective competition. A derogation may be applied for and granted at any time, even before notification or after the transaction.

5.   The validity of any transaction carried out in contravention of paragraph 1 or 2 shall be dependent on a decision pursuant to Article 6 (1) (b) or Article 8 (2) or (3) or on a presumption pursuant to Article 10 (6).

This Article shall, however, have no effect on the validity of transactions in securities including those convertible into other securities admitted to trading on a market which is regulated and supervised by authorities recognized by public bodies, operates regularly and is accessible directly or indirectly to the public, unless the buyer and seller knew or ought to have known that the transaction was carried out in contravention of paragraph 1 or 2.

Article 8

Powers of decision of the Commission

1.   Without prejudice to Article 9, all proceedings initiated pursuant to Article 6 (1) (c) shall be closed by means of a decision as provided for in paragraphs 2 to 5.

2.   Where the Commission finds that, following modification by the undertakings concerned if necessary, a notified concentration fulfils the criterion laid down in Article 2 (2), it shall issue a decision declaring the concentration compatible with the common market.

It may attach to its decision conditions and obligations intended to ensure that the undertakings concerned comply with the commitments they have entered into *vis-à-vis* the Commission with a view to modifying the original concentration plan. The decision declaring the concentration compatible shall also cover restrictions directly related and necessary to the implementation of the concentration.

3.   Where the Commission finds that a concentration fulfils the criterion laid down in Article 2 (3), it shall issue a decision declaring that the concentration is incompatible with the common market.

4.   Where a concentration has already been implemented, the Commission may, in a decision pursuant to paragraph 3 or by separate decision, require the undertakings or assets brought together to be separated or the cessation of joint control or any other action that may be appropriate in order to restore conditions of effective competition.

5. The Commission may revoke the decision it has taken pursuant to paragraph 2 where :

(a) the declaration of compatibility is based on incorrect information for which one of the undertakings is responsible or where it has been obtained by deceit ; or

(b) the undertakings concerned commit a breach of an obligation attached to the decision.

6. In the cases referred to in paragraph 5, the Commission may take a decision under paragraph 3, without being bound by the deadline referred to in Article 10 (3).

Article 9

Referral to the competent authorities of the Member States

1. The Commission may, by means of a decision notified without delay to the undertakings concerned and the competent authorities of the other Member States, refer a notified concentration to the competent authorities of the Member State concerned in the following circumstances.

2. Within three weeks of the date of receipt of the copy of the notification a Member State may inform the Commission, which shall inform the undertakings concerned, that a concentration threatens to create or to strengthen a dominant position as a result of which effective competition would be significantly impeded on a market, within that Member State, which presents all the characteristics of a destinct market, be it a substantial part of the common market or not.

3. If the Commission considers that, having regard to the market for the products or services in question and the geographical reference market within the meaning of paragraph 7, there is such a distinct market and that such a threat exists, either :

(a) it shall itself deal with the case in order to maintain or restore effective competition on the market concerned ; or

(b) it shall refer the case to the competent authorities of the Member State concerned with a view to the application of that State's national competition law.

If, however, the Commission considers that such a distinct market or threat does not exist it shall adopt a decision to that effect which it shall address to the Member State concerned.

4. A decision to refer or not to refer pursuant to paragraph 3 shall be taken :

(a) as a general rule within the six-week period provided for in Article 10 (1), second subparagraph, where the Commission, pursuant to Article 6 (1) (b), has not initiated proceedings ; or

(b) within three months at most of the notification of the concentration concerned where the Commission has initiated proceedings under Article 6 (1) (c), without

taking the preparatory steps in order to adopt the necessary measures under Article 8 (2), second subparagraph, (3) or (4) to maintain or restore effective competition on the market concerned.

5. If within the three months referred to in paragraph 4 (b) the Commission, despite a reminder from the Member State concerned, has not taken a decision on referral in accordance with paragraph 3 nor has taken the preparatory steps referred to in paragraph 4 (b), it shall be deemed to have taken a decision to refer the case to the Member State concerned in accordance with paragraph 3 (b).

6. The publication of any report or the announcement of the findings of the examination of the concentration by the competent authority of the Member State concerned shall be effected not more than four months after the Commission's referral.

7. The geographical reference market shall consist of the area in which the undertakings concerned are involved in the supply and demand of products or services, in which the conditions of competition are sufficiently homogeneous and which can be distinguished from neighbouring areas because, in particular, conditions of competition are appreciably different in those areas. This assessment should take account in particular of the nature and characteristics of the products or services concerned, of the existence of entry barriers of of consumer preferences, of appreciable differences of the undertakings' market shares between the area concerned and neighbouring areas or of substantial price differences.

8. In applying the provisions of this Article, the Member State concerned may take only the measures strictly necessary to safeguard or restore effective competition on the market concerned.

9. In accordance with the relevant provisions of the Treaty, any Member State may appeal to the Court of Justice, and in particular request the application of Article 186, for the purpose of applying its national competition law.

10. This Article will be reviewed before the end of the fourth year following that of the adoption of this Regulation.

Article 10

Time limits for initiating proceedings and for decisions

1. The decisions referred to in Article 6 (1) must be taken within one month at most. That period shall begin on the day following that of the receipt of a notification or, if the information to be supplied with the notification is incomplete, on the day following that of the receipt of the complete information.

That period shall be increased to six weeks if the Commission receives a request from a Member State in accordance with Article 9 (2).

2. Decisions taken pursuant to Article 8 (2) concerning notified concentrations must be taken as soon as it appears that the serious doubts referred to in Article 6 (1) (c) have been removed, particularly as a result of modifications made by the undertakings concerned, and at the latest by the deadline laid down in paragraph 3.

3. Without prejudice to Article 8 (6), decisions taken pursuant to Article 8 (3) concerning notified concentrations must be taken within not more than four months of the date on which proceedings are initiated.

4. The period set by paragraph 3 shall exceptionally be suspended where, owing to circumstances for which one of the undertakings involved in the concentration is responsible, the Commission has had to request information by decision pursuant to Article 11 or to order an investigation by decision pursuant to Article 13.

5. Where the Court of Justice gives a Judgement which annuls the whole or part of a Commission decision taken under this Regulation, the periods laid down in this Regulation shall start again from the date of the Judgement.

6. Where the Commission has not taken a decision in accordance with Article 6 (1) (b) or (c) or Article 8 (2) or (3) within the deadlines set in paragraphs 1 and 3 respectively, the concentration shall be deemed to have been declared compatible with the common market, without prejudice to Article 9.

Article 11

Requests for information

1. In carrying out the duties assigned to it by this Regulation, the Commission may obtain all necessary information from the Governments and comptent authorities of the Member States, from the persons referred to in Article 3 (1) (b), and from undertakings and associations of undertakings.

2. When sending a request for information to a person, an undertaking or an association of undertakings, the Commission shall at the same time send a copy of the request to the competent authority of the Member State within the territory of which the residence of the person or the seat of the undertaking or association of undertakings is situated.

3. In its request the Commission shall state the legal basis and the purpose of the request and also the penalties provided for in Article 14 (1) (c) for supplying incorrect information.

4. The information requested shall be provided, in the case of undertakings, by their owners or their representatives and, in the case of legal persons, companies or firms,

or of associations having no legal personality, by the persons authorized to represent them by law or by their statutes.

5. Where a person, an undertaking or an association of undertakings does not provide the information requested within the period fixed by the Commission or provides incomplete information, the Commission shall by decision require the information to be provided. The decision shall specify what information is required, fix an appropriate period within which it is to be supplied and state the penalties provided for in Articles 14 (1) (c) and 15 (1) (a) and the right to have the decision reviewed by the Court of Justice.

6. The Commission shall at the same time send a copy of its decision to the competent authority of the Member State within the territory of which the residence of the person or the seat of the undertaking or association of undertakings is situated.

Article 12

Investigations by the authorities of the Member States

1. At the request of the Commission, the competent authorities of the Member States shall undertake the investigations which the Commission considers to be necessary under Article 13 (1), or which it has ordered by decision pursuant to Article 13 (3). The officials of the competent authorities of the Member States responsible for conducting those investigations shall exercise their powers upon production of an authorization in writing issued by the competent authority of the Member State within the territory of which the investigation is to be carried out. Such authorization shall specify the subject matter and purpose of the investigation.

2. If so requested by the Commission or by the competent authority of the Member State within the territory of which the investigation is to be carried out, officials of the Commission may assist the officials of that authority in carrying out their duties.

Article 13

Investigative powers of the Commission

1. In carrying out the duties assigned to it by this Regulation, the Commission may undertake all necessary investigations into undertakings and associations of undertakings.

To that end the officials authorized by the Commission shall be empowered :

(a) to examine the books and other business records ;

(b) to take or demand copies of or extracts from the books and business records ;

(c) to ask for oral explanations on the spot ;

(d) to enter any premises, land and means of transport of undertakings.

2.   The officials of the Commission authorized to carry out the investigations shall exercise their powers on production of an authorization in writing specifying the subject matter and purpose of the investigation and the penalties provided for in Article 14 (1) (d) in cases where production of the required books or other business records is incomplete. In good time before the investigation, the Commission shall inform, in writing, the competent authority of the Member State within the territory of which the investigation is to be carried out of the investigation and of the identities of the authorized officials.

3.   Undertakings and associations of undertakings shall submit to investigations ordered by decision of the Commission. The decision shall specify the subject matter and purpose of the investigation, appoint the date on which it shall begin and state the penalties provided for in Articles 14 (1) (d) and 15 (1) (b) and the right to have the decision reviewed by the Court of Justice.

4.   The Commission shall in good time and in writing inform the competent authority of the Member State within the territory of which the investigation is to be carried out of its intention of taking a decision pursuant to paragraph 3. It shall hear the competent authority before taking its decision.

5.   Officials of the competent authority of the Member State within the territory of which the investigation is to be carried out may, at the request of that authority or of the Commission, assist the officials of the Commission in carrying out their duties.

6.   Where an undertaking or association of undertakings opposes an investigation ordered pursuant to this Article, the Member State concerned shall afford the necessary assistance to the officials authorized by the Commission to enable them to carry out their investigation. To this end the Member States shall, after consulting the Commission, take the necessary measures within one year of the entry into force of this Regulation.

Article 14

Fines

1.   The Commission may by decision impose on the persons referred to in Article 3 (1) (b), undertakings or associations of undertakings fines of from ECU 1 000 to 50 000 where intentionally or negligently :

(a) they fail to notify a concentration in accordance with Article 4 ;

(b) they supply incorrect or misleading information in a notification pursuant to Article 4 ;

(c) they supply incorrect information in response to a request made pursuant to Article 11 or fail to supply information within the period fixed by a decision taken pursuant to Article 11 ;

(d) they produce the required books or other business records in incomplete form during investigations under Article 12 or 13, or refuse to submit to an investigation ordered by decision taken pursuant to Article 13.

2.   The Commission may by decision impose fines not exceeding 10 % of the aggregate turnover of the undertakings concerned within the meaning of Article 5 on the persons or undertakings concerned where, either intentionally or negligently, they :

(a) fail to comply with an obligation imposed by decision pursuant to Article 7 (4) or 8 (2), second subparagraph ;

(b) put into effect a concentration in breach of Article 7 (1) or disregard a decision taken pursuant to Article 7 (2) ;

(c) put into effect a concentration declared incompatible with the common market by decision pursuant to Article 8 (3) or do not take the measures ordered by decision pursuant to Article 8 (4).

3.   In setting the amount of a fine, regard shall be had to the nature and gravity of the infringement.

4.   Decisions taken pursuant to paragraphs 1 and 2 shall not be of criminal law nature.

Article 15

Periodic penalty payments

1.   The Commission may by decision impose on the persons referred to in Article 3 (1) (b), undertakings or associations of undertakings concerned periodic penalty payments of up to ECU 25 000 for each day of delay calculated from the date set in the decision, in order to compel them :

(a) to supply complete and correct information which it has requested by decision pursuant to Article 11 ;

(b) to submit to an investigation which it has ordered by decision pursuant to Article 13.

2. The Commission may be decision impose on the persons referred to in Article 3 (1) (b) or on undertakings periodic penalty payments of up to ECU 100 000 for each day of delay calculated from the date set in the decision, in order to compel them :

(a) to comply with an obligation imposed by decision pursuant to Article 7 (4) or Article 8 (2), second subparagraph, or

(b) to apply the measures ordered by decision pursuant to Article 8 (4).

3. Where the persons referred to in Article 3 (1) (b), undertakings or associations of undertakings have satisfied the obligation which it was the purpose of the periodic penalty payment to enforce, the Commission may set the total amount of the periodic penalty payments at a lower figure than that which would arise under the original decision.

Article 16

Review by the Court of Justice

The Court of Justice shall have unlimited jurisdiction within the meaning of Article 172 of the Treaty to review decisions whereby the Commission has fixed a fine or periodic penalty payments ; it may cancel, reduce or increase the fine or periodic penalty payments imposed.

Article 17

Professional secrecy

1. Information acquired as a result of the application of Article 11, 12, 13 and 18 shall be used only for the purposes of the relevant request, investigation or hearing.

2. Without prejudice to Articles 4 (3), 18 and 20, the Commission and the competent authorities of the Member States, their officials and other servants shall not disclose information they have acquired through the application of this Regulation of the kind covered by the obligation of professional secrecy.

3. Paragraphs 1 and 2 shall not prevent publication of general information or of surveys which do not contain information relating to particular undertakings or associations of undertakings.

Article 18

Hearing of the parties and of third persons

1. Before taking any decision provided for in Articles 7 (2) and (4), Article 8 (2), second subparagraph, and (3) to (5) and Articles 14 and 15, the Commission shall give the persons, undertakings and associations of undertakings concerned the opportunity, at every stage of the procedure up to the consultation of the Advisory Committee, of

making known their views on the objections against them.

2. By way of derogation from paragraph 1, a decision to continue the suspension of a concentration or to grant a derogation from suspension as referred to in Article 7 (2) or (4) may be taken provisionally, without the persons, undertakings or associations of undertakings concerned being given the opportunity to make known their views beforehand, provided that the Commission gives them that opportunity as soon as possible after having taken its decision.

3. The Commission shall base its decision only on objections on which the parties have been able to submit their observations. The rights of the defence shall be fully respected in the proceedings. Access to the file shall be open at least to the parties directly involved, subject to the legitimate interest of undertakings in the protection of their business secrets.

4. In so far as the Commission or the competent authorities of the Member States deem it necessary, they may also hear other natural or legal persons. Natural or legal persons showing a sufficient interest and especially members of the administrative or management bodies of the undertakings concerned or the recognized representatives of their employees shall be entitled, upon application, to be heard.

Article 19

Liaison with the authorities of the Member States

1. The Commission shall transmit to the competent authorities of the Member States copies of notifications within three working days and, as soon as possible, copies of the most important documents lodged with or issued by the Commission pursuant to this Regulation.

2. The Commission shall carry out the procedures set out in this Regulation in close and constant liaison with the competent authorities of the Member States, which may express their views upon those procedures. For the purposes of Article 9 it shall obtain information from the competent authority of the Member State as referred to in paragraph 2 of that Article and give it the opportunity to make known its views at every stage of the procedure up to the adoption of a decision pursuant to paragraph 3 of that Article ; to that end it shall give it access to the file.

3. An Advisory Committee on concentrations shall be consulted before any decision is taken pursuant to Article 8 (2) to (5), 14 or 15, or any provisions are adopted pursuant to Article 23.

4. The Advisory Committee shall consist of representatives of the authorities of the Member States. Each Member State shall appoint one or two representatives ; if unable to attend, they may be replaced by other representatives. At least one of the representatives of a Member State shall be competent in matters of restrictive practices and dominant positions.

5. Consultation shall take place at a joint meeting convened at the invitation of and chaired by the Commission. A summary of the case, together with an indication of the most important documents and a preliminary draft of the decision to be taken for each case considered, shall be sent with the invitation. The meeting shall take place not less than 14 days after the invitation has been sent. The Commission may in exceptional cases shorten that period as appropriate in order to avoid serious harm to one or more of the undertakings concerned by a concentration.

6. The Advisory Committee shall deliver an opinion on the Commission's draft decision, if necessary by taking a vote. The Advisory Committee may deliver an opinion even if some members are absent and unrepresented. The opinion shall be delivered in writing and appended to the draft decision. The Commission shall take the utmost account of the opinion delivered by the Committee. It shall inform the Committee of the manner in which its opinion has been taken into account.

7. The Advisory Committee may recommend publication of the opinion. The Commission may carry out such publication. The decision to publish shall take due account of the legitimate interest of undertakings in the protection of their business secrets and of the interest of the undertakings concerned in such publication's taking place.

Article 20

Publication of decisions

1. The Commission shall publish the decisions which it takes pursuant to Article 8 (2) to (5) in the *Official Journal of the European Communities.*

2. The publication shall state the names of the parties and the main content of the decision ; it shall have regard to the legitimate interest of undertakings in the protection of their business secrets.

Article 21

Jurisdiction

1. Subject to review by the Court of Justice, the Commission shall have sole jurisdiction to take the decisions provided for in this Regulation.

2. No Member State shall apply its national legislation on competition to any concentration that has a Community dimension.

The first subparagraph shall be without prejudice to any Member State's power to carry out any enquiries necessary for the application of Article 9 (2) or after referral, pursuant to Article 9 (3), first subparagraph, indent (b), or (5), to take the measures strictly necessary for the application of Article 9 (8).

3. Notwithstanding paragraphs 1 and 2, Member States may take appropriate measures to protect legitimate interests other than those taken into consideration by this Regulation and compatible with the general principles and other provisions of Community law.

Public security, plurality of the media and prudential rules shall be regarded as legitimate interests within the meaning of the first subparagraph.

Any other public interest must be communicated to the Commission by the Member State concerned and shall be recognized by the Commission after an assessment of its compatibility with the general principles and other provisions of Community law before the measures referred to above may be taken. The Commission shall inform the Member State concerned of its decision within one month of that communication.

Article 22

Application of the Regulation

1. This Regulation alone shall apply to concentrations as defined in Article 3.

2. Regulations No 17 ([1]), (EEC) No 1017/68 ([2]), (EEC) No 4056/86 ([3]) and (EEC) No 3975/87 ([4]) shall not apply to concentrations as defined in Article 3.

3. If the Commission finds, at the request of a Member State, that a concentration as defined in Article 3 that has no Community dimension within the meaning of Article 1 creates or strengthens a dominant position as a result of which effective competition would be significantly impeded within the territory of the Member State concerned it may, in so far as the concentration affects trade between Member States, adopt the decisions provided for in Article 8 (2), second subparagraph, (3) and (4).

4. Articles 2 (1) (a) and (b), 5, 6, 8 and 10 to 20 shall apply. The period within which proceedings may be initiated pursuant to Article 10 (1) shall begin on the date of the receipt of the request from the Member State. The request must be made within one month at most of the date on which the concentration was made known to the Member State or effected. This period shall begin on the date of the first of those events.

5. Pursuant to paragraph 3 the Commission shall take only the measures strictly necessary to maintain or store effective competition within the territory of the Member State at the request of which it intervenes.

6. Paragraphs 3 to 5 shall continue to apply until the thresholds referred to in Article 1 (2) have been reviewed.

([1]) OJ No 13, 21. 2. 1962, p. 204/62.
([2]) OJ No L 175, 23. 7. 1968, p. 1.
([3]) OJ No L 378, 31. 12. 1986, p. 4.
([4]) OJ No L 374, 31. 12. 1987, p. 1.

Article 23

Implementing provisions

The Commission shall have the power to adopt implementing provisions concerning the form, content and other details of notifications pursuant to Article 4, time limits pursuant to Article 10, and hearings pursuant to Article 18.

Article 24

Relations with non-member countries

1. The Member States shall inform the Commission of any general difficulties encountered by their undertakings with concentrations as defined in Article 3 in a non-member country.

2. Initially not more than one year after the entry into force of this Regulation and thereafter periodically the Commission shall draw up a report examining the treatment accorded to Community undertakings, in the terms referred to in paragraphs 3 and 4, as regards concentrations in non-member countries. The Commission shall submit those reports to the Council, together with any recommendations.

3. Whenever it appears to the Commission, either on the basis of the reports referred to in paragraph 2 or on the basis of other information, that a non-member country does not grant Community undertakings treatment comparable to that granted by the Community to undertakings from that non-member country, the Commission may submit proposals to the Council for an appropriate mandate for negotiation with a view to obtaining comparable treatment for Community undertakings.

4. Measures taken under this Article shall comply with the obligations of the Community or ot the Member States, without prejudice to Article 234 of the Treaty, under international agreements, whether bilateral or multilateral.

Article 25

Entry into force

1. This Regulation shall enter into force on 21 September 1990.

2. This Regulation shall not apply to any concentration which was the subject of an agreement or announcement or where control was acquired within the meaning of Article 4 (1) before the date of this Regulation's entry into force and it shall not in any circumstances apply to any concentration in respect of which proceedings were initiated before that date by a Member State's authority with responsibility for competition.

This Regulation shall be binding in its entirety and directly applicable in all Member States.

Bibliography

Aaronson, R. (1992), 'Do companies take any notice of competition policy?', *Consumer Policy Review*, 2/3, pp. 140–5.

Anderlini, L. (1987), 'Manager-managed firms', Economic Theory Discussion Paper No. 115, University of Cambridge.

Anderson, S. and D. J. Neven (1992), 'Merger waves', mimeo, Brussels.

Bain, J. (1956), *Barriers to New Competition*, Cambridge, MA: Harvard University Press.

Baumol, W., Panzar, J. and R. Willig (1988), *Contestable Markets and the Theory of Industry Structure*, New York: Harcourt Brace Jovanovich.

Bernheim, B. and M. Winston (1990), 'Multimarket contact and collusive behavior', *Rand Journal of Economics*, Vol. 21, No.1, Spring, pp. 1–26.

Boner, R. and R. Krueger (1991), 'The basics of anti-trust policy: a review of ten nations and the European communities', Technical Paper No. 160, Washington, DC: World Bank.

Boyer, K. D. (1992), 'Mergers that harm competitors', *Review of Industrial Organization*, Vol. 7, pp. 191–202.

Bresnahan, T. F. and P. C. Reiss (1991), 'Entry and competition in concentrated markets', *Journal of Political Economy*, Vol. 99, No. 5, pp. 977–1009.

Brittan, L. (1990), 'The law and policy of merger control in the EC', *European Law Review*, pp. 352–3.

Caillaud, B., Jullien, B. and P. Picard (1993), 'Competing vertical structures: precommitment and renegotiation', mimeo, CEPREMAP, Paris.

Caves, R. E. (1991), 'Corporate mergers in international economic integration', in Giovannini, A. and C. Mayer (eds), *European Financial Integration*, Cambridge: Cambridge University Press.

Coase, R. (1972), 'Durability and monopoly', *Journal of Law and Economics*, Vol. 15, pp. 143–9.

Coate, M. B. and F. S. McChesney (1992), 'Empirical evidence on FTC enforcement of the Merger Guidelines', *Economic Inquiry*, Vol. XXX,

April, pp. 277–93.

Commission of the European Communities (1990), 'Community merger control law', *Bulletin of the European Communities*, Council Regulation (EEC) No. 4064/89, Supplement 2/90, Luxembourg: Office for Official Publications of the European Communities.

Commission of the European Communities (1992), *XXIst Report on Competition Policy*, Luxembourg: Office for Official Publications of the European Communities.

Crémer, J. (1992), 'Arm's length relationships', IDEI, University of Toulouse, mimeo.

Culyer, A. (1989), 'The normative economics of health care finance and provision', *Oxford Review of Economic Policy*, Vol. 5, pp. 34–58.

de Jonquieres, Guy and Andrew Hill (1992), 'Sources of change for mergers', *Financial Times*, 23 July, p. 16.

Diamond, P. and J. A. Mirrlees (1971), 'Optimal taxation and public production', *American Economic Review*, Vol. 61, pp. 8–27, 261–78.

Downs, A. (1957), *An Economic Analysis of Democracy*, New York: Harper & Row.

Drèze, J. (1992), 'La capitale de l'Europe, le marché et les pouvoirs locaux: murmures d'analyse et d'anticipation économique', *Comptes Rendus de la Societé Royale d'Economie Politique de Belgique*, 470, March, pp. 3–55.

Easterbrook, F. (1983), 'Antitrust and the economics of federalism', *Journal of Law and Economics*, Vol. 26, pp. 23–50.

Emerson, M. *et al.* (1988), *The Economics of 1992: The EC Commission's Assessment of the Economic Effects of Completing the Internal Market*, Oxford: Oxford University Press.

Evans, L. and S. Garber (1988), 'Public-utility regulators are only human: a positive theory of rational constraints', *American Economic Review*, Vol. 78, No. 3, pp. 444–62.

Fairburn, J. and P. Geroski (1992), 'The empirical analysis of market structure and performance', in Fairburn, J. and J. Kay (eds), *Mergers and Merger Policies*, Oxford: Clarendon Press, Second Edition.

Farrell, J. and C. Shapiro (1990), 'Horizontal mergers: an equilibrium analysis', *American Economic Review*, Vol. 80, No. 1, pp. 107–26.

Fishwick, F. (1989), 'Definition of monopoly power in the antitrust policies of the United Kingdom and the European Community', *Antitrust Bulletin*, Fall, pp. 451–88.

Fishwick, F. and T. Denison (1992), 'The geographical dimension of competition in the European Single Market', December, mimeo.

Foster, C. D. (1993), *Privatization, Public Ownership and the Regulation of Natural Monopoly*, Oxford: Blackwell.

Franks, J. and C. Mayer (1989), *Risk, Regulation and Investor Protection: The Case of Investment Management*, Oxford: Oxford University Press.

Franks, J. and C. Mayer, (1992), 'Corporate control: a synthesis of international evidence', April, mimeo.

Froeb, L. M. and G. J. Werden (1991), 'Residual demand estimation for market delineation: complications and limitations', *Review of Industrial Organization*, Vol. 6, No. 1, pp. 33–48.

Froeb, L. M. and G. J. Werden (1992), 'The reverse *Cellophane* fallacy in market delineation', *Review of Industrial Organization*, Vol. 7, No. 2, pp. 241–7.

Fudenberg, D. and J. Tirole (1991), *Game Theory*, Cambridge, MA: MIT Press.

Gatsios, K. and P. B. Seabright (1989), 'Regulation in the European Community', *Oxford Review of Economic Policy*, Vol. 5, No. 2, pp. 37–60.

George, K. and A. Jacquemin (1992), 'Dominant firms and mergers', *Economic Journal*, Vol. 102, January, pp. 148–57.

Geroski, P. (1991), 'Domestic and foreign entry in the United Kingdom: 1983–1984', in Geroski, P. and J. Schwalbach (eds), *Entry and Market Contestability*, Oxford: Blackwell.

Glais, M. (1992), 'L'application du reglement communautaire relatif au controle de la concentration: premier bilan', *Revue d'Economie Industrielle*, Vol. 60, pp. 94–115.

Good, D. *et al.* (1991), 'The structure of production, technical change and efficiency in a multiproduct industry: an application to U.S. airlines', Working Paper No. 3939, Cambridge, MA: National Bureau of Economic Research, December.

Green, R. and D. M. G. Newbery (1992), 'Competition in the British electricity spot market', *Journal of Political Economy*, Vol. 100, pp. 929–53.

Grossman, S. and O. Hart (1980), 'Takeover bids, the free-rider problem and the theory of the corporation', *Bell Journal of Economics*, Vol. 11, pp. 42–64.

Hampton, C. (1992), 'Nestlé–Perrier appeal', *Business Law Brief, Financial Times*, December, p. 6.

Harberger, A. C. (1954), 'Monopoly and resource allocation', *American Economic Review*, Vol. 44, May, pp. 77–87.

Haspeslagh, P. and D. Jemison (1991), *Managing Acquisitions, Creating Value through Corporate Renewal*, New York: The Free Press.

Hausman, J., Leonard, G. and J. Douglas Zona (1992), 'Competitive analysis with differentiated products', mimeo.

Hawk, B. (ed.) (1991), *International Mergers and Joint Ventures*, Ardsley-on-Hudson, NY: Transnational Juris Publications.

Hayek, F. (1944), *The Road to Serfdom*, University of Chicago Press.

Heidenhain, M. (1991), 'Merger control in the Federal Republic of Germany', in Cromie, S. (ed.), *Merger Control in Europe*, London: IFR Books.

Henderson, J. J. and R. E. Quandt (1980), *Microeconomic Theory*, New York: McGraw-Hill.

Hicks, J. (1935), 'Annual survey of economic theory: the theory of monopoly', *Econometrica*, Vol. 3, pp. 1–20.

Hill, A. and Paul Betts (1992), 'Air France free to buy Sabena stake', *Financial Times*, 6 October, p. 22.

Hirschman, A. O. (1970), *Exit, Voice and Loyalty*, Cambridge, MA: Harvard University Press.

Holmstrom, B. and P. Milgrom (1990), 'Multi-task principal-agent analysis: incentive contracts, asset ownership and job design', SITE Working

Paper #6, Stanford University.

Hughes, A. (1992), 'Mergers and economic performance in the UK: a survey of the empirical evidence 1950-1990', in Fairburn, J. and J. Kay (eds), *Mergers and Merger Policies*, Oxford: Clarendon Press, Second Edition.

Jackson, Tony and de Jonquieres, Guy (1992), 'Brussels expected to opppose ICI swap deal with Du Pont', *Financial Times*, 12 September, p. 1.

Jacquemin, A. (1990), 'Horizontal concentration and European merger policy', *European Economic Review*, Vol. 34, May, pp. 539–50.

Jenny, F. (1992), 'The efficiency defence under the EC Merger Regulation', Conseil de la Concurrence, mimeo.

Jensen, M. and K. Murphy (1990), 'Performance pay and top management incentives', *Journal of Political Economy*, Vol. 98, pp. 225–64.

Kahn, M. (1971), 'Collective bargaining on the flight deck', in Levinson, H., Rehmur, L., Goldberg, J. and M. Kahn (eds), *Collective Bargaining and Technological Change in American Transportation*, Evanston, IL: North-Western University Press.

Klibanoff, P. and J. Morduch (1993), 'Local public goods provision with externalities, local information and local autonomy', MIT, mimeo.

Krueger, A. O. (1974), 'The political economy of the rent-seeking society', *American Economic Review*, Vol. 64, June, pp. 291–303.

Kühn, K.-U., Seabright, P. B. and A. Smith (1992), 'Competition policy research: where do we stand?', *Centre for Economic Policy Research Occasional Papers*, No. 8.

Kwoka, J. (1989), 'The private profitability of horizontal mergers with non-Cournot and maverick behavior', *International Journal of Industrial Organization*, Vol. 7, pp. 403–11.

Laffont, J.-J. (1993), 'The new economics of regulation ten years after', *Econometrica*, forthcoming.

Laffont, J.-J. and J. Tirole (1992a), 'Should governments commit?', *European Economic Review*, Vol. 36, April, pp. 345–53.

Laffont, J.-J. and J. Tirole (1992b), 'Cost padding, auditing and collusion', *Annales d'Economie et de Statistique*, No. 25–26.

Laffont, J.-J. and J. Tirole (1993), *A Theory of Incentives in Procurement and Regulation*, Cambridge, MA: MIT Press.

Linklaters & Paines (1992), *Competition Law Bulletin*, Autumn.

Little, I. M. D. and J. A. Mirrlees (1974), *Project Appraisal and Planning for Developing Countries*, London: Heinemann.

McGowan, F. and P. B. Seabright (1989), 'Deregulating European airlines', *Economic Policy*, No. 9, pp. 283–344.

McGowan, F. and P. B. Seabright (1992), 'Regulation in the European Community and its impact on the UK', in Kay, J., Mayer, C. and D. Thompson (eds), *Privatization and Deregulation: the UK Experience*, Oxford: Blackwell.

Meeks, G. (1977), *Disappointing Marriage: A Study of the Gains from Merger*, Cambridge: Cambridge University Press.

Mookherjee, D. (1984), 'Optimal incentive schemes with many agents', *Review of Economic Studies*, Vol. 51, No. 3, pp. 433–46.

Morrison, S. and C. Winston (1986), *The Economic Effects of Airline*

Deregulation, Washington, DC: Brookings Institution.

Neven, D. J. (1992), 'Regulatory reform in the European Community', *American Economic Review, Papers and Proceedings*, Vol. 82, pp. 98–103.

Noll, R. G. (1989), 'Economic perspectives on the politics of regulation', in Schmalensee, R. and R. Willig (eds), *Handbook of Industrial Economics*, Amsterdam: North-Holland, Vol. 2, pp. 1253–587.

Olson, M. (1965), *The Logic of Collective Action*, Cambridge, MA: Harvard University Press.

Perry, M. K. and R. H. Porter (1985), 'Oligopoly and the incentive for horizontal merger', *American Economic Review*, Vol. 75, No.1, pp. 219–27.

Persson, T. and G. Tabellini (1993), 'Designing institutions for monetary stability', Milan, IGIER, mimeo.

Pestieau, P. and H. Tulkens (1992), 'Assessing and explaining the performance of public enterprises: a matter of ownership or of competition?', mimeo, February.

Ravenscraft, D. J. and F. M. Scherer (1987), *Mergers, Sell-offs, and Economic Efficiency*, Washington, DC: Brookings Institution.

Rose-Ackerman, S. (1981), 'Does federalism matter? Political choice in a federal republic', *Journal of Political Economy*, Vol. 89, No. 1, pp. 152–65.

Rosenthal, D. (1992), 'Competition policy in the EC', in Hufbauer, G. (ed.), *Europe 1992: An American Perspective*, Washington, DC: Brookings Institution.

Salant, S., Switzer, S. and R. Reynolds (1983), 'Losses due to merger: the effects of an exogenous change in industry structure on Cournot-Nash equilibrium', *Quarterly Journal of Economics*, Vol. 98, May, pp. 185–99.

Salop, S. C. (1987), 'Symposium on mergers and antitrust', *Journal of Economic Perspectives*, Vol. 1, No. 2, pp. 3–12.

Scheffman, D. T. and P. T. Spiller (1987), 'Geographic market definition under the *U.S. Department of Justice Merger Guidelines*', *Journal of Law and Economics*, Vol. 30, pp. 123–47.

Scherer, F. M. and D. Ross (1990), *Industrial Market Structure and Economic Performance*, Boston: Houghton Mifflin.

Schmalensee, R. (1987a), 'Horizontal merger policy: problems and changes', *Journal of Economic Perspectives*, Vol. 1, No. 2, pp. 41–54.

Schmalensee, R. (1987b), 'Interindustry studies of structure and performance', in Schmalensee, R. and R. Willig (eds), *Handbook of Industrial Economics*, Amsterdam: North-Holland.

Schumann, L. (1988), 'State regulation of takeovers and shareholder wealth: the case of New York's 1985 Takeover Statutes', *Rand Journal of Economics*, Vol. 19, pp. 557–67.

Schwartz, M. and R. Reynolds (1983), 'Contestable markets: an uprising in the theory of industry structure: comment', *American Economic Review*, Vol. 73, pp. 488–90.

Seabright, P. (1990), 'Can small entry barriers have large effects on competition?', Discussion Paper No. 396, Centre for Economic Policy Research, London.

Shleifer, A. (1985), 'A theory of yardstick competition', *Rand Journal of Economics*, Vol. 16, pp. 319–27.

Siragusa, M. and R. Subiotto (1991), 'The EC Merger Control Regulation: the Commission's evolving case law', *Common Market Law Review*, 28, pp. 877–934.

Sleeuwagen, L. (1986), 'On the nature and significance of collusive price leadership', *International Journal of Industrial Organization*, Vol. 4, June, pp.177–88.

Smith, A. and A. J. Venables (1988), 'Completing the internal market in the European Community: some industry simulations', *European Economic Review*, Vol. 32, September, pp. 1501–25.

Stigler, G. J. (1950), 'Monopoly and oligopoly by merger', *American Economic Review*, Vol. 40, May, pp. 23–34.

Stigler, G. J. (1971), 'The theory of economic regulation', *Bell Journal of Economics*, Vol. 2, pp. 3–21.

Stigler, G. J. (1988), *Memoirs of an Unregulated Economist*, New York: Basic Books.

Stragier, J. (1993), 'The competition rules of the EEA Agreement and their implementation', *European Competition Law Review*, Vol. 14, pp. 30–8.

Tiebout, C. M. (1956), 'A pure theory of local expenditures', *Journal of Political Economy*, Vol. 64, October, pp. 416–24.

Tirole, J. (1988), *The Theory of Industrial Organization*, Cambridge, MA: MIT Press.

Tirole, J. (1993), 'The internal organization of government', *Oxford Economic Papers*, forthcoming.

US Department of Justice and Federal Trade Commission (1992), *Horizontal Merger Guidelines*, 2 April.

Vermaelen, T (1992), 'Corporate restructuring: evidence from the stock market', in Cool, K., Neven, D. J. and I. Walter (eds), *European Industrial Restructuring in the 1990s*, London: MacMillan.

Vickers, J. (1985), 'Delegation and the theory of the firm', *Economic Journal*, Vol. 95, Conference Papers, pp. 138–47.

Vickers, J. and G. Yarrow (1988), *Privatization: An Economic Analysis*, Cambridge, MA: MIT Press.

Viscusi, K., Vernon, J. and J. Harrington (1992), *Economics of Regulation and Antitrust*, Lexington, DC: Heath.

Vogel, D. (1986), *National Styles of Regulation*, Ithaca, NY: Cornell University Press.

White, L. J. (1987), 'Antitrust and merger policy: a review and critique', *Journal of Economic Perspectives*, Vol. 1, No. 2, pp. 13–22.

Williamson, O. E. (1968), 'Economies as an antitrust defense: the welfare tradeoffs', *American Economic Review*, Vol. 58, pp. 18–36, 1372–6.

Willig, R. (1991), 'Merger analysis, industrial organization theory, and merger guidelines', *Brookings Papers on Economic Activity* (Special isue on Microeconomics), pp. 281–332.

Index

accountability, 171–2, 178, 219
actual entry, 43, 45, 57
Advisory Committee on
    Concentrations, 98, 107,
    217–18, 229, 234, 277–8
Agnelli group/family, 122–3, 127
allocative efficiency, 32–6, 62, 116
Anderson, S., 31
anti–trust policies, 148
    merger analysis, 16, 23–4, 29, 40,
        48, 59, 61
    merger decisions, 79, 81, 87, 90,
        111
    regulatory capture, 169, 179, 184,
        193, 195
appraisal of concentrations, 270–71
assessment of dominance, 57–63, 77,
    93, 101–16
Austrian School 10
autonomy (joint ventures), 84, 85

bargaining process, 78, 204–5, 225–6
    problem, 151–5
    solutions, 156–60
Baumol, W., 40
Bernheim, B., 83
Betts, Paul, 124
Boner, R., 193, 220
Boyer, K. D., 29
brands, 98, 113, 114, 126, 127

Bresnahan, T. F., 10, 30, 32
Britain, 81, 167, 182, 187, 215–17,
    219, 238
Brittan, Sir Leon, 1, 106, 193
Brown Shoe Co v. United States 370
    US (294), 31, 62
Bundeskartellamt, 81, 106, 145, 167,
    169, 187, 198, 216–17, 219–20,
    233–4, 236, 238
burdens of proof, 169, 203, 205–6,
    231
bureaucratic capture, 165, 185, 193
business plans, 82
buyer power, 77,
    106, 111–12, 226

candidate market, 55–6, 90–91
cases, *see separate index*
Caves, R. E., 31
CE12 nationality breakdown, 263
centralization, 3, 237–8
    regulatory powers, 176–82
CES sub-utility function, 27
classification (statistics)
    according to categories of
        products, 254–6
    according to cross-border/
        non cross-border operations,
        257
    according to type of

concentration, 254
of companies according to origin,
256
Clayton Act, 31
Coase, R., 154–6, 159
Coate, M. B., 58, 60, 61, 167, 185,
195
collective bargaining, 38–9
collective dominance, 29, 106–7,
111, 223
collusion, 137
merger analysis, 42–3, 51–2, 61–2
merger decision, 83, 106, 119,
126–7
Common Agricultural Policy, 175
common veto powers, 81–3, 89
company origin, 256
competition, 189–90
actual, 105
additional, 125–8
agency, 64–5, 190, 206, 233
'conditions of', 92–3, 99
criteria for assessment, 204–5
efficiency defence and, 201–4
perfect, 17
potential, 40–44, 45, 59, 112–16
role, 9–13
Competition Directorate, 1, 64, 106,
140, 141, 146, 148, 186, 193,
214, 216, 221, 233
concentration
Advisory Committee, 98, 107,
217, 218, 229, 234, 277–8
classification according to type,
254
control of, 4–5, 268–72
definition, 78–90
market power and, 31–2, 57–9
suspension of, 266, 273
types of, 265
concentrative joint ventures, 76–80,
84–90, 148–9
concessions, 225
'conditions of competition', 92–3, 99
Conseil de la Concurrence, 216, 217,
220
consensus approach, 169–70, 234
consumer surplus, 32–3, 34–5, 37

consumer surveys, 55–7, 66, 96, 98–9
contestability, 40–44, 59–62
convex function (regulatory powers),
183–4
cooperative joint ventures, 78–80,
84–5, 90
coordination (joint ventures),
85–6, 90
cost-price relationship, 17–22, 29,
34, 46
cost overruns, 187
cost savings (efficiency), 116–17
costs
fixed, 40–44, 205
information, 64–5, 175, 189
marginal, 17–21, 24, 32–5, 38–9
of market power, 36–40, 42–5
production, 40–44, 98, 159, 205
regulatory capture, 192–6
social, 37, 72–3, 168
sunk, 40–44, 48, 60, 114, 205
transaction, 112–13, 118, 120,
141–2
transport, 98–9, 113, 114, 198
welfare (of market power), 32–45
Court of First Instance, 125, 128, 222
Court of Justice, 18–19, 30, 84, 106,
222, 277
Crémer, J., 189
cross-border cases, 99, 257, 264
cross-border effects, 237
cross-price elasticity of demand,
20–26, 28, 47, 91, 94, 98
Culyer, A., 166
customer surveys, 55–7, 66, 96,
98–9

de Jonquieres, Guy, 126, 128
deadweight loss, 32–3, 39, 40
decentralization, 2–3, 237
regulatory powers, 176–82
decisions
chronological list, 245–52
criteria, 216, 221
final, 259–61
powers of, 273–4
publication of, 278
statistics, 252–66

time limits, 5, 274–5
see also merger decision (of EC)
delegation, 171–2, 183
demand
  elasticity, *see* elasticity of
    demand
  for product groups 55–6
  seasonal fluctuation, 92
  substitution, 23, 48–51, 53–4,
    90–94, 96, 241
Denison, T., 52–3, 91
Department of Justice (USA),
  16, 52–3, 60–62, 65, 167, 184,
  215–16, 218, 224
deregulation, 42, 171, 185–6
Director General of Fair Trading,
  215, 216
discount factor, 65–7, 69, 73
discretionary bargaining, *see*
  bargaining process
'dissatisfaction index'. 143–4
division of responsibility, 231–6
dominance, 4–5, 137, 241
  assessment, 57–63, 77, 93, 101–16
  collective, 29, 106–7, 111, 223
  market power and, 17–19
dual price index, 27
duopoly behaviour, 127
'Dutch clause', 198

Easterbrook, F., 177, 179
econometric techniques, 55–7, 241
economies of scale, 13, 17, 60, 168
economies of scope, 60
efficiency, 239–40
  allocative/productive (trade–off),
    32–6, 62, 116
  defence, 5, 13, 62, 77, 116–17,
    201–4, 235
  dominance and, 62–3
  gains, 190, 203, 204, 235
  offence, 62, 77, 116–17
  productive, market power and,
    36–40
EFTA nationality breakdown, 263
elasticity of demand, 54, 95, 241
  cross-price, 20–26, 28, 47, 91, 94,
    98

  market power and, 16, 20–25, 29
  own-price, 16, 19, 21–2, 24–8, 34,
    45, 47–9, 55–6, 90–91
Emerson, M., 194
entry
  actual, 43, 45, 57
  barriers, 41, 60–61, 97, 99, 113–15,
    119, 123–5, 159, 205
  contestability and, 40–44, 59–62
  facilitating, 123–5
  lags, 60–61, 112–13, 114
  potential, 57, 60–61
  potential competition and 40–44,
    112–16
  re-entry, 86
  threat of, 43, 57, 113
entry into force (Merger
  Regulations), 279
European cases, *see separate index*
European Commission
  Court of Justice, 18–19, 30, 84,
    106, 222, 277
  decisions, *see* merger decisions
    (EC)
  market definition, 16, 52–7
  merger policy (design), 163–207
  Merger Regulation, *see* Merger
    Regulation (EC)
ex ante transparency, 174, 188,
  220–21, 230–31
ex post transparency, 174, 188, 220,
  231
exclusive access, 120
executives (terms of appointment),
  82
exit, 86, 178

Fairburn, J., 32
Farrell, J., 29, 35
Federal Trade Commission (USA),
  111, 184, 216
final decisions, 259–61
Financial Services Act (1986), 166
fines, 276
firms, reaction of, 136–7
  surveys response, 138–49
first-mover advantage, 153–4
Fishwick, F., 52–3, 91

fixed costs, 40–44, 205
foreclosure, 120
'forum shopping', 7
Foster, C. D., 164
France, 216–17, 220
Franks, J., 166
free-rider problem, 38
Fundenberg, D., 153, 157
functional autonomy, 85

game theory, 61
Gatsios, K., 177, 179, 195
generic regulation, 182–6
geographic market, 50, 53–5, 77, 91,
    97–101, 159, 205, 240–41, 261
George, K., 19
'German clause', 198
Germany, 81, 106, 145, 167, 169, 187,
    198, 216–17, 219–20, 233–4,
    236, 238
Geroski, P., 32, 61
Gladstone, William, 164
Glais, M., 195
Good, D., 39
government, 10–11, 190–92
    capture, 193, 194, 195
Green, R., 44
Grossman, S., 38

Hampton, C., 128
Harberger triangles, 9, 38–9
Hart, O., 38
Hausman, J., 47
Hawk, B., 87
Hayek, F., 176
Heidenhain, M., 29, 106
Herfindahl-Hirschman index,
    29–30, 33, 34–5, 58–9, 108–11
Hicks, Sir John, 36
Hill, A., 124, 126
Hirschman, A. O., 178
Holmstrom, B., 182
horizontal mergers, 58–9, 118,
    120–23
House of Commons Select
    Committees, 171
Hughes, A., 201

implementation, 129–30, 279
'incentive compatibility', 169
incentive schemes, 38
independence (regulatory capture),
    152, 173–4, 175–6, 187–8, 191
industrial leadership, 84, 87–9, 90
industrial policy, competition and,
    12–13
industry capture, 193–4, 199,
    203–4, 224, 225
information, 190, 277
    asymmetries, 153–5, 165, 168–70,
        172, 174, 178, 180–82, 197, 203,
        206
    burden of proof, 169, 203, 205–6,
        231
    costs, 64–5, 175, 189
    requests for, 275
    sources of relevant, 55–7
institutional changes, 231–6
'inter-service' meetings, 218
interest groups, 3, 163–6, 168, 172–5,
    194, 224–5
international spillovers, 3, 198
investigations, 215–16, 218–21, 275
investigative powers, 275–6

Jackson, Tony, 128
Jacquemin, A., 19, 62
Jenny, F., 116
Jensen, M., 40
joint control, 78, 81–4, 89–90, 132
joint ventures, 76–81, 84–90,
    119–21, 148–9
judicial review, 217, 222–3, 277
jurisdictions, 278
    strategic choice of, 79–80, 89–90

Kahn, M., 38
Klibanoff, P., 177, 180–81, 197
Krueger, A. O., 37, 137, 193, 220
Kühn, K.-U., 187
Kwoka, J., 23

Laffont, J.-J., 46, 165, 168, 172
laissez-faire, 10–11, 168
language of procedure, 262
law firms (survey response), 146–9

'legitimate interests' clause, 198
Linklaters & Paines, 106, 114, 126
lobbying activities, 142–3, 164–5,
    183–4, 186, 188, 194, 196, 218
local public goods, 177–8
loyalty discounts, 73

Maastricht Treaty, 2, 176
McChesney, F. S., 58, 60, 61, 167,
    185, 195
McGowan, F., 39
'Mandy Rice-Davies problem', 169,
    174, 203
marginal costs, 17–21, 24, 32–5, 38–9
market
    definition, 47–57, 77, 86–7,
        100–101
    failure, 171, 177
    position, 101–11
    relevant, 24–5, 47–8, 53, 90–101
market-wide effects, 28–31
'market context', 101, 104
market power
    definition, 15–16, 17–32
    impact of merger (assessed), 45–63
    welfare costs, 32–45
market shares
    actual competition and, 105
    Herfindahl-Hirschman index,
        108–11
    market power and, 25–8
    significance, 101–4
Marx, Karl, 164
Mayer, C., 166
merger
    market-wide effects, 28–31
    policy design, 163–207
    refusals, 152–3, 154–5
merger analysis, 15–16
    changes, 240–42
    market power (defined), 17–32
    market power (welfare costs),
        32–45
    mergers, impact of, 45–63
    procedures, 63–6
    simple model, 67–73
merger assessment (criteria), 201–6
merger control

analysis, *see* merger analysis
European (case for), 196–201
importance of, 11–12
see also Merger Regulation (EC)
merger control (procedure)
    EC's strength/weakness, 223–6
    international comparison, 214–23
    stages, 231–6
merger decisions (of EC), 76–7
    concentration, 78–90
    concluding remarks, 131–4
    dominance, 101–16
    efficiency, 116–17
    relevant market, 90–101
    remedies, 117–31
Merger Guidelines (USA), 16, 29, 35,
    46, 50–53, 58–60, 62, 220
Merger Regulation (EC), 1–5
    bargaining process, 151–60
    decisions, *see* merger decisions
        (EC)
    evaluation, *see* merger analysis
    merger control procedures,
        214–26
    options for change, 229–42
    reaction of firms, 136–49
    regulatory capture, 192–206
    terms of (review), 236–40
    text of, 268–79
Merger Task Force, 1, 64, 117, 128,
    151
    merger control procedures,
        214–216, 218–21, 223–5
    modifications, 229–37, 239–41
    reaction of firms, 136, 138–42,
        144–8
    regulatory capture and, 187,
        199–200, 204
Milgrom, P., 182
Ministry of Economic Affairs
    (France), 216, 220
monitoring activities, 129–30
Monopolies and Mergers
    Commission, 81, 167, 182, 187,
    215–16, 219, 238
Monopolkommission (Germany),
    217
monopoly, 48–9

'hypothetical monopolist', 50–51,
55, 90
power, 9, 11–12, 37, 38–40
pricing, 32–3, 38–9, 40
rents, 40–44, 127
welfare losses, 9
Mookherjee, D., 182
Morduch, J., 177, 180–81, 197
Morrison, S., 42
Multi-Fibre Arrangement, 175
Murphy, K., 40

NACE codes, 253
national capture,
194, 218, 224, 225
national preferences (geographic
markets), 97
nationality breakdown, 262–3
negotiation
bargaining process, 78, 151–60,
204–5, 225–6
strategies (merger decisions), 130
neighbouring markets (joint
ventures), 87
Neven, D. J., 31, 177
Newbery, D. M. G., 44
no-competition clause, 86
Noll, R. G., 165
non-member countries, relations
with, 279
notification, 273
merger control procedure,
214–215, 216
statistics, 252, 258, 265

Office of Management and Budget
(USA), 171
*Official Journal of the European
Communities*, 278
oligopoly, 30–31, 34–5, 42, 51, 59,
106–7, 111, 128
original equipment (OE) market, 92
own-price elasticity of demand, 16,
19, 21–2, 24–8, 34, 45, 47–9,
55–6, 90

penalty payments, 276–7
Persson, T., 173

Pestieau, P., 39, 119
political
cost, 190–91, 234
independence, 173–4
pressures, 218–19
potential competition, 40–44, 45, 59,
112–16
potential entry, 57, 60–61
predatory behaviour, 187–8
predatory pricing, 21, 46
prenotifications (statistics), 253
price-cost relationships, 17–22, 29,
34, 46
prices, 55–6
coordination, 30–31, 32
differential, 98–99
monopoly, 32–3, 38–40
predatory, 21, 46
principal-agent relationships, 182–5
procedural transparency, 175, 220
product
categories, 254–6
characteristics, 86–7, 94–6, 241
demand, 16, 20–25
differentiation, 20, 22, 57
substitution, *see* substitution
product market
definitions, 50, 53–4, 77, 91–6, 159,
205, 240–41
geographic market and
(distinction), 77, 97–8
rents, 37
production costs, 40–44, 98, 159, 205
productive efficiency
allocative efficiency and
(trade-off), 32–6, 62, 116
market power and, 36–40
professional secrecy, 277
profit, 9, 10–11, 39
market power and, 32–8
maximization, 24, 25–6, 49
public choice theory, 10
public goods, local, 177–8
public procurement, 114, 119
Public Procurement Directive, 119
publication of decisions, 278

quantity index, 27

Ravenscraft, D. J., 201, 203
re-entry, exit and, 86
referrals, 78, 266, 274
reforms (options), 229–42
regulatory barriers, 113
regulatory capture, 3, 46, 159, 242
    concluding remarks, 206–7
    European policy, 192–206
    theory of, 163–92
regulatory objectives, 186–92
regulatory powers
    assignment of, 176–82
    functional separation, 182–92
Reiss, PC., 10, 30, 32
'relative majority', 80–81
relevant market, 24–5, 47–8, 53,
    90–101
remedies (merger decisions), 77,
    117–31
rent-seeking activities, 10–11, 137,
    186
'rent dissipation', 36
rent sharing, 119, 168
Report on Competition Policy
    (XXIst), 78, 91, 97, 99, 104
reputation effect, 154–8 *passim*, 205
research and development, 37
resources (of competition agency),
    64–5
review (by Court of Justice), 277
Reynolds, R., 41
Rose-Ackerman, S., 177, 179
Rosenthal, D., 79, 194
Ross, D., 40

Salant, S., 29
Salop, S. C., 62
scale economies, 13, 17, 60, 168
Scheffman, D. T., 55
Scherer, F. M., 40, 201, 203
Schmalensee, R., 52, 60
Schwartz, M., 41
scope of activity (joint ventures), 87
scope economies, 60
Seabright, P. B., 39, 177, 179, 195
secret agreements, 83–4, 89–90
Secretary of State for Trade and
    Industry, 215, 216

sectoral regulation, 182–6
Shapiro, C., 29, 35
Sherman Act, 52
Shleifer, A., 182
Single Market Programme, 194
Siragusa, M., 62
Sleeuwagen, L., 30
Smith, A., 27
Social Charter, 128
social costs, 37, 72–3, 168
social welfare, 48, 152, 202
sole control, 78, 80–84, 88, 89
speed of investigation (merger
    analysis), 65–73
Spiller, P. T., 55
spillover effects, 3, 87, 179–81, 197,
    198, 199–200, 237–8
statistics of (decisions), 252–66
Stigler, G. J., 28, 164, 176
sub-utility function, 27
subcontracting, 120
Subiotto, R., 62
subsidiarity principle, 176–7,
    199–200
substitution
    demand, 23, 48–51, 53–4, 90–94,
        96, 241
    supply, 23–4, 48–51, 53, 55, 77,
        91–4, 97, 99–100, 241
sunk costs, 205
    of entry, 40–44, 48, 60, 114
supply, 23–4, 48–51, 53, 55, 77, 91–4
    241
    geographic markets and, 97,
        99–100
surveys (response)
    of firms, 138–46
    of law firms, 146–9
suspension of concentration, 266,
    273
synergy effects, 36, 116, 168

Tabellini, G., 173
takeover, threat of, 192
Tebbit Guidelines (1984), 219
technological spillovers, 87
Thatcher, Margaret, 175
'third force', 125, 127

threat of entry, 43, 57, 113
Tiebout, C. M., 177, 178–9, 180
Tirole, Jean, 17, 46, 153, 157, 165, 172, 187
'tournaments' (incentive schemes), 38
transaction costs, 112, 113, 118, 120 141–2
transparency, 78
 bargaining process, 152, 158–60
 merger control procedures, 219–20, 222, 224–6
 options for change, 229–31, 236, 240
 regulatory capture, 159, 188–9, 191–2, 194–6, 204–5
transport costs, 98, 99, 113, 114, 198
Treaty of Rome, 18, 53, 79, 185
triggering event (cases), 5, 215
Tulkens, H., 39, 119
turnover
 calculation of, 272
 thresholds, 198–200, 226, 236–9
'two-thirds rule', 199

United States, 31, 35, 46
 Department of Justice, 16, 52–3, 60, 61–2, 65, 167, 184, 215–16, 218, 224

 Department of Transportation, 184–5
 Federal Trade Commission, 111, 184, 216
 market definition procedure, 16, 50–52
 Merger Guidelines, 16, 29, 35, 46, 50–53, 58–60, 62, 220
United States/E. I. du Pont de Nemours and Co. 351 (US 377), 51–2

Venables, A. J., 27
vertical mergers, 113, 118–20
Vickers, J., 83
Viscusi, K., 171
Voluntary Export Restraints, 175

wages (collective bargaining), 38–9
welfare
 costs (of market power), 32–45
 economics (of regulatory capture), 166–7
 losses (monopoly), 9
 see also social welfare
White, L. J., 52
Williamson, O. E., 33
Willig, R., 53
Winston, C., 42
Winston, M., 83

Index of European cases

ABB/BREL (221), 103, 104, 109

ABC/GDE/Canal + /WH Smith TV(100), 86, 95–6

Accor/Wagons-Lit (126), 118, 120, 123

Aerospatiale/Alenia/de Havilland (53), 1, 63, 102, 104–5, 108–9, 112–13, 117, 238

Aerospatiale/MBB (17), 81

Air France/Sabena (157), 88, 102, 108–9, 112, 118, 123–5, 129, 130, 239

Alcatel/AEG Kabel (165), 103, 106, 110, 111, 114

Alcatel/Telettra (42), 102, 104, 108, 111, 112, 113–14, 118–19, 133

Apollinaris/Schweppes (93), 82

Arjomari/Wiggins Teape (25), 81

AT and T/NCR (50), 62, 116, 117

Avesta/British Steel/NCC/Axel Johnson (239), 82–3

British Airways/TAT (259), 95, 118, 124–5, 129, 130, 133, 239

Conagra/Idea (10), 82

Courtaulds/SNIA (113), 93, 95, 102, 104, 108, 110, 112, 114, 118, 120, 133

Digital/Kienzle (57), 103, 109

Digital/Philips (129), 110

Draeger/IBM/Hmp (101), 86, 101

Du Pont/ICI (214), 103, 104, 110, 115, 118, 125, 128, 129–30

Elf/BC/CEPSA (98), 82, 100

Ericsson/Kolbe (133), 85, 88–9

Eridania/ISI (62), 99

Fiat/Ford (9), 118, 123

Fortis/La Caixa (254), 88

Herba/IRR (188), 86

Hoffman-La Roche, 18

IFINT/EXOR (187), 122

Ingersoll Rand/Dresser (121), 82

La Redoute/Empire (80), 94–5, 133

Linde/Fiat (256), 88

Lucas/Eaton (149), 81–2, 87, 94–100, 113

Magneti Marelli/CEAs (43), 80, 92, 97–8, 102–3, 109, 118, 120–23, 133

Mannesmann/VDO (164), 110

Mediobanca/Generali (159), 83–4

Metallgesellschaft/Safic Alcan (146), 93, 95, 133

295

Nestlé/Perrier (190), 30, 59, 103–4,
106–7, 109, 111, 114–15, 118,
125–8, 130, 223
Northern Telecom/Matra (249), 88

Otto/Grattan (70), 94–5, 100

Pan Am/Delta (130), 116
Pepsi Co/Kas (298), 94
Philips/Thomson/Sagem (293), 83

Renault/Volvo (4), 96–7, 102, 104–5,
109

Saab/Ericsson Space (178), 82
Sanofi/Sterling Frug (72), 82, 93

Sextant/BGT-VDO (290), 116
Solvay-Laporte/Interox (197), 98–9

Tetra Pak/Alfa-Laval (68), 96, 102,
108
Thomson/Pilkington (86), 88
Thorn EMI/Virgin (202), 106–7, 110
*TNT/Canada Post, DBP Postdienst,
La Post and Sweden Post* (102),
114, 118, 119–20, 239

Varta/Bosch (12), 81–2, 85, 92, 99,
103, 104–5, 118, 120–21, 129,
133, 238
Viag/Continental Can (81), 18,
111–12